The

Good
Car
Guide

Quentin **Willson**

BBC BOOKS

Published by BBC Books,
an imprint of BBC Worldwide Publishing,
BBC Worldwide Limited, Woodlands,
80 Wood Lane, London W12 0TT

First Published 1995

ISBN 0 563 37089 0

Designed by Edward Moody Design Limited, Leicester

Printed and bound in England by Clays Ltd, St Ives plc

Cover printed by Clays Ltd, St Ives plc

To Helen

Contents

SECTION eleven

INDEX

Introduction
Good *Car* Guide
95-96

Welcome to the second edition of the *Top Gear Good Car Guide* – everything you'll need to know about buying a new or used car. Here are detailed, down-to-earth descriptions of most new cars on the market and buying profiles of the more worthwhile secondhand ones, plus how to negotiate, what to look for, how to pay and what not to buy. It's all here, in accessible, non-technical language - the only book of its type. Compulsory reading for anybody about to plunge into the motor market.

Separating emotion and cars may be hard, but winning at the buying game is really all about shrewd and humourless accounting. All cars consume money, but the real skill lies in minimising the financial loss. Every car buyer needs to ponder some ticklish and potentially expensive questions. How much will I lose? What's it going to cost to run? Is the thing really such a good deal after all? Ignore the all-important subject of money and you'll wish you'd never bothered.

You won't come across pages of purple praise in the *Good Car Guide*, but you will find plenty of sensible, level-headed, money-saving tips. Follow our step-by-step advice, and there's a strong chance you'll save thousands rather than hundreds and buy yourself a car that will neither wither in worth nor bleed you dry. And remember – the world is full of cars, so take your time, know your chosen models, and, if you're not sure, just walk away. Good luck and good hunting.

Image

When the big car makers conduct research to find out what we like or dislike about their products, they hold clinics and seminars where carefully targeted customers fill out furlongs of questionnaires. For some time now, observers have had a sneaking suspicion that the answers people give are only what they think they're *supposed* to say. They won't admit on paper, or possibly even to themselves that, when the impression they have of the driver

BUILT TO GO PLACES ...*FAST!* Daimler V8 S.P. 250

‘The marketing men repeatedly tell us that it's not what a car does but how it looks that matters most in the final buying decision’

of a particular make and model mirrors their own ambition, they immediately want to go out and buy that car. They subconsciously espouse the image it projects.

Of course, safety, longevity, reliability and all those other eminently sensible considerations figure in the buying process, but the marketing men repeatedly tell us that it's not what a car does but how it looks that matters most in the buying decision. Whether we own up to it or not, most of us harbour a strong subconscious motivation to see ourselves projected through what we drive.

Cars aren't just reasonable machines to be used reasonably by reasonable people, they're symbols of power, wealth, sex and speed. We don't just drive cars, we wear them, because, if we're honest, the way to be distinctive in society is to drive a distinctive car.

Car manufacturers have learnt a lot since the Austin 3 litre. Fancy using a car for a brochure with a number plate like that...

A flash motor with a high image permits two forms of pretence. First, it allows the driver to pretend that he's a new and better person, and second it creates the illusion that he *is* that person. It's the old existentialist principle that you can't be something without pretending to be it first. The underlying motive for buying a car with image is to assert oneself in a society which has given itself over to the motor car. Among the symbols that define our position in the social order, few are more forceful than the motor car. It's highly visible, extremely mobile currency everyone understands.

Subliminal messages

For years, manufacturers have unashamedly traded on the image their cars project. Jaguar spent millions on racing in the 50s and 60s to project an image of sporting oneupmanship. BMC's Morris Oxford and Cambridge were aimed at establishment respectability, named after universities steeped in cultural heritage and middle class conformity. BMW and Audi hypnotised buyers into believing the 3 Series and the Quattro spelt instant membership to the apres-ski and high-tab restaurant set with a free gold Amex card in the glovebox. This is subliminal marketing at its most refined, penetrating consumer consciousness until reality blurs into fantasy. A form of image engineering that creates lapel badges for aspirational buyers to exhibit as talismans of discrimination and style.

> **All cars give off little messages. Audi Quattros and the BMW 3 Series spelt instant membership to the apres-ski, high-tab restaurant set with a free gold Amex card in the glovebox**

DE **LOREAN** - one dream that went horribly wrong

They were pedling the
same **dreams** in 1950.
The *Corvette* was
for the batchelor
whose **Levis** were
feeling the **strain**

For the **man about town**
the *Jaguar Mk7* was
the **zenith** of
achievement

Hand-built for
racing, the 1950s
Jaguar D Type with
its sleek lines
epitomised the
peak of **sensual
power**.
The subliminal
suggestion of sex
made Jaguars the
perfect **Cad's Car**

Image

Creating **the illusion**

If you're not convinced, let's take a closer look at how one car manufacturer turned its image round virtually overnight. In 1982 the typical Audi driver was a middle-aged, grey-suited white collar administrator and consumers perceived the Audi range as functional and workmanlike, in other words, very dull. The impending launch of the new and very advanced Audi 100 meant that the marque's image needed some serious polishing up. Their advertising agency, Bartle Bogle Hegarty, coined the now legendary strapline 'Vorsprung durch Technik', or progress through technology. Arguably more memorable than any other campaign, consumer perception of the range did a volte-face. Not content with this clever coup, the marketing magi decided it was time for a holiday.

> In 1982 consumers perceived Audi cars as workmanlike but very dull. 'Vorsprung durch Technik', progress through technology, launched the new, and very advanced Audi 100. Consumer perception of the range did an instant volte-face

Remember that soft-focus TV ad with the sun-washed Iberian villa, the turquoise pool, the wonderfully leggy girl and the frog frisking in the blue water? The Schmidts, assured the cerebral-sounding voice-over, drive a sluggish, thirsty car and are still miles away from their villa. The Rheinhardts on the other hand, drive an Audi 100 and, while the Schmidts are slogging somewhere between San Sebastian and Seville, the Rheinhardts, a chic and careless couple, are already lazing at the water's edge sipping cocktails in the best cinematic tradition. The punchline ran: 'And the moral of the story is, if you want to get on the beach before the Germans, you'd better buy an Audi 100.' Sales soared and, more significantly, the image of the Audi owner was recast into an eager, young and well-heeled professional. The Audi 100 became an intensely desirable social accessory.

Audi 100 became the favourite transport of the middle classes

Other manufacturers, keen to give the image of their products a similarly successful invigoration, quickly followed Audi's example. BMW came up with their powerful 'Ultimate Driving Machine' and Vauxhall their persuasive 'Once Driven Forever Smitten'. Volvo, desperate to move away from their well-worn imagery of worthiness and safety, did much to improve their market positioning with their campaign for the new 850 – 'Drives Like It's Alive'. These are all expert, carefully considered advertising thrusts calculated to energise product image, suggesting that the act of purchase and ownership will liberate us from our inadequacies and daily cares.

Image and **desirability**

A high image not only makes new cars desirable, it can keep values of secondhand ones strong as well. Marketing sleight-of-hand exerts a strong influence on new car buyers, but four or five years down the line some of the bons mots have faded into obscurity and a used car's desirability depends on how much residual effect is left over from the original marketing campaign. Mercedes use the copywriter's art to enormous effect with straplines like 'Engineered Like No Other Car'. The implication is that the life expectancy of a Mercedes is much greater than any other car.

Mercedes-Benz
Engineered like no other car.

M622 DNV

BMW'S ULTRA-VIOLET FILTER STOPS YOUR BODY GOING PINK, HOWEVER LONG YOU STAY IN THE SUN.

Image

They also aggressively market the appeal of their used cars, and the whole process of ongoing image burnishing helps to shore up and control resale values of even four- and five-year-old examples.

Negative images

In a market-place as self-perceptive and relentlessly materialistic as this, there are bound to be some casualties. Take the Escort XR3i. Launched in 1981 amid a glow of smart and showy sportiness, it quickly became synonymous with comfortable middle-class achievement. But the triteness of mass appeal began to sully its sparkle, with VW's trendy Golf and Peugeot's pert 205 GTi competitors fast gaining ground. By the early 90s the once elegant Escort had become a regional lout's plaything, crashed, thrashed and stolen with all the panache of an old shoe. Small wonder that used values are abysmal, insurance premiums astronomic and buyer resistance ferocious.

Remember the 80s phenomenon of the city-slick commodity broker cleaving through suburbia in his Guards Red Porsche 911? The roundy-round Porsche, once symbolic of the zenith of entrepreneurial achievement, suffered a

■ PEUGEOT 205 GTI

similar but less savage humiliation. After years of supremacy as the power and the glory of automotive attainment, the 911 found itself suddenly startled by the dawn of the caring 90s. Social responsibility was in and conspicuous consumption was out. Instantly, it seemed, the 911 became a brash and belligerent weapon wielded by people temperamentally unfit to drive anything larger than an electric razor. Its speed, irresponsibility and barefaced arrogance had ostracised it in a recession-weary society that had turned its back on extravagance and oblivious opulence. As a result used prices collapsed.

So next time you buy a car, new or secondhand, pause for thought and choose something with a positive and prominent image. An informed and reasoned decision about its market status will ensure minimal loss when you come to sell. Remember the rule of thumb - image dictates desirability, which in turn limits depreciation. The ambiguous and poorly defined image of a Fiat Croma, Renault 25, Vauxhall Carlton or VW Passat will always undermine their resale potential. Cars with a feeble image like Ladas, Yugos, Renault 21s and Seat Marbellas shed their value like crumbling masonry. But the carefully positioned image of the Land Rover Discovery, Mitsubishi Shogun, Mercedes Estate or BMW 3 Series will always guarantee a gentle and containable depreciation curve. In a word, image is all.

> **Next time you buy a car, new or second-hand, pause for thought and choose something with a positive, prominent image to ensure minimum loss when you come to sell**

THE LATEST MODEL FROM YUGO

—

THE LOWEST PRICE IN BRITAIN*

Power

Unlike the Americans, British new car buyers have never had access to a warts-and-all list of the good, the bad and the ugly. Until now, that is. For the second year running *Top Gear*, with the help of US-based market research company JD Power, have published a unique Car Customer Satisfaction Index – and the results make interesting reading. Like the fact that Britain's car industry is ten years behind the USA when it comes to customer satisfaction, that British buyers still favour Japanese cars for their reliability and high degree of customer service, and that some of the best sellers, the cars you'd expect to come top, actually don't do very well at all.

Stateside Surveys

In America, JD Power has as much clout as any car boss. The surveys are both admired and feared and car manufacturers buy the data contained in the reports not only because it gives them detailed information about cars and dealers, but because it can uncover faults they themselves have missed. When he started his surveys, Power was accused of being the puppet of Japanese car makers, because so many oriental cars ranked high. Power ensured that his research was overseen by a leading group of statisticians and they found nothing wanting. Now, in the US, Power is considered the benchmark of car quality and consumers take his verdicts very seriously indeed. And the point of the whole thing, helping the industry to make better cars, seems to work. In less than ten years the percentage of American owners saying that they're 'very satisfied' with their cars has soared from 59 per cent to 73 per cent. The manufacturers who listen to what Power says and try to improve their products reap plenty of benefits. In a 1989 US survey, Power announced that the Buick LeSabre had jumped from 44th to 2nd place. Sales of the LeSabre promptly doubled.

Thanks But *No Thanks*

JD Power tried to launch his satisfaction surveys in Europe as early as 1988 but was met with a wall of hostility. European firms told him outright they didn't want him around. But *Top Gear* did. And in May 1994 the first results of the *Top Gear–JD Power Car Customer Satisfaction Survey* were announced, sending shock waves throughout the entire British motor industry. *Top Gear* approves of Power's hard-headed statistical approach which cuts through the marketing hype to give a true picture of how cars perform in the hands of that most important person, the consumer. Only by repeating such surveys year after year will consumers actually be given a voice and manufacturers realise that they're building cars not for the industry but for the people who drive them. Sounds daft, but car manufacturers have been so used to a producer-controlled market that they don't realise how powerful the consumer actually is.

How **it Works**

The JD Power Survey covers every aspect of car ownership. From how smooth the engine is, parts and service back-up, ownership costs and warranty, right down to how rude or polite you found the receptionist at your local dealer. The six-page questionnaire has forty multiple-choice questions and takes around half an hour to fill in. The results are specially processed by the company's powerful computer system using a specially written statistical analysis programme. The survey looks at how happy people are with their cars after a year or eighteen months of ownership. Which is why in the first survey drivers of J registered cars were invited to contribute and in the second year it was K plate cars.

Secrecy

In America the Freedom Of Information Act gives JD Power and other firms unimpeded access to names of new car buyers. Britain on the other hand is one of the most secretive countries in the world about releasing information, and the Data Protection Act seeks to prevent the DVLA and car manufacturers releasing details of car ownership to independent bodies. Which is where *Top Gear* comes in. By making an appeal for voluntary information on TV, the programme received over 40,000 telephone requests for questionnaires, neatly side-stepping the restrictions of the Data Protection Act. Over 17,000 respondents were sent six-page questionnaires and over 10,000 were returned completed, giving details of 70 models and 30 makes, representing a solid 92% of the entire UK market.

Interesting *Reading*

Some models didn't quite meet the criteria of the survey because not enough drivers had responded to make the results statistically accurate. In those cases the make rather than the model was given a ranking. In the first year insufficient Jaguar drivers responded, but in the second year enough completed questionnaires to give Jaguar a specific position. Apart from the physical reliability and performance of the cars, it emerged that customer service and after-sales support is becoming ever more important to British consumers. Only just over half of British car buyers think that their dealers are doing a better job than they did in the past, while 13 per cent think they've actually got worse. Only 7 per cent of British dealers offer servicing on the spot rather than by appointment and just 47 per cent of dealers ring up customers as soon as their car is ready for collection. Most surprisingly, a pitiful 13 per cent of British dealers ring up their customers to make sure they're totally satisfied.

The **Results**

Of the 70 different models, an astonishing nine of the top ten come from the Land Of The Rising Sun, which is bad news for European car makers. Worse news is that Oriental cars are getting even better. But remember – the survey isn't just about the reliability, performance or image of a car. It covers the whole ownership experience, which is why cars like the Mondeo, Fiesta and Escort have such lowly rankings – Ford's dealer network needs to try much harder.

The same is true of Vauxhall with the Cavalier, Astra, Corsa, Calibra and Frontera which are all way down the list. Often it's simple things which let both the car and manufacturer down. In the Calibra's case the service receptionists don't communicate clearly, whereas with the Frontera it's having to go back to the garage several times because repairs were unsatisfactory. Each problem area pulls a car's score down dramatically.

The **Top Ten**

1   **Toyota Corolla**
    Top of the heap for the second year. Corolla owners are extremely satisfied with their cars and their dealers. Over 50 per cent said they'd definitely buy another.

2 Honda Civic

Apart from a few misgivings over service costs and warranty, Civic owners seem well pleased. Few problems, strong back-up and helpful dealers give the Civic second place.

3 Mitsubishi Colt

Two from the top is Mitsubishi's little Colt. Owners were particularly taken with its performance and sweet-revving engine and reckoned Mitsubishi dealers nice people.

4 Mazda 323

323 owners told us they had experienced very few problems, and any the car did have were sorted out with only one visit to the dealer. Only discouraging word was a general feeling that Mazda's service costs were a bit strong.

5 Proton 1.3/1.5

Cheap and cheerful, the Proton exceeded the industry average on performance. Owners praised its engine and transmission smoothness and its hardy build quality. Thirty-eight per cent said they'd buy another.

6 Honda Accord

Accord owners liked the way Honda dealers looked after them and promptly and courteously sorted out any glitches. But they did say that the Accord's performance, acceleration, handling and fuel economy could be better.

7 Honda Concerto

Again, Honda's attitude to customer care and their efficient servicing network gave the Concerto a strong position. It was only held back from a higher rating by average performance and warranty.

8 Toyota MR2

Another Toyota that owners were well pleased with. The MR2 scored highly because of its no-nonsense reliability, brisk performance and all those friendly Toyota dealers.

9 Toyota Carina

The Carina was favoured for its reliability, long warranty and dealer back-up. Only downside was the performance, which owners thought could be a touch more refined.

10 Mazda 626

Owners told us that 626s are fine cars to drive but service and customer care could be better. Less than speedy resolution of warranty problems seems to be one of the 626's few shortcomings.

The *Middle Fifty*

11 **Nissan Micra**	13 **Skoda Favorit**
12 **Nissan Sunny**	14 **Subaru Legacy**

15	Isuzu Trooper		38	Peugeot 405
16	Mercedes 200/300		39	Peugeot 205
17	Mercedes 190		40	Rover Metro
18	Saab 9000		41	Fiat Tempra
19	Daihatsu Fourtrak		42	Peugeot 106
20	Hyundai Lantra		43	Peugeot 309
21	BMW 3 Series		44	Ford Mondeo
22	Jaguar XJ6		45	Seat Toledo
23	Rover 200		46	VW Golf
24	BMW 5 Series		47	Ford Fiesta
25	Citroen BX		48	Rover Montego
26	Rover 400		49	Vauxhall Cavalier
27	Audi 80		50	Citroen AX
28	Citroen ZX		51	Renault 19
29	Nissan Primera		52	VW Polo
30	Volvo 440		53	Renault Clio
31	Volvo 940		54	Range Rover
32	Renault 21		55	Land Rover Discovery
33	Rover Maestro		56	Vauxhall Astra
34	Suzuki Vitara		57	Fiat Tipo
35	Vauxhall Nova		58	Vauxhall Astra
36	VW Passat		59	Rover 800
37	Fiat Panda		60	Fiat Uno

The **Bottom Ten**

61 **Vauxhall Calibra**

Real problems with servicing back-up and not enough communication between dealer and customer. Owners did say they thought the servicing costs were modest for a sports coupe.

62 **Vauxhall Carlton**

The Carlton's fine, it's the dealers that are the problem. Owners complained about lack of estimates before servicing work was done, clear explanation of charges and slow delivery of parts. Scored well for low incidence of faults, though.

63 **Citroen XM**

The only Citroen in the bottom ten, availability of parts and quality of servicing work pulled the XM's score right down. Owners didn't complain about the car's performance, but about the way they were treated.

64 Ford Granada

One of four Fords in the bottom ten, the Granada scored badly
because of poor parts and service, quality of workmanship and not
sorting repairs properly first time round.

65 Ford Sierra

Poor performance across the board, with the worst feature of all
being service costs. Owners didn't like Ford dealers' attitude, abilities
and communication skills. They also thought servicing cost too high.

66 Lada Samara

Samara owners rate their dealers, but the car itself has too many
niggling problems. But honourable mention for running costs,
servicing, attitude of service receptionists and warranty.

67 Rover Mini

Thumbs up for the Mini's handling and fuel economy but thumbs
down on customer care and warranty.

68 Ford Orion

The Orion scored so miserably because of its performance. Handling
and engine were marked down by users who also thought it had too
many faults.

69 Vauxhall Frontera

Frontera was punished because of its dealers. There were too many
problems during the warranty period and dealers couldn't fix things
first time round. Service costs were reasonable.

70 Ford Escort

Britain's best seller had the lowest score in every area of car - and
dealer-related performance except service costs. The latest Escort is a
much better car - let's hope Ford dealers measure up too.

Before you
make a
move

Should I buy **new** or **used**?

In the end, deciding between a new or a slightly used car is up to you. But research shows that many people are guided by prejudice rather than hard information.

You feel good when you buy new. No-one has used the car before, you simply stroll into the dealer, pick one out and, in an ideal world, it won't go wrong. It'll be immaculate, have covered almost no miles and even smell new. But you'll pay a hefty price for the privilege.

New cars depreciate fast. Some by as much as 50 per cent in their first year. As soon as you drive that spanking new car off the forecourt, the meter starts to run. You can kiss goodbye to upwards of £2000 as soon as your name appears on the registration document. And that's just on a family car like a Mondeo or Escort. It'll hurt a lot more on a BMW or an Audi.

The wisdom of buying new is quietly questioned these days, and the phenomenon of the nearly-new car has been born. Canny private buyers and far-sighted companies have seen the sense of buying a few-month-old tiny mileage car as an alternative to a brand new model, and have made some very solid savings as a result. Often, nearly-new cars can be as much as £5000 cheaper than the brand new model, yet look and drive just as well. There are very few bad cars these days and buying new simply to avoid unreliability or the prospect of breakdowns is a bit over-cautious.

17

Another reason people opt for brand new cars is simply the snob value. Being the first in the cul-de-sac with the brand new year letter may sound like fun, and the neighbours may well be impressed, but it's the bloke who beats the system by buying a cracking used car at half the price who is really the winner.

Like it or not, cars are all about money. Never forget this. Mobility needn't cost an arm and a leg and, when I see some of the cost per mile figures of some new cars, it makes me blanch. It's perfectly possible to buy a decent used car that does everything a new one will – except cost a lot. Unkind commentators will remark that having to trawl round garages and scan used car advertisements is a lot of hassle. Some secondhand cars such as Shoguns, BMW 3 Series and Mercedes can be hard to find. But if you're prepared to put in the effort and be patient, more often than not you'll save the cost of a serious Caribbean holiday.

If the choice was left to me, I'd never buy new – I couldn't bear all that depreciation. In the last analysis, buying new is the easiest, least painful and most expensive option, but never the most intelligent.

The **cost** of **depreciation**

Some cars depreciate like falling girders, while others level off after a few years. Choosing a car that holds its value is crucial and making the wrong buying decision can cost you plenty.

All new cars drop in value as soon as you pass through the showroom door. Put part of that down to car tax, VAT, delivery charges and the manufacturer's and dealer's profit margins – costs that aren't part of the car's real value, but one-off payments to the treasury, the factory and the dealer. Even if your new car has never turned a wheel, it may still be worth only three-quarters of what you wrote on the cheque just five minutes earlier.

'**Perhaps the single most important factor is image, a difficult thing to define, but essential to healthy residual values**'

So what factors make some cars depreciate more drastically than others? There are several reasons, and the salesman certainly isn't going to tell you. Poor build quality, unreliability, sluggish performance and lacklustre image all push values down the slippery slope quickly. If a car is seen as fast, economical, fashionable and well made, buyers hold it in fierce esteem, supply becomes limited and values firm up. That means they enjoy slower depreciation.

Perhaps the single most important factor is image, a difficult thing to define, but essential to healthy residual values. Use the word fashion instead of image and we get a bit closer to a clear definition. Most people

10 **truths** about **depreciation**

1
Buying from a **dealer** means you give him the first chunk of your **depreciation** in the form of his profit margin, which is instantly lost. If you're buying used, go to the classifieds and pay as near to trade price as you can

2
Buy a **current** model shape. When a new model appears, old shapes become less desirable and values quickly fade

3
Choose a car with a good **mechanical** reputation, reasonable servicing costs and a **fashionable** image

4
Attractive, fashionable colours such as red, black or metallics are always more **desirable**. Colour can represent as much as 20 per cent of a car's **value**. Drab beiges, browns and greens are far less saleable

5
Buy the **highest** specification you can afford. Nobody wants base models. Sports and high-spec cars are **always** at a premium because more people **want** them

6
A **good** condition, low-mileage, few-owner car will hold its value much better than a high-mileage tatty example. Condition is **everything**

7
Engine **size** is important. 850 Minis and 950 Fiestas don't go. A 1.6 Cavalier is **better** than a 1.4

8
Cars which purport to be stylish, but are not, **depreciate** quickly: Fiat Uno Turbo, Renault 21 Turbo, Vauxhall Belmont SRi, MG Metro Turbo etc. **None** of them has a clearly defined image

9
Body **shape** matters. Hatchbacks are more desirable than saloons. Two-door Sierras and Cavaliers don't sell as well as five-door cars. Mercedes estates sell better than saloons. Everybody **wants** convertibles in fine weather

10
Larger saloons marketed as **prestige** models often have an expensive new list price and can lose **half** their value in the first year. High tech options alone will not necessarily protect a car's residual **value**

buy cars for all the wrong reasons – the heart rules, not the head. As a possession, the motor car makes more of a statement about your personality than anything else you own. People choose a particular car for what it says about them. A BMW shouts wealth, modernity and style. A Porsche 911 says speed, power and money, while a Volvo implies safety, respectability and control. Successful marques have a definite image – they actually deliver what they promise and they're seen as fashionable – and they have motoring credibility. But when a car has an uncertain and unfashionable image, depreciation is painful.

Eastern bloc cars like Ladas and FSOs depreciate quickly because they have no image. They don't set out to be fashionable – they're just no-frills, low-cost motoring. The Nissan Bluebird is one of the most reliable cars on the road, but it has a confused, lacklustre image and isn't desirable. Result – heavy depreciation.

Running costs and reliability also play a part in the equation. Alfa Romeos have bags of style but used to suffer very poor residuals because of rust and poor build quality. Values are much better since Alfa boosted the image of the whole range with the stylish and reliable 164.

Citroëns, apart from the 2CV, were plagued with lousy residuals because of their mechanical complexity and high maintenance costs. The CX was a fine car but virtually worthless after three years. When it went wrong, often only a main agent and a considerable sum of money could fix it – the only honorable way out was to scrap the car. But now Citroën have the accomplished Xantia in their model line-up and wilting secondhand values are a thing of the past.

Options to take and to avoid

Optional extras make little difference to the secondhand value of most cars. Only expensive and significant options – sunroofs and air conditioning, for instance – add any value at all to used cars, and even then it may only be improved desirability rather than a financial advantage. Despite what the salesman says, specifying a litany of extras on your new car could be like pouring money down the drain. The new-car buyer confronted with a list of options resembling the Gettysburg Address must decide which make good buying sense and which are merely valueless add-ons.

'A list of extras that reads like the Gettysburg Address could be serious money down the drain'

*Which options have **lasting value** and which **don't**?*

Options that actually boost a used car's value are not, surprisingly, the ones that cost the most in the first place – automatic transmission (essential on some prestige cars), air conditioning, leather trim, alloy wheels, power steering, ABS, sunroof and electric windows. But they'll still cost more than they'll return at trade-in time.

At the other end of the scale there are the bagatelle options that add nothing to the value – rear centre armrest with ski bag, illuminated vanity mirror, mud flaps, cassette storage holder, outside temperature gauge, cruise control, dashboard wood inserts and eight-speaker stereo.

Let's assume you're a hedonist and have specified leather trim on your new VW Golf GTi. In the showroom you'll pay the thick end of £2000 for hide, but in the classified ads, two years down the line, your Golf may be worth a few hundred more than the other bloke's. Add air conditioning to your new Granada Ghia and you'll bump the invoice price up by £1000. Come part-exchange time and, if you're lucky, the salesman may allow another £200 on the book value, but no more. Ask for ABS on some new cars and it'll cost you £900, but don't expect to see much more than £150 back when you come to sell a year later.

Why options **aren't a big deal** *on used cars*

More and more manufacturers, particularly those from the land of the rising sun, are loading their cars with standard equipment, and buyers are coming to take certain things for granted – power steering and ABS, for example. Understandably they're reluctant to pay extra for what comes as standard on other cars. The secondhand motor trade know that in most cases options don't really sell cars, they just help them along, so they resist costing them out individually.

Instead, they calculate in reverse. If a BMW 3 Series doesn't have alloy wheels or a sunroof, it attracts a price penalty – as much as £700. In fact, in the trade guides some cars are valued on the basis that they have metallic paint, sunroofs and alloy wheels. If they don't, they make the appropriate deductions. An XR3i with electric windows, ABS and heated windscreen is a handy thing to have, but it's not significantly more valuable than the stock item – just more attractive.

> **Prestige cars with lower or poverty spec become orphans. It's no good ordering a new Jag with a manual gearbox; the car won't only be worth less, it'll be very difficult to sell at all**

When options are **essential**

Some cars do need certain options to appeal to the used market. Because buyers have become used to highish levels of specification, cars with lower or poverty spec become orphans. It's no good ordering a new Jaguar with a manual gearbox. Used buyers will always go for the Jag with automatic, and the car without won't only be worth less, it'll be very difficult to sell at all.

Specifications of new and used cars have patterns, because customers have established preferences. Most BMW 730s have air conditioning and leather specified by first owners, so if you're about to sign a cheque for a used one that boasts neither, think again. A specless 730 is bad news. If you fancy a Sapphire Cosworth, get into one with leather trim – the market sees that as the better buy.

Consumer option patterns create a level of expectation on certain models. Just as automatics are preferable on prestige cars, so is metallic paint because that's the norm. These days anything without a sunroof is a poor relation. And if you come across a big car without power steering, leave it alone – most other buyers will.

Options when **buying new**

Ordering a car that hasn't yet been built means you may have to pay full whack for your creature comforts. These days list prices are not carved in stone, and you should still be able to get a decent deal on a well specified car. But the shrewd move is to buy a demonstrator or something that's already in the showroom with the options you want. Then you can take the salesman to task over the added cost and haggle your way round it.

Options when **buying used**

Don't be persuaded to pay major money for add-ons. Factory fitted optional equipment does little to boost used values, despite what Mercedes and BMW salesmen might have you believe. Used buyers can play the option game better than anybody for one simple reason. The options are historical. They're already on the car and the seller's hardly going to rip them off before he sells. Use them only as a negotiating lever.

Colour **sells** cars

It's surprising that many car buyers don't give colour much thought. But colour choice isn't just a question of vanity; it's one of desirability and can affect the used value by as much as 10 per cent. Nobody could argue that driving a red car will magically enrich your life, but choosing red instead of grey means that you safeguard an important element of the car's secondhand value. Bright-looking cars in mainstream, attractive colours sell faster and for more money than dull-looking ones.

The clued-up buyer is likely to have firm views on car colour and won't choose anything that looks remotely uninteresting. He wants his car to make a statement, to imply that he has discrimination and taste. To this bloke, owning a tower block grey Sierra is like wearing flares – he just won't do it. He won't go for anything too garish, either, like a canary yellow VW Corrado. His choice of colour will be a part of his buying decision and it will probably be red, black, white or an assertive metallic. What's more, he'll only consider buying something in a socially acceptable or fashionable shade. So hearing-aid beige is definitely out.

Saleable *and* **unsaleable** *colours*

How do you know which colours are regarded as saleable and which aren't? While the motor trade is well aware of the influence of colour on car values, they're unlikely to take the trouble to explain the concept before you hand over the money for that navy blue Montego. Various colour-blind car manufacturers, for reasons best known to themselves, continue to paint their products in questionable shades that have scant regard for majority tastes. As a used-car buyer you need to familiarise yourself with what are acceptable colours so you don't end up with something nobody else wants.

Colour and *prestige* cars

Executive and luxury cars are even more susceptible to the colour effect. On a Mercedes, BMW or Jaguar, colour should reflect the car's prestige and higher purchase price. The association should be one of elegance and value. To buy a luxury car finished in flat blue or grey is defeating the object of the exercise – heads will not turn. Try it yourself. Look at an ivory Mercedes estate and compare it to a dark metallic one. The darker car looks lower, sleeker and more expensive.

You don't often see Rolls-Royces and Bentleys in lacklustre colours. Invariably they're painted in restrained but upmarket blues and greens or light metallics like Georgian Silver or Willow Gold. The Rolls colour list reads like a Hatton Garden inventory: Black Pearl, Onyx Green, Opal Green, Silver Chalice and Garnet Red. Jaguar, which used to offer some emetic choices in the 1970s, now have a fine selection. The names alone sound rarified: Sovereign Gold, Tungsten, Silver Birch, Bordeaux Red and Westminster Blue. Making the wrong colour choice on a prestige car not only means a heavy financial penalty, it could also mean the difference between selling and not selling.

Metallic or *solid* colour?

Metallics are more desirable than solid colours and listed on most new cars as an extra-cost option. The disadvantage of metallics is their lack of durability. Matching up paint repairs is more difficult, too given the more complicated structure of metallic two-pack paint. A vandal scratch on a car in a solid colour can easily be 'blown in' locally without having to go through the lengthy and expensive process of masking, preparing and painting the whole panel.

With metallics, blowing in small areas is rarely possible without drawing undesirable attention to the panel being repaired. Some metallics have a base colour coat which is then covered by a clear lacquer to give depth and shine. With age, or if repairs are poor, the lacquer coat can lift and peel, which means the whole panel has to be resprayed.

The car **buyer's guide** *to* **colour**

Select mainstream, emphatic shades with majority appeal. Safe choices are red, black and white. Metallics are good news, especially the darker more powerful tones like graphite, dark metallic blue and metallic red. Metallic light green has a high buyer resistance for no other reason than some old wives' tale about green being unlucky. Dark green suits some prestige models better than others, but on ordinary saloons it's generally considered a disadvantage. Dark brown, unless metallic, isn't fashionable and is likely to encounter buyer resistance. Navy blue is seen as flat and uninteresting and without positive associations.

Problem colours to avoid at all costs are light, nondescript shades like off-white, beige, grey and light brown. Anything remotely anaemic should be left alone.

How to **buy** a **new** car

Where **new cars** come **from**

You could be forgiven for thinking that all new cars are bought from just one outlet – the franchised dealer. Not so. You can buy new from several other sources: car brokers or multi-franchise dealers – who operate more than one franchise – or you can import a new foreign car yourself or through a car import specialist.

Usually, however, new cars are sold directly by manufacturers' appointed sales agents – car dealers who operate that particular franchise. Some foreign cars are imported by what's known as a concessionaire or importer – a company set up to distribute those cars to dealers. The trouble is, you can't buy directly from the importer or manufacturer, but have to take your chances with the traditional dealer network.

A new car dealer will usually order, or be expected to stock, a representative range of a manufacturer's product. If he can sell you a car he has in stock, all well and good, but if he doesn't have the model you're looking for, he'll have to order it either directly from the manufacturer or through what's known as an inter-dealer transfer. When a second dealer is holding the car you want, your man will buy it from him to sell on to you. So if you want a particular specification or colour scheme, you will probably have to wait longer.

Car **brokers**

Buying from a franchised or multi-franchised dealer is the least risky route. Buying from a car broker may be cheaper but you aren't as well protected.

Car brokers buy in bulk and are more able to offer a discount to the customer. And because they don't usually operate from showrooms, they don't incur dealers' overheads and expenses, so they can pass these savings on to you. In fact, you may never even see the broker you deal with. The car will be ordered through him and delivered to your nearest franchised dealer. So these are the points to watch with car brokers:

✓ Financial risk. We've heard of several car brokers going bankrupt, some taking their clients' money with them. Not all brokers can be assumed to be financially healthy.

✓ Brokers don't carry demonstrators or stock, so you'll be expected to take a test drive with your local dealer.

✓ Car brokers are not interested in part-exchanges, just a cash sale, so you'll have to sell your own car first.

✓ Some brokers order through normal dealers while some import their cars from abroad. Make quite sure that the car you've ordered is not a direct import. You could have all sorts of problems with the warranty and a non-UK specification.

✓ If you're paying a deposit, pay it to the franchised dealer, from whom the broker is ordering the car. That way, if the broker goes bust, you stand a decent chance of getting your deposit back.

✓ Never pay a car broker the full amount up-front. Pay the dealer – you'll have legal title if anything goes amiss.

Personal *imports*

Importing a car from abroad is never as simple or convenient as buying from a dealer. There's no part-exchange opportunity, for example, and unless you're fluent, using a foreign language to order complicated colours and specifications can end in tears. The lines of communication between two countries separated by water mean long delays, and arranging finance in somewhere like France or Germany may be tricky. Do your sums well and ask yourself whether the price of the aggravation is worth it, because the savings on car imports are not that great.

Remember:

✓ A personal import will nearly always have 'previously registered/used abroad' on the V5 or registration document. The used market considers this a stigma and it can put subsequent buyers off. Unless the V5 says 'declared new at first registration in Great Britain by Manufacturer/Sole Import Concessionaire', the car is likely to be a personal import and its secondhand value will be affected accordingly.

✓ Some personal imports may have what's known as continental specification. The headlamps may dip to the wrong side, the engine may be tuned to run on a lower grade of fuel, bumper heights may be different and we've even heard of left-hand drive being converted to right-hand drive without the buyer's knowledge. You don't want a foreign spec car.

✓ Warranties can differ, too. A car sold in Spain and then imported to Great

Britain may not be covered by any British warranty at all. So remedial work under warranty may have to be carried out by a Spanish dealership. A nightmare that's best left to the imagination. At the very best, if your personal import does enjoy a warranty that's valid in the UK, you may still have to cope with glacial service managers giving preference to their own 'loyal' customers.

✓ The bill for importing a car needs shrewd and humourless accounting. You may feel that your continental holiday offsets the cost, but don't forget you'll still have to pay VAT at 17.5 per cent plus the cost of shipping. Then there are exchange rates to consider. A weak Swedish Kroner means cheap Saabs and Volvos. A strong Deutschmark means villainously expensive Mercedes, VWs, Audis, BMWs and Porsches. Getting caught by shifting exchange rates in the middle of a transaction can easily wipe out any savings.

Old versus **new** models

Make sure you're not sold a run-out model without realising it. Manufacturers know well in advance when they're planning to bring out a new model and try to shift the old ones double quick. Sometimes they introduce keenly priced special edition models to stimulate sales. Ask the salesman if there's a new model around the corner and don't even think about paying anything like list price for something that's about to be replaced. It'll only hurt come part-exchange time.

Paying the **right price**

Unlike butter, new cars are not sold for a fixed price. Most new car dealers have a margin of up to 20 percent to play with and in this country new car discounting is widespread. A realistic discount can be anything between 6 per cent on, say, a BMW – notoriously difficult to buy at a significant discount – and up to 15 per cent on a more commonly discounted Fiat or Ford.

Don't wait to be offered a discount, ask for one. Traditionally, the British car buyer finds bargaining uncomfortable but the discount system exists, so use it. The best tactic is to play one dealer off against another and shop around for the highest discount. The cheapest cars are the ones already in stock. Dealers would much rather sell you a car they have on hand than order from another dealer or the manufacturer. If a car's in the showroom for longer than 100 days, they'll be very keen to move it.

Improve your negotiating position by not having an unattractive part-exchange. It always pays to sell your own car first and go in with cash or a clean finance agreement. While it's possible to walk out of a showroom with something like 12 per cent, don't expect that from everybody. Cars in high demand, like Range Rovers, Mitsubishi Shoguns and BMW 3 Series, won't usually be discounted by much, and sometimes not at all. By the same token some Japanese manufacturers are limited by import quotas and won't give any discount.

When to buy **new**

Never buy in January. Fifty per cent of all cars sold are bought by companies, and January is one of the peaks of their buying cycle. Dealers are busy at this time sorting out company purchases and in a discounting mood.

Like any market, the new car market has highs and lows which you can use to your advantage. There are certain calendar rules which you must obey to make the best deal.

A better time to buy. The January sales rush will have subsided and some dealers will be twiddling their thumbs. Good deals can be made.

Even better in March. Used and new car sales are slow and the January rush will be a memory. Dealers will be looking for an earner.

Not a good time to buy convertibles because approaching good weather increases demand. However, 4x4 demand is slackening because the snow's gone.

Don't buy now. The sun brings a wave of optimism and new sales pick up slightly.

August approaches. Dealers will be anxious to clear stock in preparation for the August mahem. A good time to start thinking about buying. Generous deals should be in the offing.

July

Excellent time to buy if you're not bothered about next year's registration letter. Dealers will now be desperate to meet forthcoming August sales targets and everybody's waiting for the new year letter. You should have the pick of the showroom. But see that you get a discount that makes up for not having the new letter. The advantage of next year's letter can be as much as £500 on a secondhand family saloon, and up to £1000 on a Jaguar or BMW.

August

Don't buy now. Dealers are usually bullish at this time of year and understandably reluctant to give unnecessary discounts. They'll also be working flat out and may not give you the attention you deserve.

September

A shrewd time to buy. The August novelty is over and dealers are looking for a pot of tea before Christmas. They're nearly always on monthly or three-monthly targets and eager to do business at the end of these months. The best quarterly target to go for is the September 30 deadline - try the week before.

October

Plenty of deals about. Private buyers tend to be distracted by Christmas and showrooms are eerily quiet. Discounting tends to be fierce, except on 4x4s as winter looms.

November

The trade is in the doldrums. There's very little new car activity on the horizon until January 1, so dealers should welcome you with open arms. A good time to buy a draughty or leaky convertible.

December

Make your deal now. Dealers will have little profit opportunity until the beginning of the new year and should cut their margins to the bone. If you're clever, you'll buy as near to Christmas as possible and get the dealer to hang on to the car and register it in the new year. That way you get the latest year on the registration document.

The effect of **discounts** *on* **resale**

If a manufacturer aggressively discounts a particular model the lower price is bound to be reflected in that car's secondhand value. Let's say Rover decide to discount the Metro 1.4 L by 20 per cent across the board. Market dynamics dictate that all discounted Metro 1.4Ls will therefore be worth 20 per cent less than non-discounted Metros, simply because they cost less in the first place. Cars heavily discounted by the manufacturers are always picked up in the industry used car price guides and down-valued accordingly. Find out if you're actually getting a genuine discount from the dealer or just a manufacturer's special offer. Run-out models are often shifted this way, so do your homework carefully.

Discounts on **demonstrators**

Greater savings can be made by buying a demonstrator, which is still a new car on the current registration letter but has just a few thousand miles notched up. Ask your dealer first if he's got a demonstrator on offer of the particular model you want. It'll have the dealer's name in the registration document as the first owner, but that shouldn't affect its used value.

Discounts on **nearly new** *cars*

Manufacturers fight to get on the much vaunted Top Ten Sales list. The number of cars sold is measured in actual cars registered rather than the number physically passing to new owners. For years, car manufacturers have been registering cars *en bloc* to boost sales figures. They then sell these cars off to the trade in special closed auctions, sometimes with only a few hundred miles on the clock. Cars like these are virtually brand new, still covered by the manufacturer's warranty, carry the relevant manufacturer's name in the V5 and make particularly canny purchases for the private buyer. So it always pays to ask the dealer if he has any nearly new, current year letter, tiny mileage models available. The savings can be huge.

Getting the **price down**

✓ Ask for a discount as soon as you talk numbers

✓ Shop around and look for good discount deals with several dealers

✓ Play off one dealer's discount against another's

✓ Avoid having a part-exchange if possible. It puts you in a stronger bargaining position

✓ Make sure the discount you're offered is a genuine dealer discount and not a manufacturer's special offer on a run-out model

✓ Ask if the dealer has a low-mileage demonstrator in your chosen model

✓ Ask about tiny mileage, nearly new, same-plate cars

Size of **dealer network**

If you're buying from a franchised dealer, check there are at least a couple of servicing outfits in your area. There's nothing worse than having a duff car that has to be ferried 50 miles to and from a dealer. It also helps to have another franchise close by if the one you're dealing with proves to be unsatisfactory or – not unheard of – incompetent. Not all manufacturers have large dealer networks. Ferrari, for example, only has 18 dealers, Alfa Romeo 74, Lotus 28 and Aston Martin a mere 10 nationwide.

Don't pay too much for *extras*

Money spent on extras and accessories on a new car won't boost its secondhand value (see pp20–22). In fact, very few extras make any financial difference to a car's used price. While it's tempting to splash out on bits and bobs to personalise your new car, watch it – you could be throwing money down the drain. Resist any pressure from the salesman to tack on superfluous knick-knackery – remember he's on commission and wants the numbers on the bottom of his order to be as big as possible.

Sale **or** *return*

Some major manufacturers are now offering buyers a trial period to test and evaluate their new car choice. This can be anything from a couple of weeks to a whole month, with the option of a full refund or exchange vehicle if the customer is not completely satisfied. This kind of scheme is excellent news for the punter, but do be certain you've got full redress if you're not happy with the car. Watch the small print about how many miles you can do, what constitutes 'normal wear and tear' during your trial and, above all, make sure you're not liable for the full purchase price if your shiny new acquisition is damaged or stolen.

Automatic **versus** *manual*

On bigger luxury and prestige cars there is one factory fitted option always worth having – automatic transmission. Some big cars must be automatic if they're not to suffer a used price penalty. On some, mainly Mercedes, BMW 5 and 7 series and Jaguars, the manual variants can be worth as much as £1500 less than the automatics. A typical case is the Mercedes 190E. Manual 190Es aren't popular because of the heavy, lorry-like quality of the gear change, and used prices are much lower because used buyers always prefer the 190E automatic.

Price **rises**

What do you do if the price of the new car you've ordered rises before you've paid for it? You've two options. Either stump up the higher price or pull out of the deal and get your deposit refunded. Legally, your contract with the dealer is broken if the price rises, so you're quite within your rights to cancel the order. Generally, though, most dealers won't lose a sale over a price rise of a few per cent, so it's worth holding out and insisting that you pay the pre-increase price. If the dealer won't play ball, take your business to someone who will.

Checking out your **new car**

Before you actually accept delivery of your new car, make sure it's exactly what you ordered and doesn't have any faults. Getting your money back once you've driven away can be notoriously difficult, so take time, (before you leave the showroom), to check out your purchase. Ask yourself these questions:

✓ Are the bodywork and trim the colour you ordered?

✓ Are there any flaws in the paint finish like runs, scratches or mismatched colours on body panels? Are there any scuffs or other marks caused by sloppy pre-delivery treatment?

✓ Check that all the electrical equipment works – windows, central locking, radio, etc.

✓ As part of your pre-delivery inspection, take the car for a 20-minute test drive. A stiff gear change could mean the car has yet to loosen up, but a rattle from the engine might not be so simple. Warm the car up fully and open all the doors, windows, bonnet and boot. Check it over as if it was a secondhand car.

✓ If you do find any minor faults, insist they're put right immediately. Don't be fobbed off until the first service.

✓ If a major mechanical fault develops, let your dealer know immediately. Your legal contract is with him, not the manufacturer or importer. If you want to reject the car, don't let the dealer persuade you to have it repaired – this could prejudice your right of rejection. Leave the car with the dealer and keep a record of all correspondence – you may need it in court.

✓ If the dealer fails to put the problem right, go to the manufacturer. If they don't help, take your grievance to your local Trading Standards Office. Car manufacturers don't like bad publicity, so make plenty of noise until you're satisfied.

New **car scams** to watch for

New car dealers usually don't stoop to the tricks of the used car trade, but occasionally they have been known to try the odd bit of wool-pulling. Here are some of the more popular try-ons:

The disconnected **speedometer**

When a car is being delivered, driven on trade plates from one dealer to another, it has been known for unscrupulous dealers to disconnect the speedometer so the delivery mileage isn't recorded. When you check your new car over, look for stone chips on the bonnet and road grime under the wheel-arches, which may suggest your new car has already worn a groove in several motorways.

The price **confusion**

After agreeing a figure when taking the order, some dealers can tack on a couple of hundred pounds to the invoice price while you're not looking.

When you come to collect the car they explain away the unfortunate anomaly as confusion. See that the dealer writes down the total on the road price when you make your order. That way you can prove the mistake is the dealer's and not yours – so it's his problem.

Delivery charges

Make sure the price the dealer quotes you is the on the road price, which includes delivery, number plates and road tax. Delivery charges are a particularly unfair cost borne by the customer and cover the delivery of the new car to the dealer and his pre-delivery inspection or PDI. This can be as much as £400. There can't be many other manufacturers of consumer products who charge to have them delivered to retail outlets, so check delivery charges, the on the road or OTR price and what it includes.

Phantom extras

If your new car arrives with extras you didn't choose, don't be pushed into paying for them. Occasionally, a dealer will present a car to a customer with a sunroof, set of mud flaps or ski-bag that wasn't ordered, hoping he won't mind. It's the dealer's fault, so don't be told you should stump up any more money.

Special **editions**

A manufacturer's special or limited edition is usually a lower spec model with a few extras such as sunroof, fancy wheels and plusher trim. Limited editions are used to make certain models more attractive when sales are slow or a model is about to be replaced. Some dealerships make their own special editions which aren't worth any extra secondhand. We've seen Fiat Unos and Tipos – with garish stick-on body graphics, tacky plastic wheel trims and a pop-up glass sunroof – masquerading as something special with a special price tag. Avoid this type of dealer 'Limited Edition' at all costs. Buy the standard item or nothing at all.

Minimum **part-exchange**

You've seen the advertisements – £1500 Minimum Part-Exchange. Watch offers like this very carefully. They mean the dealer is prepared to flatter you with a subsidised price for your part-exchange. What he's not telling you is that the subsidy comes from his profit margin on the new car, which you'll be paying. Taking this route means it's difficult to know exactly how much discount you're actually getting. It also makes it hard to compare one dealer's offer with another. Far better to know you're getting a fair percentage off the list price than some artificially inflated price for your old car.

Extended **warranties**

Dealers also extract profit by selling extended warranties. While any form of extra cover on your new car is a good idea, some manufacturers have recently been offering a three-year warranty as standard, instead of the traditional 12-months. Mitsubishi were the first to pioneer this with their Diamond Care Three-Year Warranty. They were followed by Daihatsu, Hyundai, Jaguar, Lexus, Lotus, Mazda, Nissan, Rolls-Royce and Toyota, all offering three-year cover. With as many manufacturers as this throwing in a longer warranty, it's only a matter of time before everybody follows suit. Our advice is not to pay extra for any extended warranty, but to press for it to be included in the deal anyway. Some warranties can cost up to £500, so it's a handy negotiating point.

Warranty **cop-outs**

Another warranty scam to watch for is a three-year guarantee which is only the standard one-year manufacturer's warranty with two further years of much reduced cover tacked on. Sometimes you just get AA or RAC breakdown cover or holiday help abroad. Check that your extended warranty covers the car against all manufacturer's faults and defects for the full three years. Some give full details of their extended guarantees, while others can be advertised without qualification and are not as extensive as you might think.

Pre-delivery inspections

The Motor Agents Association Code of Practice states that every new car must have a pre-delivery inspection with written details available to potential buyers. One study showed that only 54 per cent of MAA members actually provide this information. With manufacturers extending the first service to as much as 10,000 miles from the date of first registration, there's a growing trend in the trade to skimp the PDI and put any faults right at the first service, which can sometimes be as much as a year away from the date of purchase. Before you hand over any money, get hold of a written copy of the PDI. If anything does go wrong and the dealership hasn't picked up that particular fault, you've got documentary proof that the work should have been carried out properly and wasn't.

Not so new

With new cars being stockpiled because of reduced demand, there are literally thousands furring up the system, sitting round for as long as a year before they're delivered. Ask the dealer the exact build date of the car you're about to buy and steer clear of anything that was built longer than six months ago. Cars don't like standing still for very long and you shouldn't be buying something that's been languishing in a compound for 12 months exposed to the elements. We know of one major manufacturer who's been stocking certain 'new vehicles' for as long as two years and is actually having to recondition them before sale.

A-z of new cars

a-Z **A**lfa Romeo

Service interval: *5-12,000*
Warranty: *36-months/60,000. 8-year anti-corrosion.*
74 dealers

145

Clever design and interesting to drive but lacks poise at the limit

Ratings

image	*Unconventional*
value	*Plenty*
quality	*Getting there*
depreciation	*Buy a lottery ticket*
comfort	*There are worse*
resale	*We'll see*
durability	*Untried*
driving	*Entertaining*

Best **b**uys

1.6L
Low cost fun

1.7 16 valve
Performance and luxury

Star **b**uy

1.6L
Max speed 114
0–60 11.5
Mixed mpg 34.3

For
Verve, Italianate individuality, generous space and equipment, safety features, zesty performance, 3 year warranty

Against
Lively ride, wayward handling, expensive ownership

Overall
Alfa's avant-garde addition to the 2.4 children market. Distinctive, perky, moderately pretty and bristling with features seldom seen on a tiny hatch. ABS, locking, windows, mirrors and PAS all standard but the sunroof's extra. Goes quickly but can handle skittishly. Highish insurance at Group 10. Looks like a vast improvement on the 33. Only time will tell if image and market acceptance can strengthen enough to erase a record of punitive depreciation and dodgy build. 1.6L likely to be a favourite

In a **W**ord
Bravissimo!

155

155 likely to depreciate fast as it hasn't won many friends

For

Smooth, supple and handles well. Distinctive and unusual Italian looks. Narcotic to drive, with lovely engine and race-bred sound effects. True 5-seater and very separate

Against

Hardly a pretty face. Cabin a bit synthetic. Poor driving position, leg and headroom. Depreciation not brilliant, so brand new purchase could cost you dear. One year old makes most sense

Overall

Brave assault on BMW 3-series market. Well-furnished, separate and distinctive, but probably still too quirky for mainstream British tastes. Fine chassis though. 4x4 Q4 extremely sure-footed

Ratings

image	*Off-focus*
value	*Only average*
quality	*Not bad*
depreciation	*Heavyish*
comfort	*Okay*
resale	*Tricky*
durability	*Fair*
driving	*Interesting*

Best **b**uys

2.0i Twin Spark
Low cost fun

2.5 V6 Sport
Performance and luxury

Q4
Speed and grip

Star **b**uy

1.8 Twin Spark
Max speed 124
0–60 10.3
Mixed mpg 33

In a **W**ord
Not a BMW 3-series beater

164

Classic big Alfa with brio, room and zoom. Best car in the range with sharp
handling and wonderful power plants

Ratings

image	*Stylish*
value	*Reasonable*
quality	*Getting better*
depreciation	*Not that bad*
comfort	*Cosseting*
resale	*Growing following*
durability	*Okay*
driving	*Marvellous*

Best *b*uys

2.0i Twin Spark
Economy and value

3.0 V6
Luxury and poise

Cloverleaf
Performance

Star *b*uy

164 2.0 Twin Spark
Max speed 130
0–60 9.7
Mixed mpg 36

For

Thinking man's image. A big car that drives like a small one. Crisp front wheel drive handling and buckets of poke. Individual. Glorious engines. Quick and spacious

Against

V6 model depreciates most. Dashboard requires some navigation. Still some glitches in the electrics. Build quality not yet up to BMW standards, and neither are the dealers

Overall

Fine executive alternative with plenty of style. Better than average reliability. Well-equipped. Lovely lines and disarming road manners. 24-valve engine a stormer, good resale and solid respectable middle-class image. Alfa's best effort yet

In a **W**ord
More separate than a BMW

Aston Martin a-**Z**

New *Cars*

Service interval: *5–10,000*
Warranty: *24-months/UL. 10 dealers*

DB7

Splendidly politically incorrect torpedo. Fast, elitist and megabucks to run
and buy. Last of the great leviathans

For
Mighty performance with taut and tractable
handling, rapturous looks and an aristocratic
interior

Against
No airbags, token rear space, gearstick blocks
stereo, slightly wallowy ride. Some problems
with early cars

Overall
Traditional and splendid grand tourer
reaffirming the Ford/Jaguar/Aston alliance of
superlative quality and classic craftsmanship.
Bills and depreciation will not be small but
sensory gratification and pride will be huge.
Supercharged pick-any-gear performance
from the slick manual, sporting yet civilised
point-and-squirt from the preferred self-
shifter. A true driver's car designed to flatter
and excite

Ratings
image *Elevated*
value *Don't ask*
quality *Superior*
depreciation *Hefty*
comfort *Resplendent*
resale *Always someone*
durability *Long-serving*
driving *Exhilarating*

Star buy
DB7
Max speed 159
0–60 5.9
Mixed mpg 15

In a Word
Cultured pearl

Audi

Service interval: *10/20,000*
Warranty: *36 months/60,000. 10-year anti-rust plus 3 year paint. 320 dealers*

A4

Poised, classy, affordable and rather chic, Audi's new baby casts a shadow over BMW's 3 Series

Ratings

image	*Coming on*
value	*Massive*
quality	*It's German*
depreciation	*No worries*
comfort	*For four*
resale	*Promising*
durability	*Watertight*
driving	*Involving*

Best **b**uys

1.8
Budget panache

2.6 SE
A real sleeper

2 litre TD1
Economy

Star **b**uy

1.8
Max speed 127
0–60 10.5
Mixed mpg 35.6

For

Brilliant chassis, crisp steering, almost rear wheel drive handling

Against

Lack of status, oversharp brakes, named after a road

Overall

Leagues better than the outgoing 80, with calm ride and neat handling. Lots of equipment and lots of engines. V6 2.6 a winner, 2.0-litre TDi a useful package. Better value than a 3 Series and almost as good as a C Class Merc. Easily able to rub bumpers with the best of the Brat Pack, and who knows, before very long Audi could supplant BMW as the happening car. Watch this space

In a **W**ord
Ingolstadt's ingot

Coupe

Audi coupe has grip, grunt and looks, is long lived but pricey

For

Solid and built by the same people who make Volkswagens. Quite stylish with bomb-proof mechanicals and ten year anti-corrosion perforation warranty. Sizeable rear room for a coupe. Turbo Quattro S2 very quick

Against

Choppy ride. Vocal engine. Steering lacks feel. Saloon underpinning shows through. Doesn't hold its value like a Calibra or a BMW 3 Series coupe.

Overall

Solid but over-priced. Outgunned by Calibra, Nissan 200SX, BMW 325i coupe and Mazda MX6. Feels hewn from granite, though, with long-lasting quality feel. Used values not brilliant

Ratings

image	*Classy*
value	*No bargain*
quality	*Endless*
depreciation	*Not clever*
comfort	*It's a coupe*
resale	*Iffy*
durability	*Like a rock*
driving	*Not there yet*

Star buy
16V
Max speed 129
0–60 9.7
Mixed mpg 30.9

In a Word
Could do better
for the money

A6

Fine flagship and impressive from every angle. Wonderful diesel and practical estates. We like 'em

Ratings

image	*Shoulder padded*
value	*Not bad*
quality	*Top drawer*
depreciation	*Could be worse*
comfort	*Huge*
resale	*It'll go*
durability	*Properly made*
driving	*Fine*

Best buys

2.6E
Value and class

TDi Estate
Charisma with sense

S6 Estate
Obscene speed

Star buy

2.6 SE
Max speed 130
0–60 9.3
Mixed mpg 29.6

For

Fluent lines, peerless engineering, superb turbodiesel, useful six-speed box

Against

Costly ownership, a bit clinical, austere teutonic cabin

Overall

Squeaky clean 100 successor that's a winner. Thoroughly civilised driver, generously equipped, supremely safe and completely respectable, it's a modern manager's machine, but a bit short on glam. Estates well regarded. 2.6 and 2.8 quite quick. Six-speed TDi runs on charity. Wicked S6 is the one to have. Competition for executive favours is stiff at this level, so you'll need to be well into Audis not to be seduced by a 5 Series or an E Class. We'd buy the A6 just to be different

In a Word
Drive one, you'll like it

A8

Audi's aluminium cruiser can take on the best. Superb equipment, the freshest image in town and guaranteed individuality

For
Silence, speed, sybaritic luxury, technical pre-eminence. Refreshingly different

Against
Audi badge. Unknown depreciation. Won't be cheap to run.

Overall
Exceedingly impressive top person's torpedo. Inside it's like a Roller, outside it's a rakish projectile capable of 150 mph plus in 4.2 V8 guise. Handling is unerring, appointments lavish and driving experience restorative. Basic 2.8 model a serious competitor for 5 and 7 Series BMW buyers. Majestic 4.2 4x4 a credible and distinctive S Class alternative. Shrewd buyers will look beyond its badge

Ratings
image	*The best*
value	*Appreciable*
quality	*A class act*
depreciation	*Won't be good*
comfort	*Sit back and relax*
resale	*Likely to be good*
durability	*Adamantine*
driving	*Seventh heaven*

Best buys
2.8
Individual value
4.2 Quattro
Handling and grip

Star buy
2.8
Max speed 136
0–60 11
Mixed mpg 27.2

In a Word
Very special indeed

Service interval: *12,000*
Warranty: *12-months/UL. 6-year anti-rust. 161 dealers*

Compact

BMW's Escort chaser brings the blue propellor to the Jelson estate. Nice
enough if you like that sort of thing

Ratings

image	*White sock*
value	*Add up the extras?*
quality	*Pretty good*
depreciation	*Non-existent*
comfort	*Surprising*
resale	*All day long*
durability	*Guaranteed*
driving	*Jolly*

Star **b**uy
318 Ti
Max speed 130
0–60 9.6
Mixed mpg 33.2

For
Slicker than a GTi, and almost as cheap. Predictable handling, gilt edged secondhand values

Against
Slow 1.6. Not that affordable once extras inflate the price. What will become of its image…?

Overall
Marketing finesse at its most accomplished. An aspirational plaything to suit every driveway. BMW's newest baby is a smug, we've-got-loads-of-dough rear-wheel drive hatchback with impeccable road manners, modest price tag and assertive aura. Spec's not too hot (no alloys, windows or roof) but ABS, PAS, side impacts and driver's airbag are all standard. You could buy something with more toys, but you're more interested in cutting a mild suburban dash, aren't you?

In a **W**ord
Marketing
at its most calculated

3 Series

3 Series is seriously trendy with bullet proof residuals – so depreciation is glacial. Accomplished too...

For

Feels solid and looks special. Brisk performance from all but 1.6. Class leading ride and handling, excellent diesels and super swift M3. Beat scores of buyers off when you come to sell

Against

Essential but optional equipment such as stereo and sunroof hike up the price. With Compact and sales into the company car market the 3 Series image is not what it used to be. Can BMW sell volume cars and still be 'The Ultimate Driving Machine'?

Overall

Sensible, affordable, long-term buy. Needs relatively little maintenance. Built to last, holds value well. Brilliant 5-speed auto. Useful Touring estates. Pleasing well-engineered package

Ratings

image	*Fading a bit*
value	*High*
quality	*Impressive*
depreciation	*Low*
comfort	*Okay*
resale	*A breeze*
durability	*Proven*
driving	*Impressive*

Best buys

318i
Value package

325i Coupe
Grace and pace

Star buy

318i
Max speed 125
0–60 11.3
Mixed mpg 36.7

In a Word

World's finest small saloon

5 Series

5 Series makes an interesting executive express. Touring estates much
fancied and electifying M5 fast becoming a cult car

Ratings

image	*Slipping*
value	*Worth it*
quality	*Impressive*
depreciation	*Not bad*
comfort	*Touch cramped*
resale	*Endless*
durability	*Robust*
driving	*Interesting*

Best **b**uys
525i SE
Luxury

535i Sport
Speed and style

Star **b**uy
540
Max speed 149
0–60 6.6
Mixed mpg 24.6

For
Smooth, stylish and practical saloon. Body
and mechanical longevity now proven. Image
slipping though as secondhand ones fall into
the wrong hands. Predictable maintenance
and depreciation costs

Against
Poor rear head and leg room. Enjoyable
options mean more money. Slightly too
assertive 80s image. Thinking buyers go for
an Audi…

Overall
Still has presence and flair with titanium-
tough build quality. Easily capable of
100,000 miles without incident. Smaller
engined 520 and 525 and estates hold value
longest, best with auto and SE pack. Diesels
good news. 540 best of bunch. Sensible good
value long-term buy. Due to be replaced soon

In a **W**ord
Best in class

7 Series

7 Series despite face lift is getting a bit long in the tooth. Such corpulence
is out of kilter with the caring, sharing 90s

For

Tremendous quality, space, equipment and
presence. Wonderful comfort and more
gadgets than Cape Canaveral. 740 very quick

Against

One of the highest depreciators in its class,
with running costs to match. Not as refined
as some would say

Overall

Exudes terrific authority and big money
image, but expect plenty of envy scratches
and people not letting you out at junctions.
Not as quiet or smooth-riding as a Jaguar but
better built. Elegant executive torpedo but
excellent 5-series could well be a better bet,
with much lower whole-life costs. 7 Series are
not funny come trade-in time. You pays your
money and takes your choice

Ratings

image	*Top man*
value	*If you have to ask…*
quality	*Prussian perfection*
depreciation	*Shiversome*
comfort	*Drives itself*
resale	*A bitter pill*
durability	*Forever*
driving	*Get out of my way*

Best **b**uys

730i V8
Best value
740iL
Space and luxury

Star **b**uy

740i
Max speed 155
0–60 7.4
Mixed mpg 24.4

In a **W**ord
Too big to be beautiful

840 Ci - 850 CSi

Glorious looks, equipment, finish and one of the most exclusive grand tourers around

Ratings

image	*Very slick*
value	*Not really*
quality	*Matchless*
depreciation	*Titanic*
comfort	*Rest cure*
resale	*Up to a point*
durability	*Robust*
driving	*Too insulating*

Star *buy*
840 Ci
Max speed 155
0–60 7.4
Mixed mpg 25

For
Exquisitely detailed and elegant grand tourer. Cosseting and comfortable. Awesome street cred. Stunningly beautiful and very special

Against
Expensive. Little driver involvement. Big depreciation. Cramped inside and doesn't feel that exciting at the limit

Overall
Too comfortable, plush and detached to get excited about. All but drives itself. V8 840 is best value and a better all-round buy. Porsche 928 GTS and Jaguar XJR-S might be dynamically superior to the 8 Series but somehow they don't have that Cote d'Azur magic. 850CSi has six-speed gearbox and awsome, tyre smoking 386bhp

In *a* **W**ord
Gloriously over-priced

Bentley a-z
New *Cars*

Service interval: *6,000*
Warranty: *36 months/50,000. 37 dealers*

Continental - Turbo R - Brooklands

Continental is classiest throne room around. Big, beautiful and very, very fast. Should be for a hundred and eighty seven grand!

For
Absolute aristocratic authority. Prodigious performance. Beautifully built. Much more panache than a Royce, the Bentley badge has come back in a big way

Against
Big money, big thirst, big bills, big envy

Overall
Elegant, quiet and understated plutocratic carriages with hand-built charm. Turbo R very quick (R for road-holding). Continental chic and classy. Brooklands is entry-level model at £99,000 but if you've got that much dough to blow you might as well go the whole way and have a Turbo R at £132,000. There is a certain surreal pleasure in feeling two tons of motor car hit 150mph. One day they won't be allowed to make cars like these. Shame that…

Ratings
image	*Unmatched*
value	*Not really*
quality	*Terrific*
depreciation	*Do you care?*
comfort	*Obscene*
resale	*To the right man*
durability	*Albert Memorial*
driving	*Splendid*

Best buys
Brooklands
Relative affordability
Turbo R
Grin-inspiring performance

Star buy
Turbo S
Max speed 155
0–60 5.8
Mixed mpg 12

In a Word
Absolute oneupmanship

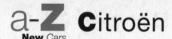

Citroën

Service interval: *9,000 (6,000 diesel)*
Warranty: *12 months/UL (XM 36 months/UL). 242 dealers*

AX

AX might be an antique but it's tremendous value, competent and much more interesting than a Fiesta

Ratings

image	*Chic*
value	*Brilliant*
quality	*Getting better*
depreciation	*Not terrible*
comfort	*All elbows*
resale	*Instant*
durability	*Average*
driving	*Competant*

Best *buys*

1.5 D Debut
Inexpensive

1.1i Forte
Cheaper than walking

Star *buy*

1.5 D Echo Plus
Max speed 98
0–60 12.7
Mixed mpg 61

For

Neat, compact, with plenty of Gallic flair. Excellent value with dealers who are prepared to negotiate. Thrifty diesel

Against

Not that roomy inside and rivals like the Micra, Corsa and Clio are making it look and feel its age. Can seem a bit tinny too

Overall

Citröen's smallest model makes an ideal budget runabout with small change ownership costs. 1.5 D incredibly frugal with 61 mpg and evergreen resale. Cheaper and more individual 106/Fiesta competitor. Outgunned in virtually every area by the new crop of super-minis, but the AX still has something they don't – individuality and class. We reckon it's a little dearie

In a **W**ord
Sensibly different

ZX

ZX is one of the best medium-sized hatches and estates you can buy, and one of our favourites. Sensible, cost-efficient and a honey to drive

For
Smooth ride that only French cars have. Poised handling, sensible price, and plenty of room especially with that sliding rear seat. Refined turbo diesels can make you believe in oil burners. Volcane TD is a diesel that goes

Against
Precious little, so don't expect much discount. There are few better hatches on the market

Overall
A splendid all-rounder, Citröen's ZX is a burster. Brilliant diesels, fiery performance from Volcane and Furio. Secondhand ones are rare and pricey. This is one car that which-ever model you choose your money will be as safe as bullion. Much much more interesting and charismatic than Ford's dreary Escort

Ratings
image	*Different*
value	*Stonking*
quality	*No problems*
depreciation	*Minimal*
comfort	*Excellent*
resale	*Buyers are queuing*
durability	*Looking good*
driving	*Crisp*

Best buys
Volcane TD
Speed and thrift
1.9 D Estate
Room and zoom

Star buy
1.9 TD Volcane
Max speed 115
0–60 10.3
Mixed mpg 47.4

In a Word
Citroën's finest hour

Xantia

Xantia is just about the only mainstream saloon on the market with a smudge of style. If you want a cracking family saloon, this is it

Ratings
- **i**mage *Classy*
- **v**alue *Pretty good*
- **q**uality *Getting better*
- **d**epreciation *Healthy*
- **c**omfort *Lots of room*
- **r**esale *Kids stuff*
- **d**urability *No problems yet*
- **d**riving *Agile*

Star **b**uy
2.0 VSX 16v
Max speed 132
0–60 9.0
Mixed mpg 31.2

For
Different, class leading ride, comely looks, very high build quality, lots of leg, head and shoulder room, clever, trick suspension, with Hydractive system the most sophisiticated of any car in its class

Against
Drone on motorways, noisy rear wiper, vocal 8-valve engines at idle. 8-valve 2.0 litre a bit underpowered. Shame that those wonderfully quirky Citroën interiors have disappeared.

Overall
Refined Cavalier and Mondeo competitor that's put Citroën on the bestsellers list. Excellent all-rounder, handsome styling, slumberland ride, and the best built Citroën yet. Handome estate versions in a showroom near you soon

In a **W**ord
A car apart

XM

XM Estates and Diesels hold value longest. Comfortable, expansive and smooth-running too. New 2.5 TD a peach

For

Individual looks, good to drive, loads of gismos, huge estates, fine diesels. Three year warrranty

Against

Depreciation, ownership costs, eccentric image, silly foot-operated handbrake

Overall

A valiant effort for Citroën's flagship, and much better than the old XM. Reliability is licked, if not the depreciation. Acres of space, wonderfully comfortable and so much more separate than Granada/Rover 800/Omega competititors. Citroën dealers are nice blokes and discounts should be the order of the day. Doesn't hold value that well, so shrewdest buy would be nearly new, tiny mileage example

Ratings

image	*Nicely quirky*
value	*Pricey*
quality	*High*
depreciation	*Not so clever*
comfort	*Expansive*
resale	*Tricky*
durability	*Pretty good*
driving	*Slumberland*

Best buys

2.0i Turbo VSX
Big car, small bills

V6 3.0 Estate
Smooth and quick

Star buy

2.5 TD VSX
Max speed 124
0–60 10.4
Mixed mpg 39.6

In a Word

Refreshingly unusual

a-Z Daewoo
New Cars

Service interval: *3-year free servicing, free courtesy car*
Warranty: *36 months/60,000. 6-year anti-rust.*
19 car centres

Nexia

Nexia is an old Astra warmed over, but offers the most comprehensive
peace of mind package of any car manufacturer in the country

Ratings
image	*None*
value	*Loads*
quality	*Not bad*
depreciation	*Won't be bad*
comfort	*Average*
resale	*Hard to say*
durability	*Okay*
driving	*Dreary*

Star **b**uy
1.5 GLi
Max speed 101
0–60 12.3
Mixed mpg 40.3

For
Angst-free motoring, standard ABS, no-haggle prices, 22 carat customer care

Against
Old-fashioned styling, unadventurous handling, poor ride, 70s dashboard

Overall
To expect the Nexia to be anything but what it is would be an act of the purest optimism. This is a tarted up Astra that comes with a truly amazing warranty and after-care package – like three years' free servicing, free delivery and lots of retail foreplay. Both models have 1.5 engines but woolly gear changes and get noisy at the limit. Handling is nose-heavy and passenger room not great. But for those who want to take the pain and fear out of car buying, Deawoo have Car Centres, not dealers

In a **W**ord
One-stop shopping

Espero

Espero is a Cavalier under the skin, doesn't look bad, has good spec and
plenty of space plus that gilt-edged warranty

For
Lots of bits, loads of room, CDi has air con

Against
Lively ride, some of the plastic's tacky, resale
prospects uncertain

Overall
Actually much better than you'd think with a
pleasing amalgam of equipment, room and
practicality. Apart from a slightly twitchy
ride and dead steering, it's okay. Engines can
moan a bit under load but all have standard
driver's airbag, side impact beams, ABS and
power steering. If you don't mind driving a
car with no image whatsoever, the Espero
really is good value at between £10,500 and
£12,200. Service them at any Halfords, pay
no delivery charges, and get a free mobile
telephone. Sounds like a good deal to us

Ratings
image	*Not really*
value	*Resounding*
quality	*Looking good*
depreciation	*Uncertain*
comfort	*Okay*
resale	*Too early to tell*
durability	*Promising*
driving	*Reasonable*

Star **b**uy
1.8 CDi
Max speed 112
0–60 10.8
Mixed mpg 34.5

In a **W**ord
King of the consumers

a-z Daihatsu
New Cars

Service interval: *6,000*
Warranty: *3 years/UL. 120 dealers*

Mira

Mira is tiny but has a big price. Fine for town toddling but pretty inept at anything else. Buy a Nissan Micra instead

Ratings

image	*Oddball*
value	*Not good*
quality	*It's Japanese*
depreciation	*Not so hot*
comfort	*Threadbare*
resale	*Hard work*
durability	*Strong*
driving	*Hopeless*

Star buy
Mira
Max speed 85
0–60 21.0
Mixed mpg 51

For
Unintimidating dinkiness, thrift, social respectability and political correctness

Against
Slow, small boot, zero image, pricey, as much fun as a luke-warm bath

Overall
Charming, but there are better small cars, such as the Corsa. Not in the Nissan Micra class and really for those who are impossibly town-bound or congenitally unable to park. It may be the best-selling mini-car in Japan but it certainly isn't here. Hard to sell as nobody knows what they are

In a Word
Buy a Micra

Charade

Charade makes lots of sense. Long warranty, oriental build quality, containable ownership costs, but howlingly dull

For

Sprightly engines, taut handling and generous spec. Sound value

Against

Shallow boot, cramped rear, engines shout when pushed hard. Not overly frugal. Geriatric image

Overall

Brisk performance but jiggly ride and nervous handling. Well-equipped and finished. Sensibly priced. Commendable 3-year warranty. We'd choose a ZX any day though

Ratings

image	*Steady*
value	*Reasonable*
quality	*Fine*
depreciation	*Tolerable*
comfort	*Okay*
resale	*Tricky*
durability	*Good*
driving	*Average*

Star **b**uy
1.3 GLXi
Max speed 103
0–60 11.2
Mixed mpg 41.8

In a **W**ord
Could do better

Applause

Silly name, plain Jane looks, average abilities. Applause is not really a
credible mainstream motor

Ratings

image	*Off-focus*
value	*Reasonable*
quality	*Solid*
depreciation	*Average*
comfort	*Okay*
resale	*Not easy*
durability	*Fine*
driving	*Lively*

Best **b**uys

1.6 GXi
Value and reliability

Star **b**uy

1.6 GXi
Max speed 115
0–60 9.4
Mixed mpg 39.7

For

Bags of equipment and plenty of room.
Workmanlike all-rounder

Against

Blunt ride and unrefined engine. High
insurance. Soulless

Overall

Faceless but sensible saloon-shaped
hatchback. Spacious and well-finished. Fast
depreciation. Pleasant driver, solid reliability,
but fails to charm. Long warranty. There are
a score of other cars we'd choose before the
Applause. This car has no right to be so
terribly dreary. Leave them to the wrinklies
with the Zimmerframes. If you're remotely
interested in your image, then this isn't the
car for you.

In a **W**ord
The slow hand-clap

Sportrak

Not pretty and pretty unrefined. Engine with 16 valves lively enough but the whole plot is let down by its tractor-like suspension

For
Reasonable mountain climbing abilities. Bullet-proof build quality and not quite so twinky as a Suzuki Vitara

Against
Disappointing on-road performance, thirsty. Joggly ride, lurid paint job and toytown looks

Overall
Not obviously trendy but business-like and tough. Nicely finished and well screwed together. Touch cramped and dreadful road ride so not a long-distance cruiser. 16v ELXi smooth and responsive. Hardly a serious form of transport unless you spend your days commuting up the North face of the Eiger. Be warned that 4x4 residuals could fall off the edge before very long. Buy a Land Rover, they're still the best

Ratings
image	*Not bad*
value	*Reasonable*
quality	*Hardy*
depreciation	*Tolerable*
comfort	*Rough and ready*
resale	*Not impossible*
durability	*Lasts well*
driving	*Dull*

Star **b**uy
1.6 ELXi
Max speed 93
0–60 13.2
Mixed mpg 28.7

In a **W**ord
Crude but cheerful

Fourtrak

One of scores of wannabee off-roaders, Fourtrak doesn't have the street cred of a Vitara

Ratings
image	*Suburban*
value	*Fair*
quality	*Well built*
depreciation	*Average*
comfort	*Not really*
resale	*Takes time*
durability	*Solid*
driving	*Unrefined*

Star **b**uy
2.8 TDS
Max speed 84
0–60 15.0
Mixed mpg 27.9

For
Reasonable off-roader. Turbodiesel has tremendous lugging power.

Against
Blunt looks, choppy ride and headstrong handling

Overall
Convincing, inexpensive 4x4 with plenty of space and fine engines. Less trendy than a Sportrak but more versatile. Does not have the Discovery/Shogun image, but used values remain firmish. Rare sight, too.

In a **W**ord
A Vitara is better

60

Service interval: *10,000*
Warranty: *3 years/60,000. 6-year paint. 92 dealers*

Viper

Viper is wonderfully anti-establishment. Irresponsible, impractical,
electrifying, conspicuous and just plain crazy...

For

Epic performance and looks, 400 bhp V10
8.0-litre engine, back-to-basics technology,
6-speed gearbox, innovative design

Against

Left-hand drive only, vestigial weather
equipment. Watch out for Plod

Overall

Latterday AC Cobra delivering gut-
wrenching performance and wild looks.
Insatiable American demand means they'll be
a rare sight here. Despite the suggestion of
brutality, it's actually an easy car to drive. For
extroverts only. Hard top very useful. Despite
the rhetoric prices haven't reached the
stratosphere. Not likely to either

Ratings

image	*Naughty*
value	*Lots of it*
quality	*Pretty good*
depreciation	*Not bad*
comfort	*Don't be silly*
resale	*Guaranteed*
durability	*Promising*
driving	*Wow!*

Star buy
Viper V10
Max speed 160
0–60 5.0
Mixed mpg 15.2

In a Word
Real wild child

Service interval: *6,000*
Warranty: *24 months/UL. 18 dealers*

348 SP/GTC

Drop dead gorgeous, the 348 is a poem in steel. The looks and sound to make grown men lie awake at nights

Ratings

image	*Stonking*
value	*It's only money*
quality	*Better*
depreciation	*Don't ask*
comfort	*Cramped*
resale	*Desirable*
durability	*Not bad*
driving	*Delightful*

Star buy
348GTC
Max speed 179
0–60 5.4
Mixed mpg 22.5

For

Intoxicating looks, wonderful engine, delightfully communicative and involving

Against

Hard ride, tiring steering – but let's not carp

Overall

Neat, compact and vivacious slingshot. Hard work at speed, but richly rewarding. Wonderfully finished, tremendous brakes and well-organised cabin. Feels gloriously special. Twitchy in the wet, not that you'd ever drive it in the rain. We reckon the GTC looks better than the Spyder and at 80 odd grand it's a hell of a lot of car for the money. Well heeled playboys only

In a Word
Pint-sized perfection

F355 Berlinetta/GTS

355 is one of the best cars in the world and even better than the 348

For

Sublime beauty, vibrant power, civilised driving position, magnificent electronic damping

Against

Mighty ownership costs, heavyish clutch, social opprobrium

Overall

The final expression of wealth, power, discrimination, sophistication and style. Rest of the world will immediately detest you. A challenging yet tractable machine that instantly repays responsible, deft and instinctive handling. PAS is crisp, suspension outstandingly cushioning and gear selection taut despite brawny clutch. Everything's adjustable, controls are finely balanced and the cabin's an artistic fusion of race-bred pedigree and technical excellence. A transport of delight

Ratings

image	*Exalted*
value	*You want more?*
quality	*Hand-crafted*
depreciation	*Who cares*
comfort	*Surprisingly good*
resale	*Too good to sell*
durability	*Matchless*
driving	*Better than drugs*

Star buy

355 Berlinetta
Max speed 183
0–60 4.7
Mixed mpg 18.0

In a Word

The apex of achievement

456

456 is major money but has pant-wetting looks and the manners of a
debutante, though 355 is better value

Ratings

image	*None better*
value	*Hardly cheap*
quality	*Fine*
depreciation	*Don't worry*
comfort	*Reasonable*
resale	*Instant*
durability	*Much better*
driving	*Amazing*

Star **b**uy
456 GT
Max speed 195
0–60 5.2
Mixed mpg 16.4

For

Gorgeous lines, 2+2, civilised equipment,
V12 performance, strutting style

Against

Price, ownership costs (insure it if you can)

Overall

Nice to see another 4-seater Ferrari.
Promising build quality, modern fittings,
useful 6-speed gearbox, well-weighted
servotronic power steering. In your face
image and at £151,000 it's no bargain.
Already the speculators have gathered like
vultures as they sense an instant classic in the
making. This is a modern Daytona without
the bad manners. If you can afford one, put
it under a dust sheet, if you can't, buy a 355

In a **W**ord
Marilyn Monroe
in metal

512

512 is Testarossa replacement. Big, wide, conspicuous and a mean, bad
mother of a motor

For

Glorious engine, sound effects, poise and
pliancy.

Against

Cramped, disorganised switchgear, but who
cares?

Overall

Once the finest supercar in the world, now
eclipsed by new F50. A revamped Testarossa,
the 512TR is an absolute burster. Awesome
mile-eating ability, leech-like grip and
perfectly civilised to boot. A real stunner and
not that dear at £131,000. Only a handful of
cars in history have had this car's wheel-arch
filling presence. Really belongs on a Miami
Vice set

Ratings

image	*Millionaires only*
value	*Not bad*
quality	*Beautiful*
depreciation	*Heavy*
comfort	*Basic*
resale	*Pretty good*
durability	*No problems*
driving	*Jaw dropping*

Star buy

512TR
Max speed 192
0–60 4.2
Mixed mpg 18.7

In a Word

Incomparable

Service interval: *9,000*
Warranty: *12 months/UL. 8-year anti-rust. 213 dealers*

Cinquecento

Cinquecento is a big small car, you can even wear a hat. One day all cars
will be this big

Ratings
image	*Chic*
value	*A bargain*
quality	*Looks good*
depreciation	*Very low*
comfort	*Roomy*
resale	*A breeze*
durability	*Okay*
driving	*Charming*

Star buy
Cinquecento SX
Max speed 87
0–60 17.8
Mixed mpg 47.6

For
Economy, room, build quality, price,
dinkiness. Wonderful Cinquecento Sporting

Against
Mid-70s interior, rubbery gear change, hard
work on motorways

Overall
Cute, charming and keenly priced. Could be
one of Fiat's best sellers. Small but feels big,
thrifty yet lively to drive. Stylish minimalist
fun. Looks well screwed together, too. Made
in Poland and bristling with clever design.
Full four seater with decent sized boot. Go
for the SX which has sunroof, central locking
and electric windows. For the money it's one
of the best small cars you can buy, with the
sort of classless image that only the Mini has.
One of Fiat's best cars this decade

In a Word
Small but perfectly formed

Panda

Panda 1000 CLX has good ride but driving position is awful. Had its day now and massively outgunned by the Cinquecento

For

Cheaper than walking and totally undemanding. Thoroughly competent shopping trolley

Against

Looks passé now. Poor resale values. Hard ride. Light on creature comforts

Overall

Fourteen years on and no longer engaging. Precious little performance or refinement, but build quality and rust resistance better than they were. Selecta is one of the cheapest automatics you can buy. Inconsequential insurance. Awesome frugality, but there are scores of much, much better small cars than this one, all of them more comfortable and refined

Ratings

image	*Small*
value	*Better used*
quality	*Reasonable*
depreciation	*Average*
comfort	*Subterranean*
resale	*Falling off*
durability	*Fragile*
driving	*Hard work*

Star buy
1000 CLX
Max speed 87
0–60 15.8
Mixed mpg 45.6

In a Word
End of an era

Uno

Uno is well-equipped, roomy and immensely practical. Build quality a million miles better than it was. Chic too

Ratings

image	*Dinky*
value	*Worth it*
quality	*Improving*
depreciation	*Average*
comfort	*Welcoming*
resale	*All right*
durability	*Proven*
driving	*Lively*

Star buy

45 Fire
Max speed 90
0–60 17.1
Mixed mpg 40

For

Neat, space-efficient and versatile. Cheap to live with. Quite stylish. Pleasing road manners

Against

Crumbling used values. Getting on in years now. Unsatisfying gear selection

Overall

Upstaged by Clio, AX and Pug 106, but still endearing. Crisp handling and responsive performance from 45 Fire engine. Impressive economy. 5-dr sells best. Uno Turbos depreciate alarmingly fast. As small cars go the Uno is fine and an extremely cost efficient purchase. Dealers will bid low come part exchange time but still a good bet on the private market. Italianate image makes it much more interesting than a Fiesta or Micra. Cheaper as well

In a Word

Cheap and able

Tipo

Teapot makes a refreshing Escort competitor. Huge room, safe and generously equipped, goes well except for diesels

For

Taut, agile, inexpensive and capacious

Against

Italianate driving position, fiddly switchgear, used values not the firmest. Quality could be better

Overall

Strong practical package that's fun to drive. Galvanised body, amazing carrying capacity. Well equipped and sensibly priced. 16–valve Sedicivalvole makes an interesting warm hatch. Good value for the money. SX versions best spec. Avoid rough and raucous diesels. Pleasing suburban image means used prices stay this side of reasonable. If it was us, we'd buy a few month old tiny mileage example and save a grand or so. Brava and Bravo 3- and 5-door hatches due to replace the Tipo soon

Ratings

i*mage* *Respectable*
v*alue* *High*
q*uality* *Some niggles*
d*epreciation* *Fair*
c*omfort* *Excellent*
r*esale* *In the end*
d*urability* *Reasonable*
d*riving* *Pleasing*

Star **b**uy
2.0ie 16valve
Max speed 123
0–60 9.3
Mixed mpg 29.3

In a **W**ord
Not your usual Earl Grey

Punto

Punto is the finest Fiat and the equal of Corsa or Micra. Cracking value for money too. GT Turbo a burster

Ratings

image *Chic*
value *Keen*
quality *Much better*
depreciation *Undramatic*
comfort *High*
resale *No problem*
durability *Improving*
driving *Interesting*

Best buys

55S
Low cost fun

GT
Power and flair

Cabrio ELX
Drop-top economy

Star buy

55S
Max speed 93
0–60 16.5
Mixed mpg 43.8

For

Modernity, safety, value, space, styling, and joie de vivre, six-speed gearbox

Against

Unyielding seats, bit heavy at parking speeds

Overall

Trendy and refined suburban shuttle fast winning friends. Giugiaro styling is seductive, space is uncannily plentiful, driving brisk and safety features extensive. Self-contained neatness a major plus point in the keenly contested supermini arena. Slight looks belie great strength and large feel. Turbocharged GT tops 125mph. Even the 55S is whizzy with a class-leading interior, decent performance, room for four and a promising resale. Great value

In a Word
Lovable little one

Tempra

Tempra is based on Tipo floorpan but is no matinee idol. Depreciation is heavy and resale likely to be hard work on all except estates

For
Comfort, room, performance, equipment, galvanised body, price

Against
Used values collapsing. Dull styling and boomy engines

Overall
Able enough booted Tipo with enormous cabin, failsafe handling and plenty of kit. Somehow doesn't have the Tipo's flair. Build quality okay, but nowhere near Cavalier Mondeo or Primera standards. Estate models the only one the market likes. Turbodiesel quick, frugal and vastly underrated. Tempra makes a decent enough hack as long as the price is right. We'd buy a nearly new, small mileage Turbo diesel and save a fortune

Ratings
image	*Lacklustre*
value	*Cheap to buy*
quality	*Only fair*
depreciation	*Heavy*
comfort	*Very good*
resale	*A struggle*
durability	*Reasonable*
driving	*Uneventful*

Best buys
1.6SX
Price and fittings
1.9Tds
Thrift and resale

Star buy
1.6 SX
Max speed 106
0–60 13.8
Mixed mpg 33.6

In a Word
Worth a look

Coupe

Striking Italianate lines, clever retro detailing, crisp handling and urgent
performance means this one's likely to be a big hit

Ratings
image *Youthful*
value *Looks a lot*
quality *Feels tight*
depreciation *Not horrendous*
comfort *It's a coupe*
resale *Cinch*
durability *Won't crumble*
driving *Engaging*

Star **b**uy
Coupe 16v
Max speed 130
0–60 9.0
Mixed mpg 30.7

For
Sporting bloodline, joyously pretty, delicate
handling, sure-footedness, classic charm

Against
Awkward gearchange, daft pedal layout, bit
claustrophobic

Overall
Charming Pininfarina-sculpted *objet d'art*
with unfailing Viscodrive traction, intelligent
and ample interior, feline litheness and
supercar beauty. More than just an ornament
– 16v performance is lusty – but pedals are
too heavily offset and gearbox unwilling to
make fast or fluent changes. A real head-
turner though with stylish and bold design
that shouts innovation from stem to stern.
2.0 litre 16-valve is quick but turbo charged
version will knock on the door of 150mph.
Just love that painted metal dash

In a **W**ord
Well stunning

barchetta

barchetta (with a small 'b') is gorgeously retrospective. Lively performance, good equipment but left hand drive only

For
Looks, doorhandles, airbag, performance, exclusivity

Against
Left hand drive, bit cramped, not cheap

Overall
Better than the MX5 and MGF the barchetta is a 90s interpretation of 60s tartmobiles complete with hooded headlamps, white gauges and period alloy wheels. Smooth 1.8 16-valve engine has 130bhp and romps to over 120mph. Front-wheel drive with five speed gearbox means handling is neat and sharp. Twin chrome tailpipes make a lovely noise. Ride is forgiving, power steering light and interior cosy. Options include passenger airbag, leather, air con and a hard top.

Ratings

image	*Classic*
value	*£14,000*
quality	*Fine*
depreciation	*Low*
comfort	*Not bad*
resale	*Easy*
durability	*No worries*
driving	*Lovely*

Star buy
barchetta 16v
Max speed 125
0–60 8.5
Mixed mpg 30

In a Word
Unadulterated good fun

Ford

Service interval: *10,000*
Warranty: *12 months/UL. 6-year anti-rust. 1,066 dealers*

Fiesta

Fiesta is well worth buying. Cheap, capable, simple to mend with lots of
safety features and power steering is a huge boon

Ratings
image *Improving*
value *Good*
quality *Fine*
depreciation *Low*
comfort *Okay*
resale *A breeze*
durability *It's a Ford*
driving *Predictable*

Best buys
1.8D
Poke and parsimony
1.6Si
Speed and practicality

Star buy
1.3LX
Max speed 94
0–60 13.3
Mixed mpg 43.4

For
Useful, spacious, high resale and
uncomplicated. Vast dealer network

Against
Sluggish 1.3, unsympathetic dealer network,
sporting versions not that hot

Overall
One of Ford's best-sellers but up against
fierce competition from Micra, Corsa and
Punto. Predictable running costs, solid
quality and strong used values keep them
selling. 1.8 diesel tough and cheap. XR2i
16V and RS1800 high fun factor but ruffian
reputation. Petrol versions a better bet than
diesel. Optional power steering well worth
having, as are driver and passenger airbags.
Due to be replaced by new model soon, so
watch depreciation

In a Word
Drama-free

Escort

Much revised new Escort is best ever. Completely reworked and completely better. About time too, this is Ford's third attempt

For

Fresh looks, neat interior, smooth ride, low noise

Against

Turbo diesel still unrefined, interior plastics not the best. At the end of the day it's still an Escort

Overall

Now at least competing with 306 and Astra after a long, long wait. Interior is more appealing, seats are better, body smoother, engine quieter and now the thing handles. Improved safety and crash protection plus revised gearing gives much more confidence. Nearly all Escorts now have power steering as standard and driver's airbag, and gone is that appalling engine drone and rock hard ride. Good rather than brilliant, we've waited five years for this new version

Ratings

image	*Improving*
value	*Reasonable*
quality	*Wait and see*
depreciation	*Predictable*
comfort	*Much better*
resale	*It's an Escort*
durability	*Not sure*
driving	*Getting there*

Best buys

1.6LX
Practicality and fittings
1.8Si
Performance and cost

Star buy

1.6Si
Max speed 110
0–60 12.2
Mixed mpg 35.8

In a Word

A long time coming

Mondeo

Mondeo is our best family car. Looks good, rides and handles well. Decent depreciation, clever design but getting a rep's car image

Ratings

image	*Sharp*
value	*Few better*
quality	*Nicely finished*
depreciation	*Looking good*
comfort	*Welcoming*
resale	*No worries*
durability	*Patchy*
driving	*Competent*

Best **b**uys

1.8i LX
Performance and refinement

2.0i GLX Estate
Space and value

Star **b**uy

V6 24v
Max speed 139
0–60 8.1
Mixed mpg 30

For
Unmatched levels of equipment, superb chassis, welcoming interior, assured handling

Against
Motorway noise, worse than average petrol economy, cramped rear, dull dealers, some quality glitches

Overall
One of the best mid-range saloons. Setting new standards in chassis refinement and safety features. Better than the Carina, Primera, 405 and Cavalier. An accomplished car which has been deservedly popular with fleet and rental companies. Ride around town is a bit jiggly and diesel engines not a patch on those of Peugeot or Citröen. V6 lump is a real beaut. If you're looking for a safe, rewarding, capable family car, this is it

In a **W**ord
Ford gets it right

Scorpio

Scorpio is Ford's new world car – but is the world ready for such groan inspiring ugliness?

For

Spacious, plenty of equipment, predictable running costs, lots of dealers. Certainly different

Against

Hardly handsome and probably too unusual for all those middle managers. This one may take a while to creep into our hearts

Overall

Now known as Scorpio only, Granada tag is history. Complete restyle is not the happiest but performance, fixtures and fittings are as good as the old model. 24-valve V6 goes well. 2.0i 16-valve Executive is probably best buy. Estates look better and will hold their value longer. How long it takes for the Scorpio to be accepted remains to be seen, but we don't reckon depreciation will be its strongest suit

Ratings

image	*Ask me another…*
value	*Not bad*
quality	*Okay*
depreciation	*No prizes*
comfort	*Parker Knoll*
resale	*Untested*
durability	*Probably good*
driving	*Fine*

Best buys

2.0i 16 valve Exec
Cost-efficient presence

2.9i 24 valve Exec
Performance and luxury

Star buy

2.0i 16 valve Estate
Max speed 131
0–60 9.6
Mixed mpg 30.4

In a Word

In the eye of the beholder

Probe

Unfortunate name. 2.0 Litre not so quick, V6 better. Really only a two-seater
and can you handle the medallion man image?

Ratings

image	*90s Capri*
value	*Reasonable*
quality	*High*
depreciation	*Not brilliant*
comfort	*Two's company*
resale	*Questionable*
durability	*US built*
driving	*Quick car*

Star **b**uy
Probe 2.5 V6
Max speed 133
0–60 8.4
Mixed mpg 27.5

For

Sensuous lines, plenty of heave, big on safety,
multi-adjustable seats

Against

Thirsty, synthetic interior, vaguish steering,
socially unacceptable image

Overall

Mazda-engined comely coupe with more
than a dash of panache. American built.
Handling is poised and balanced, ride
forgiving and performance energetic.
Available in 16v and 24v guise. PAS, ABS
and twin airbags standard. Not selling as well
as the Calibra as most companies don't
include the Probe on their preferred lists
because of its cramped interior. V6 is the one
to have and plenty of very sensible deals at
Ford dealers

In a **W**ord
Thrusting achievers only

Maverick

Maverick is friendly to drive and reasonable money. Petrol models best, but choose the diesel and you'll be overtaken by people with Zimmer Frames

For
Very car-like to drive. Five door has seven seats. A good value 4x4

Against
Slow diesel. notchy gear change, hasn't got the image of a Discovery or a Jeep

Overall
Quite refined and identical to the Nissan Terrano with the build quality that you'd expect. Looks and ride not the best and has not yet become an aspirational choice. Not many about though so at least you'd be different. High equipment levels and some good deals being done by the Ford boys who are quite frankly desperate to move metal

Ratings
image	*A bit dull*
value	*So-so*
quality	*A Nissan*
depreciation	*Could be better*
comfort	*It's big*
resale	*Not the best*
durability	*So far so good*
driving	*It's easy*

Star buy
2.4 GLX 5 door
Max speed 99
0–60 14
Mixed mpg 24.5

In a Word
Urban kerb-climber

Service interval: *10,000*
Warranty: *24 months/UL. 6-year anti-rust. 168 dealers*

Civic

High price but low depreciation. Technically clever and a very decent family car that will last forever and sell easily

Ratings

image	*Getting better*
value	*Dear*
quality	*Unmatched*
depreciation	*Horizontal*
comfort	*Lots of it*
resale	*Peach*
durability	*Endless*
driving	*Surprisingly good*

Star **b**uy
1.5 LSi 3 door
Max speed 110
0–60 9.6
Mixed mpg 38.7

For
Sweet engines, fluent handling, economy, sound resale, delight to drive. 2-year warranty

Against
Expensive, inefficient use of space, plasticky interior, ride and handling not as good as Citroen ZX or Peugeot 306

Overall
Very much a driver's car – gem-like engine, superb handling and the sort of build quality we have come to expect from Hondas. Ideal choice for those who don't care about cars. All Civics depreciate slowly, sell instantly and are surprisingly frugal. 1.5 VEi very parsimonious. Came second out of 70 cars in our *JD Power – Top Gear Customer Satisfaction Survey*, helped in no small part by all those embarrassingly charming Honda dealers

In a Word
Completely convincing

CRX

A sports car you don't have to suffer to drive. Reliable, capable, sturdy and interesting, but not much in the testosterone department

For

Engines, fun factor, economy, electric roof

Against

Shortage of low-down punch, cheap cabin, quivery ride, toytown looks

Overall

Refined and solid but not as smile-making as previous CRX. Precise power steering and disarming road manners make it a honey to drive. Cockpit cramped and synthetic and that twinky electric roof is expensive and takes up too much space. Fast and frugal, but insurance is pricey. Excellent Honda warranty. High secondhand demand and ideal posing material. Might cost a lot to buy but you'll claw most of it back when you come to sell, and the servicing bills shouldn't hurt much either

Ratings

image *Trenderama*
value *Not cheap*
quality *Legendary*
depreciation *Piffling*
comfort *Tight squeeze*
resale *All day long*
durability *Matchless*
driving *Sparkling*

Star buy
1.6i ESi
Max speed 118
0–60 9.2
Mixed mpg 37.1

In a Word
Enjoyable efficiency

Accord

Able, efficient, cheap to run but doesn't set the heart thumping. Rover 600
is based on the Accord but the Honda is the rarer of the two

Ratings

image	*Different*
value	*Not bad*
quality	*Splendid*
depreciation	*Many worse*
comfort	*No problem*
resale	*Painless*
durability	*Rock solid*
driving	*Pleasant*

Star **b**uy
2.0i
Max speed 123
0–60 10.8
Mixed mpg 33.6

For

Cost, refinement, build quality, British made, economy, quite fast, unusual

Against

A touch on the steady side but plenty of quality. Good all-rounder but somehow fails to captivate

Overall

Jolly good car whose engine compartment will only see the light of day when it's being serviced by those nice Honda people. Much more street cred than a Rover. Honda brought Rover out of the Dark Ages, and as a reward Rover did the dirty and sold out to BMW for less money than it cost to develop the Vauxhall Omega. We think that's not cricket. The Japanese, like elephants, never forget

In a **W**ord
Hard to beat

Prelude

Prelude is quick, pliant and looks the part. Secondhand values very firm and demand high

For

Looks, handling, ride and performance. Leagues ahead of its forebear and wonderfully imposing frontal aspect

Against

Coupe claustrophobia, token rear seats, quirky Red Dwarf dashboard

Overall

Stylish and beautifully formed coupe, heaps of equipment and vault-like build quality. Used prices resilient, too. 2.3i notably quick. Could become one of the cars to be seen in. Extremely interesting driver's coupe with cracking handling and urgent engines. Accommodation is strictly two's company, three's a crowd. Not many about so quite uptown image. Usual superlatives about Honda dealers apply

Ratings

image	*Fashionable*
value	*Not cheap*
quality	*Impressive*
depreciation	*Slow*
comfort	*A squeeze*
resale	*Angst-free*
durability	*Titanium*
driving	*Big fun*

Star buy

2.2 V-Tech
Max speed 140
0–60 7.1
Mixed mpg 31.4

In a Word
Vorsprung durch Honda

Legend

Legend is one Honda's finest products, the easy equal of a Merc or a BMW,
and so refreshingly different. Blisteringly quick too

Ratings

image	*Nicely understated*
value	*Lots of it*
quality	*Among the best*
depreciation	*Not terrible*
comfort	*Few plusher*
resale	*Not hard*
durability	*Resounding*
driving	*Wolf in sheeps'…*

Star **b**uy
Legend Saloon Auto
Max speed 140
0–60 9.0
Mixed mpg 26.3

For
Quality, fittings and furnishings, mellifluous engine and transmission. Built for keeps. Quiet unassuming image

Against
Dull steering, but that's about it

Overall
Pitched at a market sewn up by the Germans, the Legend is not an obvious choice for the aspirant plutocrat, yet it should be. This car is among the most reliable, well made luxury machines money can buy. Bristling with standard kit, it wants for nothing. Front-wheel drive can scramble a bit but it'll knock on the door of 145mph and requires only occassional maintenance. Usual Honda tireless build quality. Two-year warranty. If you're after a big cruiser this one is well worth mature and careful scrutiny

In a **W**ord
Seriously talented

NSX

Devlishly quick, swooping looks, utter reliability, ever so unusual, and easy enough for my mum to drive

For

Outstanding, class-leading idiot-proof supercar. Viceless, technically ingenious, glue-like grip, magic carpet ride and pocket-pleasing economy. An absolute stunner

Against

Not an Italian stallion. Does everything too well, except make the palms sweat

Overall

The shape of things to come, the NSX is the slingshot of the year. Rapid, refined and richly rewarding. Mild manners belie prodigious prowess. Tremendous V6 engine and the sort of handling balance you wouldn't believe. Because it's so good and requires little effort to propel at Olympian speeds, enthusiasts don't reckon it's entertaining enough. What do they know?

Ratings

image	*Big noise*
value	*Supercar bargain*
quality	*Terribly good*
depreciation	*Better than some*
comfort	*Surprisingly so*
resale	*In demand*
durability	*Tireless*
driving	*Sensual*

Star buy
NSX
Max speed 159
0–60 5.7
Mixed mpg 27.5

In a Word
The dog's twitcher

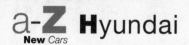

a-Z Hyundai
New Cars

Service interval: *12,000*
Warranty: *36 months/UL. 6-year anti-rust. 152 dealers*

Accent

Better than you'd think, the Accent is quite refined, has plenty of room and
an attractive price. At this money, image doesn't matter

Ratings

image	*So so*
value	*Resounding*
quality	*Quite a bit*
depreciation	*Not tragic*
comfort	*Suburban semi*
resale	*Loyal following*
durability	*Not bad*
driving	*Reasonable*

Star **b**uy
1.5 GSi
Max speed 109
0–60 11.4
Mixed mpg 45.2

For
Reliability, precise handling, pleasant ride,
willing engines, admirable spec, low price.
Three year warranty. Formidable economy

Against
No-one will be impressed. Dull interior
architecture, not brilliant performance,
clumsy gearshift

Overall
Not just another Korean bauble. Despite
spiritless looks and gutless progress this is a
cheap, friendly and refined runabout that
compares favourably to many more
expensive offerings. Equipment is excellent,
warranty formidable and ride quality
surprisingly superior. An accomplished
value-for-money package for those who don't
give a damn about the motoring pecking
order. Makes an awful lot of sense

In a **W**ord
Loads for the money

Lantra

Pleasing looks, impressive equipment. Goes, rides and handles well. It's
time to take the Koreans very seriously indeed

For

Price, equipment, space and build quality. Nice to drive as well. Lantra is much better than you think and well worth a spin round the block

Against

Pokey boot. The image is low, but so's the price

Overall

Engaging package of looks, quality, equipment, ability and price. Not a Cavalier competitor yet but distinguished by refreshing European appearance and manners. Certainly no cheapjack lash-up and with that attractive price and bullet-proof warranty you are looking at three years worry-free motoring. You could go an awful lot further and fair an awful lot worse than a Lantra

Ratings

image	*Not in the game*
value	*Yes*
quality	*Solid*
depreciation	*Not wonderful*
comfort	*Fine*
resale	*Takes a bit of time*
durability	*Tough*
driving	*Shock…it's good*

Star **b**uy
1.6 GLS
Max speed III
0–60 11.1
Mixed mpg 29.9

In a **W**ord
Getting better all the time

Sonata

Sensible package of good room, plenty of equipment and a pleasing price.
Not much fun to drive though

Ratings

image	*Blunt*
value	*Cheap enough*
quality	*Not bad*
depreciation	*Heavy*
comfort	*Okay*
resale	*Not easy*
durability	*Long warranty*
driving	*Not much fun*

Star buy
2.0 GLX
Max speed 121
0–60 10.2
Mixed mpg 42.8

For
Equipment, value economy and room

Against
Impotent image, severe ride and rubbery handling

Overall
Full of twiddly bits, but extras alone do not a prestige car make. Sonata is Hyundai's Vauxhall Omega at an Astra price, but making a foothold in the big car market isn't as easy as it looks and the Sonata is not a credible luxury car. Lantra makes more sense and is much more interesting to drive. Depreciation likely to be on the heavy side

In a Word
Big value, small image

Scoupe

Silly name but one of the cheapest coupes around. Not a patch on the competition though. Turbo goes well

For

Cheap, vaguely sporty and well-specified. Quick turbo

Against

Too softly sprung. No technocrat and hardly an oil painting

Overall

Creditable attempt at a cheap coupe at around eleven grand, but it lacks all-round refinement and isn't even on the starting line when it comes to image. Calibra might cost another six grand but it's by far the better car. Scoupe might be priced to get away but by buying it you'll just be telling the world that you can't afford the real thing. Promising reliability and long warranty

Ratings

image	*No head-turner*
value	*Cheap*
quality	*Not bad*
depreciation	*Heavy*
comfort	*Okay*
resale	*Hard work*
durability	*Looks good*
driving	*Undemanding*

Star buy

MVTi
Max speed 121
0–60 9.2
Mixed mpg 32

In a Word

A coupe without cred

Service interval: *6,000*
Warranty: *12 months/UL including powertrain.*
6-year anti-rust. 130 dealers

Trooper

Trooper is talented off-roader. No Discovery beater but still a useful bit of
kit. Identical model sold by Vauxhall known as the Monterey

Ratings
image *Confused*
value *Not terrible*
quality *Hardy*
depreciation *Okay-ish*
comfort *Plenty*
resale *Immediate*
durability *Serious*
driving *Go anywhere*

For
Butch uptown looks, Eiger-climbing lugging
power and ample accommodation

Against
Bland cabin, some trim tackiness, poor
economy from V6 petrol unit

Overall
Now almost a Shogun competitor with fine
turbodiesels and impressive all-round ability.
Competent but with Vauxhall now selling it
under another name we can't see it being
around for much longer. Depreciation could
therefore be quite painful. We'd buy a nearly-
new, tiny mileage one and save thousands

Star **b**uy
Citation 3.2S
Max speed 106
0–60 11.3
Mixed mpg 19.3

In a **W**ord
Fine,
if you like that sort of thing

Service interval: *15,000*
Warranty: *36 months/60,000. 6-year anti-rust. 92 dealers*

XJ6

XJ6 is a tremendous cocktail of speed, refinement reliability and excellence

For
Handsome graceful and poised. Britain's best loved luxury express. Build quality improved beyond all recognition. Confident 3 year warranty. Quite simply a wonderful way of wafting about

Against
Not much really. A completely transformed motor car that is a credit to Jaguar and is causing a few sleepless nights at Mercedes and BMW

Overall
Handcrafted heritage that the Germans can't rival. A pin-striped conveyance affirming establishment values. Matchless ride, pace and image. More front than Southend, and getting back towards what proper Jaguars used to be. We like them an awful lot. Not bad price either

Ratings
image	*Big money*
value	*Huge*
quality	*Getting better*
depreciation	*Many worse*
comfort	*Glorious*
resale	*Pretty good*
durability	*Endless*
driving	*So smooth*

Star buy
XJR
Max speed 151
0–60 5.8
Mixed mpg 20

In a Word
A Mercedes is better,
but only just

XJ12/Daimler Double Six

Super-silent V12 is one of Britain's finest pedigree saloons. Individual too

Ratings

image *Regal*
value *Cheapest V12*
quality *Seamless*
depreciation *Perish the thought*
comfort *Few better*
resale *Likely to be decent*
durability *Storm-proof*
driving *Effortless*

Star buy
Daimler Double Six
Max speed 155
0–60 6.8
Mixed mpg 18.4

For
Opulence, silence, refinement, class. Getting on for Rolls-Royce standards of luxury and quietness, without the ostentation. Super-swift performance with restrained dignity. And it's British through and through

Against
Depreciation, thirst, property developer image. Not the most environmentally sound buy.

Overall
Jaguar's splendid new V12 saloon is one of their best. Incredibly smooth and softly spoken with a bewitching waft factor. It's also less of a drinker than the old model at 18.4 mpg overall. Six-litre V12 plus super-slick new 4-speed auto box delivers effortless oomph – 155 mph. Much more classy and elegant than a BMW 750

In a Word
Fly the flag

XJS

Heavy-drinking V12 is gone now, shame that. But 4.0 lives on and is still a class act

For
Twenty years on and still a stunner. Growing old very gracefully. Lithe looks, top-drawer cachet and sophistication. Reassuring Jaguar warranty

Against
Politically incorrect. Strictly a 2-seater, haphazard switchgear

Overall
Least expensive of the grandest grand tourers. Premier league torpedo. Maturing well. Convertible has Côte d'Azur kudos, coupe still looks slick. Demise of V12 models due to falling demand leaves just the 4.0-litre versions, which have plenty of grunt but are far less juicy. XJS is a wonderful British dreamboat that can give most precious metal a run for its money

Ratings
image	*Pools winner*
value	*Quite reasonable*
quality	*Fine*
depreciation	*Heavyish*
comfort	*Restful*
resale	*Can be hard*
durability	*Well made*
driving	*Poised*

Star buy
XJS 4.0
Max speed 147
0–60 6.9
Mixed mpg 22.9

In a Word
Age has intensified her charm

Jeep

Service interval: *12,000*
Warranty: *36 months/60,000. 92 dealers*

Cherokee

Jeep is different, built to win a war, long warranty, inconsequential depreciation

Ratings

image	*Distinctive*
value	*Unmatched*
quality	*It's a Jeep*
depreciation	*Won't hurt*
comfort	*Cramped*
resale	*Healthy*
durability	*Unbreakable*
driving	*Good on-roader*

Star buy
4.0 Limited SE
Max speed 112
0–60 9.5
Mixed mpg 19.6

For
Value, performance, equipment, grip, image, quite quick

Against
Bit small, horrid dashboard, tacky trim, road noise, jiggly ride

Overall
Crude but endearing Discovery/Shogun alternative. Extraordinarily good value with class-leading equipment levels. Only limited space stops it from being the best off-roader. Not likely to stay as cheap as £22,000 for long. An alluring package especially with that 60,000 mile/3 year warranty. Not as much room as you'd think and that American dash takes some getting used to. But serious fun, and brash. Buy one now

In a Word
As American as a
Harley-Davidson

Service interval: *12,000*
Warranty: *24 months/UL. 6-year anti-rust. 127 dealers*

Pride

Korean-built Pride is re-badged Mazda 121. Cheap, cheerful and a steal, although handling is not its strongest suit

For
Build quality, room, engines, rummage sale prices

Against
Nauseous ride, tacky whitewall tyres, wind noise

Overall
Worthy supermini that's much more competent than you'd imagine. Class-leading amounts of space and sweet engines with peppy performance and all for less than seven grand. £6,000 1.3L makes plenty of sense. Build quality good enough to cope with driving school duffers, so why not you?

Ratings
image	*Not in the game*
value	*Outstanding*
quality	*Decent*
depreciation	*Highish*
comfort	*Okay*
resale	*Easy*
durability	*Solid*
driving	*Not terrible*

Star buy
1.3L
Max speed 91
0–60 11.6
Mixed mpg 42.6

In *a* **W**ord
Can't go wrong
at this money

Mentor

Mentor has lots of room at a reasonable price. Top seller in South Korea, if you care

Ratings

image	*Hasn't got one*
value	*Excellent*
quality	*Bit tacky*
depreciation	*Don't know*
comfort	*Pleasing*
resale	*Might be tricky*
durability	*Looks okay*
driving	*Uninspired*

Star **b**uy
1.6 GLX
Max speed 107
0–60 11.8
Mixed mpg 38.4

For
Competitive price, economy, interior space and comfort

Against
Lowly spec, drab performance, brittle feel, no sunroof, lacklustre performance

Overall
The car to be seen in. In South Korea, that is. Willing and fully functional family runabout with few vices but humdrum fittings, tragically limited options and discount house image. Superior warranty and reliable Mazda 323 power unit aren't likely to protect this commendable budget effort from buyer prejudice and dissatisfaction. But at under ten grand it's a half decent Escort-chaser. You could do worse

In a **W**ord
Worth a look

Lada a-Z
New *Cars*

Service interval: *6 months/12,000*
Warranty: *24-months/50,000. 6-year anti-rust. 200 dealers*

Riva

At under five grand it's inexpensive, but still feels like it's made from rice paper

For
Seriously cheap, hardy engines, anti-style image, 2-year warranty

Against
Late 70s concrete architecture, social security furnishings, throwaway trade-in values, non-existent build quality

Overall
One of the cheapest cars you can buy. No finesse, no street cred, but the price is right. Even better if bought year-old secondhand. Still thrown together though, and if you can cope with the niggles, fine. If not, don't bother. Not really credible in any department

Ratings
image	*You're joking*
value	*Resounding*
quality	*Passable*
depreciation	*Heavy*
comfort	*Don't be silly*
resale	*Must be cheap*
durability	*If kept serviced*
driving	*Stone Age*

Star buy
1.5SX
Max speed 100
0–60 12
Mixed mpg 36.1

In a Word
Definitely an acquired taste

Samara

If you're into yesterday's technology, don't buy a Samara, buy a Skoda instead

Ratings

image *Non-existent*
value *Cheap wheels*
quality *No*
depreciation *Oh dear*
comfort *Okay*
resale *Never simple*
durability *Forget it*
driving *Awful*

Star buy

1500 SX
Max speed 95
0–60 13.6
Mixed mpg 36.1

For

Basic price, plenty of room, long warranty

Against

Basic build quality, unhappy looks, nasty interior, bouncy suspension, crumbling used values. Awkward driving position

Overall

Not the happiest of cocktails. Saloon looks better than hatchback. No engineering tour de force and 1.1/1.3 engines underpowered. When we tested a 1.5GL, pieces detached themselves from the dash, doors wouldn't open, brakes almost caught fire and the steering wheel fell apart. Enough said…

In a Word

Flawed frugality

Niva

Niva is the cheapest 4x4 by far, but amazingly able nonetheless

For

Good traction, amazing price. Genuine 4-seater and tough too

Against

Humdrum image, build quality a bit iffy, poor on-road ride and handling, heavy on juice

Overall

Entry level 4x4 but don't expect to impress the county set. Crude and ageing design but at less than seven grand who's bothered? Niva is surprisingly good off road, but not too much cop on tarmac. Looks chunky but the interior is dire and flat out, eighty miles an hour is as good as it gets

Ratings

image	*Nope*
value	*Not bad*
quality	*Passable, just …*
depreciation	*Okay*
comfort	*Fairly basic*
resale	*In the end*
durability	*Not really*
driving	*Nothing special*

Star buy

Niva 4x4
Max speed 82
0–60 22.0
Mixed mpg 19.9

In a Word
Penny-wise off-roader

Service interval: *6,000*
Warranty: *12 months/UL*

Diablo

Crazy, awesome, silly, mad and very bad, the Diablo is the nearest thing to a Formula One racer

Ratings

image	*Off the clock*
value	*Must you ask…*
quality	*Passable*
depreciation	*Fearsome*
comfort	*It has seats…*
resale	*Who knows?*
durability	*Fair*
driving	*Mind-blowing*

Star *buy*

Diablo SE
Max speed 207
0–60 3.9
Mixed mpg 16

For

Glorious V12, 200 mph performance, Italian sound effects, unimpeachable handling, forgiving ride

Against

Hopelessly impractical, ridiculously high profile, prodigious costs

Overall

Supreme supercar. The most exciting and fastest fun-ride since Concorde. Surprisingly tractable and docile. Zillionaire image, swooping lines, Italianate idiosyncrasy. With terrifying width, incredible performance, exhilarating handling the Diablo should be on every lottery winner's shopping list. We love it to bits…

In *a* **W**ord
Bonkers

Service interval: *6,000*
Warranty: *12 months/UL. 127 dealers*

Discovery

Discovery is designer Range Rover, works well and holds value longest.
Diesels slow, V8s much better

F*or*
Green-wellie breeding, stylish versatility, solid secondhand values

A*gainst*
Build quality could be better, turbodiesel too vocal, thirsty V8, vague steering

O*verall*
Discovery is tough, trendy and much admired. Depreciation is the lowest in its class and resale instant. Build quality only average and, despite that polished image, the Disco only managed to come 55th out of 70 cars in our JD Power survey. Doesn't stop them selling though

R*atings*

image	*Slick*
value	*Big package*
quality	*Patchy*
depreciation	*Very slow*
comfort	*Plenty of room*
resale	*All year round*
durability	*Long-lasting*
driving	*Forgiving*

S*tar* **b***uy*
V8i ES
Max speed 104
0–60 13.0
Mixed mpg 18.0

I*n a* **W***ord*
Every suburban mummy
should have one

Range Rover

New Range Rover might not look as good as the old one, but is still the best of the lot

Ratings

image	*Dignified*
value	*Not really*
quality	*Better*
depreciation	*Lots*
comfort	*Cotton wool*
resale	*Huge market*
durability	*Rugged*
driving	*Mellow*

Star **b**uy
4.6 SE
Max speed 119
0–60 10.6
Mixed mpg 17.6

For
Elegance, off-road pluckiness, softer lines, more space, improved road manners

Against
Too expensive, silly mpg, transmission whine, rocky ride

Overall
Long-awaited restyle for the oldest 4x4 in town. Steering's a lot more exact, interior's commendably opulent, equipment and controls modern and comprehensive, and off-road it'll keep up with the best of them. Pleasantly rounded-off exterior hides a decent-sized living room wherein driver and passengers may abide in rarefied, refrigerated and splendid isolation. Certainly a step up from its tired and boxy forebear but the price tag needs a pause for thought

In a **W**ord
Polite poshness

Range Rover Classic

One of our better achievements that's often imitated but never bettered

For

Aristocratic aura, definitive design, inimitable institution. Big on room, refinement, gully-climbing ability. Major street cred. Clever air suspension

Against

Messy interior, big-drinking V8, no longer cheap

Overall

Twenty-five years on and still none better. Inspired mix of city-slick style and agricultural ability. Tough, swish, versatile and desirable. Diesel useful, uptown Vogue SE wants for nothing. Used values impressive. Despite the new model this one won't go away, so they now call it the Classic, which it certainly is

Ratings

image	*Class-leading*
value	*Getting expensive*
quality	*Sometimes*
depreciation	*Not terrible*
comfort	*Very swish*
resale	*Plenty of buyers*
durability	*Good*
driving	*Refined*

Star buy

Classic V8
Max speed 110
0–60 10.4
Mixed mpg 18.9

In a Word

Inimitable

a-Z Lexus
New Cars

Service interval: *6,000*
Warranty: *36 months/60,000, 3-year paint. 72 dealers*

GS 300

300 is not as good as the 400. Well built enough but not exactly happy-
looking and not nearly as refined as its big brother

Ratings
image	*Inert*
value	*There are better*
quality	*Meticulous*
depreciation	*Not bad*
comfort	*Extensive*
resale	*Okay*
durability	*Unquestionable*
driving	*Quick*

Star buy
GS300
Max speed 137
0–60 10.4
Mixed mpg 26.6

For
Awesome build quality, mechanical finesse, whisper-smooth transmission, hi-tech equipment

Against
Restricted accommodation, bumpy suspension, inadequate luggage space, large thirst, dull image

Overall
No match for the equivalent BMW or Merc. Ride is flawed by unpredictable springing on hostile surfaces, rear space is noticeably lacking and instrumentation is over-complicated. But it's a polished prestige package with grown-up performance, sumptuous levels of comfort and a superb auto gearbox. A discriminating buy that will neither disappoint nor arouse. At £33k we'd buy a second-hand LS400

In a Word
Not quite there

LS400

Super-smooth Lexus is one of the slowest depreciating luxury cars we know with huge secondhand demand. Probably the finest luxury car in the world

For
Built with millimetric precision, superb engine and gearbox, eerily quiet, painstakingly assembled, gilt-edged residuals

Against
Glum frontal aspect, disorganised dash, still no image-builder

Overall
Toyota's technocrat. Fast, able and individual. Built for keeps, bristling with knick-knackery but strangely soulless. Watertight warranty. Incredibly well engineered but a car that lacks personality which in the status-conscious luxury car market is a serious black mark. Some say it's just too quiet and insulating and Lexus engineers should start putting the noises back in. Fine if you want a car that all but drives itself. This one's not for fun

Ratings
image	*Oriental*
value	*Not cheap*
quality	*Minutely detailed*
depreciation	*Few better*
comfort	*Sleep-inducing*
resale	*Ever so easy*
durability	*Bullet-proof*
driving	*Smooth and silent*

Star buy
LS 400
Max speed 156
0–60 7.4
Mixed mpg 26.9

In a Word
Clinical perfection

Service interval: *6,000*
Warranty: *12 months/UL. 8-year chassis anti-rust.*
28 dealers

Esprit

Big performance for big money. Serious flying machine. S300 is the one to
have if you want to say hello to 170mph...

	Ratings
image	*So-so*
value	*Not really*
quality	*Only average*
depreciation	*Expensive*
comfort	*No*
resale	*Specialist buyers*
durability	*Getting better*
driving	*Wow!*

Star **b**uy
Esprit Sport 300
Max speed 169
0–60 4.5
Mixed mpg 24.9

For
Performance, handling, looks, character,
electrifying rapidity. Very different

Against
Hairdresser image, sometimes fragile build
quality, serious insurance cost

Overall
Mid-engined plastic roller-skate with gutsy
4-cylinder power plant. Welcome efforts to
improve driving position and visibility.
Maturing surprisingly well for its age but
resale can be tricky. S4 gets badly needed
power steering, tweaked suspension and a
facelift. For between £47k to £65k they ain't
cheap. For that sort of money we'd prefer
something a little better made

In a **W**ord
Potent patriotism

Service interval: *6 months/12,000*
Warranty: *5 years/100,000. 6-year anti-rust. 150 dealers*

121

Cute Mazda 121 has 3-year warranty and echoes of 50s Austin A35. Brave
effort but no match for the Nissan Micra

For

Retro looks, clever use of space, interesting
individuality, zippy engine, sterling build
quality and warranty. Fluent auto

Against

Stiff-legged handling, heavy steering,
toytown image

Overall

Charming high-roof shopping shuttle that's
well built and quite able. Very roomy, very
cute, very useful but those Enid Blyton looks
aren't for everybody. Quite a rare sight
though so depreciation reasonable and resale
easy. If you want a town toddler that's
different, this could be it

Ratings

image	*Fischer Price*
value	*A clever buy*
quality	*No worries*
depreciation	*Minimal*
comfort	*Quite big*
resale	*Easy*
durability	*Lasts and lasts*
driving	*Awful steering*

Star buy

121 GLX 1.3i
Max speed 97
0–60 11.7
Mixed mpg 43

In a Word

Little but large

a-Z Mazda
New *Cars*

323

323 has earned itself a reputation as a solid buy. Came fourth in our *Top Gear – JD Power Car Customer Satisfaction Survey*

Ratings

image	*Safe*
value	*Not bad*
quality	*High*
depreciation	*Low*
comfort	*Big*
resale	*Straightforward*
durability	*Long-lived*
driving	*Unexciting*

Star buy
1.5i GLX
Max speed 108
0–60 11.9
Mixed mpg 36.4

For

Usual hardy Mazda solidity. Undemanding to live with, big on value, slow on depreciation. Worry-free warranty

Against

Bland looks, cramped interiors, hard ride

Overall

Serious reliability and build quality. Not cheap to buy or service but very economical. Endearing all-round performer with friendly wraparound feel. Easy to drive but light on excitement. Service prices only average but very few problems. Dealers helpful, obliging and seem to know what they're doing. 1.3i looks odd with its skinny tyres. V6 version is much, much better and almost as good as VW Golf VR6

In a Word
Predictably good

626

Mazda's 626 looks well, V6 is fast, but steering lacks feel. Not as good as
Mondeo or Rover 600 though

For
Structural integrity, warranty, space, value,
equipment

Against
Anonymous, flabby ride, no panache, body
roll, slow diesel

Overall
Competent, likeable and solid but no match
for other mainstream contenders. Fine range
of engines but the whole plot is seriously
compromised by dead steering and numb
ride. Service and customer care could be
better though with quite a few warranty
claims reported. Came tenth in our JD
Power survey, liked for its performance,
reliability and economy

Ratings
image	*Sterile*
value	*Worth it*
quality	*Good*
depreciation	*Low*
comfort	*Okay*
resale	*Quick sellers*
durability	*Solid*
driving	*All over the shop*

Star buy
1.8i GLX
Max speed 119
0–60 9.9
Mixed mpg 37.5

In a Word
Plain but practical

Xedos 9

Xedos is smooth, handsome and separate and almost as good as a BMW 3
Series. Let down though by lack of passion in the driving department

Ratings
image *Upright*
value *No rip-off*
quality *Abundant*
depreciation *Average*
comfort *Enough*
resale *Debatable*
durability *Long-lived*
driving *Stolid*

Star **b**uy
Xedos 2.5i V6
Max speed 126
0–60 10.4
Mixed mpg 31

For
Quiet, fluent ride, mechanical integrity,
enviably equipped

Against
Bit faceless, heavy, could be quicker, over-
assisted steering

Overall
Mazda's executive express. Japanese
engineering at its most competent, yet
clinical and unexciting. Mind you that sweet
2.5 V6 is also used in the Ford Probe. The
Xedos 9 will do everything you ask of it
except arouse. Image is everything above
twenty grand, but this one's opted out,
preferring instead to send signals of restraint,
capability and self-effacement. But some fell
on stony ground…

In *a* **W**ord
Blameless exactitude

MX-3

MX3 looks well, sounds great but really only a two-seater. V6 a sweet-spinning device but needs more poke. Auto desperately slow

For

Distinctive looks, sound effects from V6, peerless build, fine warranty

Against

Lotus position rear seats, not as fast as you'd like, especially the 1.6

Overall

Hybrid hatch/coupe that promises more than it delivers. Rakish styling but not much grunt. Carefully built with cast-iron warranty but lacks charisma. Bit too twinky to be taken seriously and the image is a bit so-so. 1.8 makes most sense but avoid that 1.6 auto like the plague

Ratings

image	*Off-focus*
value	*Reasonable*
quality	*Impressive*
depreciation	*Low*
comfort	*Tight squeeze*
resale	*Okay*
durability	*Solid*
driving	*Not bad*

Star buy

1.8i V6
Max speed 126
0–60 8.3
Mixed mpg 30.7

In a Word

Buy an MX-5

MX-5

MX-5 is clever cocktail of 60s styling and 90s engineering. Serious rear-wheel drive fun. 1.8i is tremendous value for money

Ratings

image	*Cute*
value	*High*
quality	*Excellent*
depreciation	*Minimal*
comfort	*Two's company*
resale	*No problem*
durability	*No worries*
driving	*Appealing*

Star buy
MX-5 1.8i
Max speed 123
0–60 8.6
Mixed mpg 32.1

For

Elan, handling, quality, price, period looks. Horizontal depreciation, wonderful resale

Against

Over-assisted steering, vandal target

Overall

Old wine in a hi-tech bottle. The MG that should have been. Not that quick but loads of fun. Supple ride and taut handling. Once again the Japanese take a good idea and make it better. Real value and built for keeps, the MX-5 is a worldwide success story. In America they already have an owners club and think it's the best thing since Jayne Mansfield. A classic the instant it was born

In a Word
Highly recommended

MX-6

Seriously quick and refined with sensible price and smooth drive-train. Not much rear space so a Calibra would be more practical

For
Smooth lines, grown-up performance, melodic sounds from V6, supple chassis, affordable price

Against
Power-sapping auto, 2+1 not 2+2

Overall
Punchy performer with matinée idol looks, civilised ride and neat handling. Plenty of toys to play with and usual Mazda superlatives about fit and finish apply. Not around in any numbers so a very distinctive choice that holds its value longer than most. No horror stories about reliability and a very low warranty claim rate. If you want a separate coupe that's not as aggressive as the Probe or as predictable as the Calibra, then here it is

Ratings
image	*Smooth*
value	*Worth it*
quality	*High*
depreciation	*Low*
comfort	*Limited*
resale	*Straightforward*
durability	*Long-lasting*
driving	*Effortless*

Star buy
MX-6
Max speed 137
0–60 8.3
Mixed mpg 28.3

In a Word
Graceful grunt

RX-7

RX-7 is quick, looks nicely weird and goes well but a big drinker, harsh rider and not that popular

Ratings

image	*Slick*
value	*Expensive*
quality	*Impressive*
depreciation	*Average*
comfort	*Okay*
resale	*So-so*
durability	*Proven*
driving	*Quick*

Star buy

RX-7
Max speed 153
0–60 5.7
Mixed mpg 25.5

For

Sweeping lines, high-revving performance, individuality

Against

Noise, cost, thirst, ride quality

Overall

Dramatic looks, tenacious handling, serious go. Bewitching shape sets it apart. Heavyweight contender in the coupe stakes but at the price it should be. Considerable fun factor but you'll find the road noise and jiggly ride quite wearisome. Twin turbo power plant has plenty of urge and the handling's brilliant, when it's dry. When it's wet things get very exciting indeed

In a Word

Toast of the Rotary Club

Service interval: *6,000/12,000*
Warranty: *12 months/UL. 135 dealers*

C Class

Tremendous integrity, refinement and presence, C Class is also one of the slowest depreciating cars in the world

For
Image, longevity, resale, depreciation, economy, class

Against
180 - 200 a bit slow, base model Classic too spartan, clunky manual gearbox

Overall
Replacement for the 190 that's bigger and better. Classic is entry level, Esprit and Elegance mid-range, and Sport the BMW-chaser. 2.2s and 2.5s more interesting to drive than smaller-engined models. Not much standard kit so make sure you specify sunroof, metallic paint and automatic. Diesels okay if you like that sort of thing but not as good as BMW oil-burners

Ratings
image	*Top notch*
value	*Pricey*
quality	*Brilliant*
depreciation	*Minimal*
comfort	*Better*
resale	*Ultra desirable*
durability	*Forever*
driving	*Imperial*

Best buys
C220 Elegance
Smooth and sharp
C280 Sport
Affordable prestige

Star buy
C200 Classic
Max speed 123
0–60 11.1
Mixed mpg 32.3

In a Word
Everything that's best about Mercedes

E Class

E Class is the best Mercedes to date, challenges the BMW 5 and 7 Series
and even casts a shadow over the Merc S Class

Ratings

image	*The best*
value	*Wonderful*
quality	*Brilliant*
depreciation	*Minimal*
comfort	*Much better*
resale	*Precious metal*
durability	*Forever*
driving	*Love it*

Star **b**uy
E320
Max speed 146
0–60 7.8
Mixed mpg 28.5

For
Refinement, ride, side airbags, handling, room, equipment

Against
Lethargic 2.0 and 2.3-litre four cylinders

Overall
With new steering, bigger cabin, more safety and more refinement, this is simply a tremendous car, and one of the best luxury confections available. Six cylinder cars are better, sports suspension preferred. Best buying is the E320 which has agility, poise, comfort and endless urge. V8 and V6 planned along with electronic five speed auto. The E Class is what the S Class should have been – nimble, agile and pliant. New hatchback, coupe and estate versions coming soon

In a **W**ord
A price worth paying

116

S Class

Biggest Benz is the last word in Germanic efficiency. V8s best buys but S Class is a tad too opulent for the caring, sharing nineties

For

Technocratic pre-eminence, awesome street presence, complete credibility. Eerily smooth and silent

Against

Fat cat decadence

Overall

Class leader conveys instant respectability. V12 600SEL is the Wagnerian leviathan with comprehensive standard equipment. V8 saloons make more sense. Double glazing is standard, automatic doors mostly optional. Sexy SEC nearly a hundred grand touch. One of the most able, refined and sophisticated saloon cars money can buy

Ratings

image	*Plutocratic*
value	*If you can afford it*
quality	*Matchless*
depreciation	*Highish*
comfort	*Hedonistic*
resale	*In demand*
durability	*Cast-iron*
driving	*Smooth*

Star buy

420SE
Max speed 152
0–60 7.9
Mixed mpg 21.3

In a Word

Definitive excellence

SL

SL is smooth, slick, sensuous and built to last the millennium. Secondhand
values are like titanium and demand everlasting

Ratings

image	*Spot on*
value	*Not cheap*
quality	*Perfect*
depreciation	*Better than some*
comfort	*Fine*
resale	*Instant*
durability	*For decades*
driving	*Poserama*

Star buy
320SL
Max speed 144
0–60 8.4
Mixed mpg 23.4

For
Elegance, safety, vault-like toughness, drop-
dead looks, effortless performance

Against
V12 price. Playboy image

Overall
Essential accessory of the frightfully rich.
Chic hi-tech boulevard cruiser. Omni-
competent authority, supremely fast and
supremely safe. 600 SL may be the ultimate
boot badge, but it doesn't eclipse the 320's
all-round attraction. Heavyish first year
depreciation but used values promise to be
evergreen. Gone is the old SL's effeminacy –
this one's big, butch and wicked. 280/320
have all the looks but not quite so much
grunt

In a Word
Probably the finest
boulevardier in the world

G-Wagen

G-Wagen made from girders, but feels a touch too tractor-like. New model waiting in the wings

For

Built like a tank, almost as much panache as a Range Rover, not many about, so rare and separate

Against

Expensive, styled like a breeze-block

Overall

More able than you'd think, arguably the best built 4x4 by far. Long wheelbase models in black look macho. Pleasing automatic but diesels on the sluggish side. Add-on extras hike up price. Secondhand buying is usually the shrewdest course

Ratings

image	*Interesting*
value	*Not really*
quality	*It's a Merc*
depreciation	*Highish*
comfort	*Fine*
resale	*Not the best*
durability	*Excellent*
driving	*Go anywhere*

Star **b**uy
300GES
Max speed 102
0–60 13.0
Mixed mpg 16.7

In a **W**ord
No-nonsense mountaineer

Service interval: *9,000*
Warranty: *36 months/ UL. 6-year anti-rust. 104 dealers*

Colt

Little Colt is terribly good and heaps better than Escort/Fiesta. Secondhand
values are the other side of epic. Find one if you can

Ratings
image *Not bad*
value *Plenty of kit*
quality *Impressive*
depreciation *Slow*
comfort *Friendly*
resale *Easy*
durability *No problems*
driving *Engaging*

Star buy
1.6 GLXi
Max speed 118
0–60 9.8
Mixed mpg 38.3

For
Smooth shape, lively engines, commendable
warranty, build integrity

Against
Hard ride, drab interior, only three doors

Overall
Accomplished all-rounder with new
generation oval Euro styling. Spacious,
thrifty, undemanding and fun to drive,
especially the GTi. Useful auto option and
high level of standard spec. Not many about,
so distinctive as well. This is one of our
favourite small cars that's interesting,
beautifully built and stonking good value.
Highly recommended

In a Word
Willing and able

Galant

Galant is sturdy, blameless and ever so reliable, but lacks any kind of charisma. New model due soon...called Carisma

For
Three-year warranty, seamless build quality, splendid chassis, sweet-revving engines, high resale value

Against
Drab interiors, brillo pad seat facings

Overall
Handsome thing. Looks much better than its forebears – aggressive frontal aspect and smoother curves. Still up to the usual Mitsubishi quality with tremendous fit and finish and squeakless ride. Handling very poised in all models. 1.8 least desirable

Ratings

image	*Vastly improved*
value	*Resounding*
quality	*Enviable*
depreciation	*Low*
comfort	*High*
resale	*No problem*
durability	*Last forever*
driving	*Fluent*

Star buy
2.0 GLSi 16v
Max speed 128
0–60 9.6
Mixed mpg 33.3

In a Word
Elegant efficiency

Sigma

Sigma is groaning with gadgets and has all the integrity we've come to expect from Mitsubishi. Australian-built estate good news

Ratings	
image	*Off-focus*
value	*Pretty good*
quality	*Solid*
depreciation	*Average*
comfort	*Rest cure*
resale	*Slow*
durability	*Excellent*
driving	*Uninvolving*

For
Lots of gismos, four-wheel steering, warranty

Against
Little driver involvement, blunt image

Overall
Competent but clinical. A car that does everything well except excite its driver. Conservative styling won't woo the aspirational buyer. Limited but loyal market following

Star **b**uy
Sigma 3.0 24-valve
Max speed 141
0–60 9.4
Mixed mpg 25.6

In a **W**ord
Hi-tech sterility

Space Runner - Space Wagon

Space Wagon is big on value and big on size with a good mix of car-like manners and people-mover versatility

For

Seven-seater bargain, exalted driving position, absorbent ride, low depreciation, versatility

Against

Intrusive road noise, limited dealer supply, negligible discount, few safety features, steep price, too much plastic

Overall

Smart looks, commodious and lively performers with gilt-edged 3-year warranty. Space Wagon 2.0 makes most sense and the turbodiesel is a useful new addition to the range. Ride is good loaded or light but front wheels can go awry when too much power is applied. Sensible, practical long-term buys with no nasty surprises, although it's quite expensive for what it is. Diamond Optional Pack luxuries desirable

Ratings

image	*Mumsy*
value	*Not really*
quality	*Impressive*
depreciation	*Low*
comfort	*Loads of room*
resale	*Simple*
durability	*Robust*
driving	*Goes well*

Star buy

2.0 GLXi
Max speed 116
0–60 11.0
Mixed mpg 30.6

In a Word

Desirable real estate

Shogun

Shogun is almost as able as a Range Rover in abilities but isn't cheap, has a dull cabin and not that big on safety

Ratings
image	*Trendy*
value	*Pricey*
quality	*Impressive*
depreciation	*Class-leader*
comfort	*Superior*
resale	*All day long*
durability	*One of the best*
driving	*Endearing*

Star **b**uy
3.5 V6 24-valve SE
Max speed 116
0–60 9.5
Mixed mpg 19.0

For
On- and off-road capability. Sterling second-hand values. Ascendant image. Cast-iron build and warranty

Against
Plain cabin, high thirst on petrol V6. Lethargic diesel. Not many safety features

Overall
Getting better all the time but so is the competition. Confident, credible and comfortable climber. Growing acceptance among the smart set, so much in demand and depreciation piffling. Runner-up to the Range Rover. GLX models are best value and 3.5 V6 has serious shove. 3-drs more lively than 5-drs and auto trans saps power. Diesels are glacial and still too unrefined to impress. Super-Select transmission is the knees of the bee

In a **W**ord
Clever and classless

3000 GT

Tremendously able, fast and secure, the 3000 GT displays no histrionics but doesn't possess enough image to cut it in the supercar set

For
Speed, docility, standard equipment, technical ingenuity

Against
A bit too OTT

Overall
Deceptively fast, supple, smooth and supremely forgiving. Bristling with gadgetry like Thunderbirds electric spoilers, intelligent suspension, twin turbos and 4-wheel drive. Well-mannered, softly-spoken projectile. Not bad value at £42k and one slingshot that will hold its value, start every single time and sell convincingly secondhand. Trouble is, its heavy whiff of testosterone is a little bit too aggressive for the new age nineties. Second division footballers only

Ratings
image	*Not there yet*
value	*It's got everything*
quality	*Brilliant*
depreciation	*Not terrible*
comfort	*Quite nice*
resale	*Okay*
durability	*Long warranty*
driving	*Serious stuff*

Star buy
3000 GT
Max speed 149
0–60 5.7
Mixed mpg 24.9

In a Word
Porsche-baiter

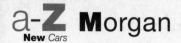
Service interval: *5,000*
Warranty: *12 months/12,000. 19 dealers*

4/4, Plus 4, Plus 8

Morgans have high fun and low depreciation. V8 is barmy and drives in the best vintage tradition. But you could grow old waiting for one

Ratings

image	*Conservative*
value	*Pricey*
quality	*Handmade*
depreciation	*Minimal*
comfort	*Okay*
resale	*Guaranteed*
durability	*Robust*
driving	*Like it used to be*

Star buy

Plus 8
Max speed 121
0–60 6.6
Mixed mpg 20.0

For

Traditional motoring, hand-fettled charm, piffling depreciation, tweedy individuality

Against

Irksome waiting list, feel-the-paint-on-zebra-crossings ride, functional cabin

Overall

Disarming design with modernish mechanicals. Relatively inexpensive and well built. 3.9 V8 Plus 8 has large fun factor but watch it in the wet. Plus 4 has containable ownership costs and just as much appeal. Cleverly packaged nostalgia with professional middle-class image. Bit of a dinosaur now and TVRs have the same retro appeal but buckets more refinement. If you can bear to wait, they're an instant, out-the-box classic

In a Word

Unspoilt by progress

MGF

Ten years too late, this is the MG we should have had in the eighties. But why oh why did they make it look like every other Japanese clone?

For

Bloodline, handling, Hydragas ride, comfort, mid-engined layout

Against

Mediocre looks, short warranty, some parts bin engineering

Overall

A tremendous effort from Rover involving no less than 239 experimental versions. At the time of writing Rover hasn't allowed anybody from the press to drive the MGF. Nevertheless we applaud its ingenuity and clever design. Rover reckon that it's better than the MX-5 and MR2 but only time will tell. With sports cars coming back, they should have made it a bit more trad, like the MX-5 or Fiat barchetta. Instead it has a rather unfortunate resemblance to the Honda Beat

Ratings

image	*Happening*
value	*Not bad*
quality	*Good*
depreciation	*Minimal*
comfort	*Okay*
resale	*Guaranteed*
durability	*Robust*
driving	*Engaging*

Star buy
MGF VVC
Max speed 130
0–60 7.0
Mixed mpg 35.0

In a Word
Modern Midget

RV8

MGR is yesterday's lunch warmed up. Fast enough but can't hide its prodigious age

Ratings	
image	*Retro*
value	*Expensive*
quality	*Okay-ish*
depreciation	*Not brilliant*
comfort	*Okay*
resale	*Unpredictable*
durability	*Not bad*
driving	*Quick car*

Star **b**uy
MGR-V8
Max speed 135
0–60 5.9
Mixed mpg 24.7

For
Nostalgia, performance, looks, breeding

Against
Vast price, old handling, real ale image

Overall
A diverting package that looks and sounds horny, but for what it is £25k looks a little steep. The market hasn't gone crazy either, with plenty for sale at sensible money. There are much better, cheaper sports cars, but if you want a V8 MG you could build your own for half the price

In a **W**ord
Old wine, old bottle

128

Service interval: *9,000*
Warranty: *36 months/36,000. 200 dealers*

Micra

Micra is one of the finest superminis with charm, poise, practicality and strong residuals

For
Cuddly looks, radical design, spacious, auto option, refinement, utterly disarming package

Against
Precious little

Overall
Accomplished abilities, technically advanced, chic and matey. Micra is a prince among small cars and much better than its forebear. With smooth ride, zesty engines and light controls it's a friendly driver, equally at home in town or on motorway

Ratings

image	*Perky*
value	*Considerable*
quality	*Hard to fault*
depreciation	*Minimal*
comfort	*Surprisingly good*
resale	*Safe bet*
durability	*Bodes well*
driving	*Fun*

Star **b**uy
1.0 LX
Max speed 90
0–60 15.2
Mixed mpg 40.6

In a **W**ord
Little cracker

Sunny

Sunny is easy to drive, live with and mend. Cramped rear though. New model soon so watch secondhand values

Ratings
image *Blunt*
value *Okay*
quality *Brill*
depreciation *Lowish*
comfort *So-so*
resale *In demand*
durability *Solid*
driving *Poised*

Best **b**uys
1.4 LX Cat 4-dr
Competitive
1.6LX Cat Estate
Inexpensive
2.0LX Diesel
Pleasing

Star **b**uy
Sunny GTi
Max speed 133
0–60 6.8
Mixed mpg 30.3

For
Formidable GTi and GTi-R, workmanlike estate but saloon is driving school dull. Unerring reliability and build quality, supple ride and mellifluous gear shifting.

Against
Drab, cramped interiors, saloon looks bland, silly name, bump steer

Overall
Potent Sunny GTi one of the best hot-shoe hatches. Easy to drive, easy to fix, long-lasting, firm secondhand values. Estate needs power steering. GTi-R has cult following. Sound all-rounder that's economical, smooth and quite rapid. Drama-free transport with a trauma-free price. Will be dropped soon when the slightly larger Almera goes on sale

In a **W**ord
Son-of-Dat
comes of age

Primera

Much misunderstood Primera makes hardy long-lived family shuttle. Strong resale, long warranty and British built

For
Euro looks, oriental build quality, peppy engines, natty handling, calm ride, thoughtful fascias, pleasing equipment, predictable running costs

Against
Diesels need turbos, estates have wallowy ride, bit light on personality

Overall
Fine refreshing fleet contender to run-of-the-mill Sierra/Cavalier variants. Likely to last longer, too. Refined, roomy and rewarding. Distinctive image, and still a rare sight. Ford set the Primera as a yardstick for the Mondeo, which is praise indeed. Big model range of useful, capable cars. Worth a drive

Ratings
image	*Separate*
value	*Very good*
quality	*Best in class*
depreciation	*Pleasing*
comfort	*Calming*
resale	*Easy*
durability	*Robust*
driving	*Sprightly*

Best buys
1.6 LX Estate
Cost and capacity
1.6 LS
Value package
2.0 GSX
Plush and potent

Star buy
1.6 SLX
Max speed 113
0–60 11.9
Mixed mpg 35.1

In a Word
The alternative family car

100 NX

100 NX looks better than it is and there are many better pint-sized coupes

Ratings

image	*Blousey*
value	*Okay*
quality	*Fine*
depreciation	*Small*
comfort	*Not bad*
resale	*An acquired taste*
durability	*Robust*
driving	*Predictable*

Star buy
100NX
Max speed 118
0–60 10.7
Mixed mpg 40.1

For

Usual Japanese solidity, rare sight, clever targa top, dapper looks

Against

Only 90 bhp, soggy ride, lacks personality

Overall

Sensibly priced, but don't expect much in the thrills department. Pretty party frock conceals only average performance and handling. Swanky enough but a touch too camp for our tastes. Much in the Corsa/Tigra mould and more of a dubious lifestyle accessory than a proper car. Pretty light on street cred too. We wouldn't if we were you

In a Word
Suburban trinket

200 SX

Excellent 200 SX offers huge value and performance, plus long warranty and big-time entertainment

For

Vigorous performance from delightful turbo, deft handling, forgiving ride, irresistible price tag

Against

Small boot, rear passengers have a tough time, synthetic interior, over-assisted steering, less than able dealers

Overall

Probably the quickest car in its price band with highly entertaining road manners. Uncommon rear drive surprisingly effective. Peerless value and, if you can ignore the 200 SX's blunt looks, this is a seriously engaging motor, easily as good as a Honda Prelude or Ford Probe

Ratings

image	*Quiet*
value	*Unbeatable*
quality	*Impressive*
depreciation	*Not terrible*
comfort	*Tight fit*
resale	*Okay*
durability	*Brilliant*
driving	*Ab fab*

Star buy
200SX
Max speed 146
0–60 6.4
Mixed mpg 25.3

In a Word
Epic value

133

QX

Quick, quiet and comfortable, Nissan's executive flagship boasts everything
except personality

Ratings

image	*Not in the game*
value	*Pretty good*
quality	*Near perfect*
depreciation	*Unproven*
comfort	*Fine*
resale	*Reasonable*
durability	*Endless*
driving	*Beguiling*

Star buy
2.0 V6 SE
Max speed 125
0–60 11.3
Mixed mpg 30.3

For

Perky V6 engines, economy, solidity, different, brilliant warranty

Against

Dull looks, dull character

Overall

A valiant effort from Nissan but in a fiercely aspirational market segment luxury cruisers need to offer more than just mechanical integrity. The QX is neither distinctive nor emotionally captivating. A fine car nonetheless but not one that will carve itself a space in the high flyer's car park. Competition is stiff with benchmarks like Vauxhall's Omega hard to beat. Very few will be imported so it'll be very separate but depreciation might not be its strongest suit. For those who don't want to shout too loud, the QX is ideal

In a Word
A shortage of charisma

Patrol

Patrol is one of the toughest off-roaders. Turbo diesel is the one to have but its sheer bulk may intimidate

For

Kalahari-crossing capabilities, don't-mess-with-me image, bomb-proof build, generous warranty

Against

Armoured personnel carrier styling, parade ground image, Sherman Tank thirst

Overall

Big, rugged and a real gulley-climber, but it can't compete in the snooty off-roader club. Shogun and Range Rover may cost more but they are more refined, more desirable and hold their value longer. Better on safari than at the hunt ball. Deceptively small inside and certainly not as accommodating as its considerable girth might suggest. Unbreakable though and the off-roaders in Dubai reckon it's even better than a Range Rover

Ratings

image	*Beefcake*
value	*Not bad*
quality	*Tremendous*
depreciation	*Lowish*
comfort	*A touch cramped*
resale	*No problem*
durability	*Made from girders*
driving	*Capable*

Star buy

GR 4.2D SGX
Max speed 87
0–60 20.7
Mixed mpg 24.0

In a Word
Trans-continental
expeditions only

Serena

Clever use of space but awful driving position and Social Services minibus looks. Huge thirst as well

Ratings

image	*Not really*
value	*Okay*
quality	*It's a Nissan*
depreciation	*Heavy*
comfort	*Boomy*
resale	*In the end*
durability	*No complaints*
driving	*Like a van*

Star buy

2.3D SLX
Max speed 84
0–60 26.5
Mixed mpg 31.3

For

Versatility, value, visibility

Against

Noisy, thirsty, slow and dull

Overall

Do we really want to drive round in a van with windows? The people carrier explosion hasn't happened and looking at the Serena you can understand why. Alas, it has precious little to recommend it with fairly poor depreciation, as low as 20 mpg from the petrol versions, unacceptable levels of cockpit noise and all the pzazz of an old shoe. If you must have one of these dire devices, try an Espace

In a Word

A Transit is better

Terrano II

Terrano is also sold as rebadged Ford Maverick. Clumsy looks and howling diesel spoil the effect

For

Comfortable, impressive spec, well behaved, refined

Against

Wheezy performance, excitable handling, heavy on the juice, uncharismatic

Overall

Nissan-badged Maverick designed by Nissan. Not much in the way of the street appeal that sells off-roaders to town-bound suburbanites, but capable and practical on- or off-roader. Power is disappointing and fuel bills on the expensive side. Equipment, cabin, controls and driving position have a distinctly estate-like feel. Not one to impress your friends but more of a genuine 4x4 than many of its type

Ratings

image	*Blunt*
value	*Acceptable*
quality	*Polished*
depreciation	*Not ruinous*
comfort	*Reasonable*
resale	*Average*
durability	*Hardy*
driving	*Run-of-the-mill*

Star buy

2.4 SLX
Max speed 99
0–60 14.0
Mixed mpg 24.5

In a Word

Off the mark

Service interval: *12,000*
Warranty: *12 months/UL. 6 year anti-rust. 402 dealers*

106

Roomy, pretty, capable and fun, the 106 is one of the best small cars around
with fine ride and zesty engines

Ratings
image *Classy*
value *Very good*
quality *Okay*
depreciation *Low*
comfort *Cramped*
resale *Easy*
durability *No problems*
driving *Disarming*

Best buy
XR 1.4i
Value package

Star buy
Rallye 1.3i
Max speed 118
0–60 9.3
Mixed mpg 35.4

For
Handling, magic-carpet ride, trendy looks,
generous room, precise steering. Peppy XSi

Against
XN models 4-speed only and very basic, stiff
throttle response, awkward pedal layout, XSi
slightly skittish at limit. Not much room in
the back

Overall
One of the best small hatchbacks. Has verve,
flair and practicality. Excellent 1.4 Citroën
AX diesel engine. A cracking little car likely
to achieve the same higher than average used
prices of the 205. Unassisted steering is heavy
on the hands, XSi goes well but cheaper,
lighter Rallye delivers more excitement

In a Word
Top tiny

205

Despite its classless, timeless looks 205 is nearing the end of the road. 1.9 GTi versions already being hailed as emergent classics

For
Style, refinement, handling, ride. Still looks modern after 10 years. Now deleted GTi highly desirable and fiercely admired

Against
Some French flimsiness, panels susceptible to denting, expensive used prices, overrated diesels

Overall
Still a superb small car despite the much more modern competition. Bags of image, fun to drive, well finished. 106 and 306 are replacing the 205 but neither has the sort of fine handling balance that made the 205 such a mould-breaker. Nice automatic option, horizontal depreciation, wonderful turbo diesels

Ratings

image	*Sloane Ranger*
value	*Great*
quality	*Not bad*
depreciation	*Don't worry*
comfort	*Plenty*
resale	*Instant*
durability	*Proven*
driving	*Charming*

Best **b**uys
205 1.8D Turbo
Enjoyable economy
205 1.6 auto
Value package

Star **b**uy
1.8 D Turbo 5-dr
Max speed 108
0–60 12.2
Mixed mpg 47.0

In a **W**ord
Farewell My Lovely

306

306 has magic cotton wool ride and composed handling. Booted Sedan
looks good and Cabrio is a real stunner

Ratings

image	*Steady*
value	*High*
quality	*Solid*
depreciation	*Low*
comfort	*Fine*
resale	*Good news*
durability	*Likely to be okay*
driving	*Undramatic*

Best *b*uys
1.6 XR
Cost and practicality
2.0 XSi
Speed and grip

Star *b*uy
1.9 XTDT
Max speed 111
0–60 12.4
Mixed mpg 46.3

For
Safety, comfort, practicality, room, ride and
handling, high resale

Against
Hatchback looks bland, S16 disappointing

Overall
Accomplished and able but not as interesting
as 106/205/405 brethren. Reasonable
equipment, quite refined and undeniably
practical. Shamelessly targeted at an
undemanding suburban market – like the
309. But in the medium-sized car sector it's
one of the best with plenty of comfort and
ability. Insurance low, dealers pretty good
and hardly a discouraging word to be heard

In a **W**ord
Jolly good,
but a Citroën ZX is better

405

405 is refined, reliable and a delight to drive. Economical, comfortable and massively big inside but new Quasar hatchback and saloon due any minute

For

Crisp handling, quality ride, endearing economy, Pininfarina-sculpted lines, excellent diesels, vast estates. Standard air-con on all but base

Against

Sometimes fragile build quality, although it is improving. No folding rear seat, limited front headroom, ageing slightly despite minor facelift

Overall

Still one of the most rewarding fleet cars to drive with faultless road manners. Fine engine range includes some of the best diesels around. Estates and oil-burners hold value longest. Turbo diesels make most sense. Driver's airbag standard across the range. Highest spec cars depreciate fastest. Estates look best. Due to be replaced any minute

Ratings

image	*Unusual*
value	*Good*
quality	*Variable*
depreciation	*Average*
comfort	*Soft-riding*
resale	*Not bad*
durability	*Lovely*
driving	*Pleasing*

Best **b**uys

GLX 1.6i Saloon
Family friend
GLXDT 1.9 Estate
Thrift and size

Star **b**uy

1.8i GLX Saloon
Max speed 115
0–60 11.7
Mixed mpg 37.1

In a **W**ord
Better to drive than a
Mondeo

605

Pug 605 is Peugeot's best kept secret. But the only problem is everyone thinks it's a 405

Ratings

image	*Lacklustre*
value	*Great secondhand*
quality	*Okay*
depreciation	*Above average*
comfort	*Very smooth*
resale	*Limited*
durability	*Solid*
driving	*Interesting*

Best buys

SR dt
Size and thrift

SVE 3.0
Quiet and quick

Star buy

SRD Turbo 2.1
Max speed 119
0–60 11.8
Mixed mpg 43.2

For

Acres of room, bundles of equipment, lively diesel, quick and plush 3.0 litre. Smooth-riding, fluent handling, quiet grown-up looks

Against

Over-sensitive brakes and steering, too visually similar to smaller 405 sister. Iffy secondhand values

Overall

The 405 writ large. Capable, comfortable big car choice, but not aggressive enough to woo the image-builders. Sophisticated, elegant and restrained. Heavy initial depreciation, so a nearly-new used buy seems the best way. Automatics sap too much power. Diesels very economical. All models have standard driver's airbag and ABS. SVT upwards has air con too

In a Word
Thinking man's Granada

Service interval: *6,000/12,000*
Warranty: *24 months/UL. 10-year anti-rust + 3-year paint.*
33 dealers

968

968 is reworked 944 and loads better. 968S makes best buy but Club Sport is the real jewel in the crown

For
Sleek, sensuous, superb chassis, impeccable handling, six-speed gearbox. Classy cabriolet. Budget priced Club Sport

Against
Messy switchgear. Gets pricey once you add the options. Tiptronic auto box ratios too high

Overall
Not just a 944 in taffeta. Superior handing, power, technical evolution with 240 bhp and 3.0 litres squeezed into 4 cylinders. Possibly the only Porsche with a socially acceptable image now. Excellent value new and even better secondhand with commendably low running costs and decent depreciation. If you fancy one now, go out and buy a Club Sport as it'll soon be deleted as Porsche dealers make room for the new Boxster

Ratings
image *Glitzy*
value *Pretty good*
quality *Immaculate*
depreciation *Reasonable*
comfort *Not bad*
resale *Straightforward*
durability *Rock solid*
driving *Thrilling*

Star buy
968 Club Sport
Max speed 157
0–60 6.2
Mixed mpg 27.4

In a Word
Satisfaction guaranteed

143

911

911 is a real class act with improved handling and tidied up interior. New Turbo is the dog's whatsit

Ratings

image	*Big and bad*
value	*Who cares…?*
quality	*Superb*
depreciation	*High*
comfort	*Bit basic*
resale	*Easy*
durability	*One of the best*
driving	*Addictive*

Star **b**uy
Carrera 4 Coupe
Max speed 168
0–60 5.5
Mixed mpg 25.1

For

Classic bloodline, ageless shape, glorious flat-six engine and sound effects, adamantine build quality, white-knuckle performance

Against

Mad price tags, city broker image

Overall

Supreme confection of speed, poise, looks and grip. 4-wheel drive Carrera 4 almost viceless. Awesomely fast Turbo not for the meek. All the reliability and solidity of a Golf and no histrionics. Secondhand values strengthening all the time making the 911 probably one of the most satisfying and practical supercar packages money can buy. Some say the new model has lost its endearing raw quality but we reckon it's now a perfect blend of tradition and technology

In a **W**ord
Sublime supercar

928

928 has awesome mile-swallowing ability, grown-up image and tremendous 5.4 litre grunt. Still looks brilliant after 15 years

For
Smooth, effortless acceleration. Withering mid-range punch, clear-the-fast-lane appearance, masculine superiority

Against
Roundy-round looks, jiggly ride, wearisome road noise, vast price, embarrassing envy factor, predatorial image

Overall
Probably the best grand tourer in the world. Wickedly fast and irresponsible. Built for keeps with magnificent 5.4 V8. Claustro-phobic cockpit, chaotic dashboard, but too much tyre rumble. GTS was a classic the day it was born and secondhand ones look wonderful value and worth keeping. Make your mind up now because it won't be around for much longer.

Ratings

image	*Plutocratic*
value	*73 grand*
quality	*Beautiful*
depreciation	*Painful*
comfort	*Noisy*
resale	*Not terrible*
durability	*Hewn from stone*
driving	*Narcotic*

Star buy
928 GTS
Max speed 161
0–60 5.6
Mixed mpg 19.9

In a Word
Master racer

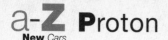

a-Z Proton
New Cars

Service interval: *6 months/24,000*
Warranty: *24 months/50,000. 6-year anti-rust + 6-year powertrain. 230 dealers*

1.3/1.5

Malaysian-built confection of 1984 Mitsubishi Lancer. Looks crap but well built with a suitcase full of warranties

Ratings

image *Steady*
value *Very cheap*
quality *Passable*
depreciation *Average*
comfort *Okay*
resale *So-so*
durability *Reasonable*
driving *Able*

Best buys

1.3 GE
Cheap if not cheerful

1.5 SL Aeroback
Undemanding and cost-effective

Star buy

1.5 SL
Max speed 103
0–60 13.0
Mixed mpg 37.6

For

Unbeatable value, reasonable capabilities. Properly screwed together, civilised levels of equipment, friendly

Against

Dated, low-rent image

Overall

Deservedly popular amalgam of low-cost and practical virtues. Yesterday's Mitsubishi Lancer warmed up. Generally favoured by the elderly as a sort of modern day Triumph Acclaim. Easy to drive, good dealers but whole life costs can be quite high due to heavy early depreciation. Another far eastern compromise car with all the street cred of a misfiring moped but, with prices starting at £7,500, who's bothered?

In a Word

More pros than cons

Persona

Lots of standard kit, modern looks, willing engines and decent handling
make the Persona a commendable buy

For
Economy, practicality, accommodation, impressive after-sales package

Against
Choppy ride, cheapjack interior, muddled switchgear

Overall
Worthy Daihatsu/Hyundai competitor with dependable power unit and drive-train but staid image and rickety trim. Undemanding driver offering laudable levels of spec and space for the price. Watch the excitable and over-sensitive ride, but space, warranty, oriental efficiency and user-friendliness more than compensate. New three-door model due later this year

Ratings
image	*Mundane*
value	*Considerable*
quality	*Sound*
depreciation	*Average*
comfort	*Restful*
resale	*Not bad*
durability	*Solid*
driving	*Take it steady*

Best buys
1.5 GLi
Value package
1.6 SEi
Poshest Proton

Star buy
1.5 GLi
Max speed 108
0–60 12.1
Mixed mpg 38.5

In a Word
A to B without tears

Service interval: *6,000/36,000*
Warranty: *12-months/UL. 8-year anti-rust. 270 dealers*

5

Slovenian-made R5 may be reaching pensionable age but at a whisker over five grand it's a steal

Ratings
image — *Chic*
value — *Few better*
quality — *Okay*
depreciation — *Many worse*
comfort — *Bit basic*
resale — *Pretty good*
durability — *Proven*
driving — *Entertaining*

Star buy
Campus Prima
Max speed 89
0–60 16.0
Mixed mpg 36.6

For
Value, Frenchness, character, mateyness

Against
Stone age technology, sounds a bit busy, precious few creature comforts

Overall
One-model-only range – Campus Prima – is still able to charm despite considerable age. At such an alluringly low price (cheaper than a Kia Pride) it's one of the few budget small cars with any sort of credibility. Still looks good and is amusing to drive with plenty of hatchback practicality. Low ownership costs plus easy resale make Renault's antique an extremely sensible buy

In a Word
Biggest small bargain

Clio

Clio looks trendy with bags of room but driving position leaves a great deal to be desired

For

Natty packaging, sensible levels of equipment, plenty of space, chic image, wonderful chassis, 16v elan, smooth ride

Against

Awkward driving position, some tinniness, nervous at the limit. 1.2 slow, clumsy clutch and gearchange

Overall

Smart shopping shuttle with engaging abilities. 1.9RN one of the best diesel superminis. 16v exceptional value for money. Charming auto only on 1.4RN and Baccara. Williams 16-valve is a real whizz-kid. Driver's airbag standard on RT and top models but £250 cost option on others. Passenger airbag only available on Prima diesel 1.9RL

Ratings

image	*Hip*
value	*Excellent*
quality	*Okay*
depreciation	*Very low*
comfort	*Cosy*
resale	*No trouble*
durability	*Looking good*
driving	*Perky*

Best buys

1.4RN
Value package
1.9RT Diesel
Price and frugality

Star buy

Williams 2
Max speed 134
0–60 7.7
Mixed mpg 32.3

In a Word

Corsa and Micra are better

19

R19 is old hat now and pretty anonymous but ride, handling and use of space redeem things, a bit

Ratings

image *Boring*
value *There are better*
quality *Patchy*
depreciation *Heavy*
comfort *Not bad*
resale *Hard work*
durability *Not brilliant*
driving *Just*

Best buys

16V Executive
Speed and cost
1.9 RN Diesel
Thrift and capability

Star buy

1.4 RT 5-dr
Max speed 108
0–60 12.2
Mixed mpg 42.0

For

Practicality, cost, ride, handling, equipment

Against

Faceless image, sometimes fragile build quality, initial depreciation

Overall

Better-looking now after badly needed facelift, but range still lacks sparkle and credible image. 16V highly regarded, swish Cabrio looks good but rattles a lot, diesels none too refined. Secondhand values nothing to shout about. Reasonable levels of equipment but driver's airbag standard only on RT and Executive. No passenger airbag available. One of the least capable and cost-effective cars in this sector

In a Word

Only average

Laguna

Laguna is a little disappointing and looks like so many other cars of this ilk.
Gone is Renault's wonderful individuality

For
Luxury car feel, perky performer

Against
Higher than average ownership costs, interior feels cramped, uncertain market. Bland looks. Thirsty V6

Overall
Much vaunted (by its makers) 21 replacement that's a shade heavy on the pocket and none too easy on the eye. Renault's UK share of the fleet and family markets has always been precarious, held back by ambiguous image and expensive maintenance. The Laguna's accessibility and flexibility should help, but fierce discounting and even fiercer competition from Cavalier/Mondeo and the like will be a tough nut to crack. Laguna estate promised any minute now

Ratings
image	*Indefinite*
value	*Ample*
quality	*Fine*
depreciation	*Parlous*
comfort	*Expansive*
resale	*Chancy*
durability	*Sturdy*
driving	*Okay*

Star buy
1.8 RT
Max speed 108
0–60 14.2
Mixed mpg 34.8

In a Word
It's all turned out a bit
average

Savanna

Hugely ancient, the Savanna endures because of its seven seats and huge load area. Looks and driving are not its good points

Ratings

image	*Frumpy*
value	*Cheap 7-seater*
quality	*Not perfect*
depreciation	*Quite desirable*
comfort	*For all the family*
resale	*Fast seller*
durability	*Not bad*
driving	*Predictable*

Star **b**uy
2.0 RT
Max speed 124
0–60 10.4
Mixed mpg 32.2

For

Load-carrying capacity, 7-seat option, smooth ride, vast interior

Against

Low on spec, quirky build quality, plain Jane face

Overall

Still one of the roomiest family estates. Cult following. Sheer capacity eclipses any shortcomings in style. Diesels useful devices with strong secondhand values. No driver's or passenger airbag available. Strangely robust used values because of its middle class, large family appeal. Nice, low mileage ones will make all the money, and then some. Fine as a scaled down people carrier but remember, as an estate, it's woefully outclassed by the competition

In a **W**ord
Like a very old
chaise-longue

Safrane

Safrane is tremendously comfortable with scores of gadgets but, like the R25 before it, not an impressive big car choice

For

Refinement, build quality, equipment, plush cabin, fine driving position, smooth V6

Against

Leisurely performance, jerky gearbox, woolly steering, heavy depreciation, main agent parts and service prices, messy switchgear

Overall

Rover 800, Citroën XM, Granada, Saab 9000 competitor that's better than you'd think, but let down by glacial 2.0-litre with lacklustre performance. V6 the one to have. Previous build shortcomings appear to have been licked. Depreciation likely to follow R25 pattern. Big and roomy but image in a market segment thick with self-conceit will always hold it back. Low spec cars – RT/RN 2.2 – best value

Ratings

image	*No*
value	*Not bad*
quality	*Much better*
depreciation	*Difficult*
comfort	*Welcoming*
resale	*In the end*
durability	*Quite good*
driving	*Pleasant enough*

Star buy

V6 RXE
Max speed 132
0–60 10.2
Mixed mpg 23.8

In a Word

Good but could be better

a-Z Renault
New *Cars*

Espace

Espace is still one of the best MPVs with car-like manners, fashionable
image and class-leading used values

Ratings
image *Private school*
value *Best of the bunch*
quality *Can be iffy*
depreciation *Inconsequential*
comfort *A three-piece suite*
resale *Beat off the buyers*
durability *Proven*
driving *Surprisingly fluent*

Star buy
2.0 RT
Max speed 107
0–60 13.6
Mixed mpg 28.0

For
Amazingly versatile, sprightly and doesn't feel
or look like a van

Against
In all-seater format you must leave the
luggage at home. Not cheap, thirsty V6

Overall
One of the finest people carriers around.
Uptown, private school image. Bullish
secondhand values, made to last, handsome
too. Very able family transport but watch for
the odd build quality gremlin. There's an
outraged group of Espace owners who have
formed a disgruntled owner's club. No
passenger or driver's air bag available, and
ABS is an annoying £850 cost option on all
but V6

In a Word
Room with a view

A610

A610 is fine all-round road rocket but a little fragile with fairly serious depreciation. Different but flawed

For
Looks, poised handling, plastic body, 4-seat, turbo oomph

Against
Limited luggage space, off-focus image, jittery secondhand values

Overall
Quick, pretty and individual, the A610 is the alternative supercar. Low profile styling belies considerable abilities. Almost as able as a 911, but many thousands cheaper. Properly made now too, but watch it at part-exchange time. On paper it looks like value at £30,000 but it can't escape its humdrum body badge. That's an awful lot of dosh to pay for a Renault

Ratings
image	*Alternative*
value	*Pretty good*
quality	*Only average*
depreciation	*Hurtful*
comfort	*4-seater*
resale	*Tricky*
durability	*Bit flimsy*
driving	*Big fun*

Star buy
A610
Max speed 165
0–60 5.7
Mixed mpg 26.9

In a Word
Drastic plastic

Service interval: *6,000*
Warranty: *36-months/50,000. 37 dealers*

Silver Spirit III/Silver Spur III

Spirit still the last word in snob value but image out of kilter with the
New Age Nineties

Ratings
image *Acquired taste*
value *Hardly...*
quality *Gilt-edged*
depreciation *Perish the thought*
comfort *Hedonistic*
resale *Ever desirable*
durability *Rock of ages*
driving *Unruffled*

Star **b**uy
Silver Spirit III
Max speed 134
0–60 9.3
Mixed mpg 16.0

For
Refinement, appurtenances of gracious living, traditional values, effortless grace

Against
Pools winner overtones, conspicuous bulk, not involving enough, shameless thirst and price tag

Overall
Socially unsound exclusivity for the insecure. Splendidly dated, marvellously irrelevant motoring monarch. Handling and ride now far superior to previous Roly Polys. Uncannily quiet and cosseting. A unique blend of elegance and engineering. Spur is even more luxurious than Spirit. But how long can such hugely expensive motor cars – £100,000 plus – remain in production with technical marvels like the Mercedes 600 chewing its coat tails?

In a **W**ord
Blithe Spirit

Corniche IV

Corniche IV is now special order only, which is hardly surprising with a £166,000 price tag

For
Presence, composure, fin de siecle elegance

Against
Unpardonable cost and thirst. Not what you might call tasteful

Overall
The most expensive and outrageous sun lounger money can buy. Wonderfully opulent with meticulous detailing but looks more at home on Sunset Boulevard than Sunderland High Street. Fair to say that depreciation is likely to be the other side of catastrophic. But with no serious London parties or social soirees to go to anymore, one has to ask, what the hell's the point?

Ratings
image	*Hollywood*
value	*Don't be silly*
quality	*Seamless*
depreciation	*Unthinkable*
comfort	*I should say so*
resale	*Sultan of Brunei*
durability	*Cathedral*
driving	*Milk and honey*

Star **b**uy
Cornich IV
Max speed 130
0–60 9.3
Mixed mpg 17.0

In a **W**ord
As politically incorrect
as they come

Service interval: *12,000*
Warranty: *12/months/UL. 6-year anti-rust. 700 dealers*

Mini

Mini is still a polished little package and enormous fun. Cooper is even better and all are splendidly classless

Ratings
image *Pert*
value *Good*
quality *Okay*
depreciation *Slow*
comfort *Basic*
resale *Simple*
durability *Well tried*
driving *Beguiling*

Star buy
Cooper 1.3i
Max speed 92
0–60 13.8
Mixed mpg 38.9

For
Fun, personality, nostalgia, chuckability, thrift, classlessness, interior room

Against
Mad switchgear, stone-age ride, almost zero luggage space, poor gearbox

Overall
Dinky but dated. Hardly a practical purchase but surprisingly popular and terribly endearing despite beign 36 years old. There are better small cars, but few with as much cheek. Mini Sprite is cheap at £6,200, Cooper a bargain at eight grand but Mini Cabriolet mad money at £12,500 – ugly too. No power steering, no airbags, no ABS, but auto option on Mayfair at a considerable £985. They say they'll drop it, but with all things sixties so chic, we wonder when?

In a Word
Still crazily desirable after all these years

100

Rover 100 is just a reworked Metro, and feels it too. Punto and Micra much better. Cabriolet is dog ugly

For

Softer body styling, cleaner controls, brighter interior, tighter safety and security

Against

Superannuated design and concept, Metro by another name, airbags extra

Overall

Skilful but transparent exercise in cosmetic surgery. Cheaper and better specced than its predecessor. Peugeot-powered 1.5 diesel unit is quicker, while 1.1s get fuel injection for slightly nippier progress. Likely to sell on looks rather than usefulness. Able shopping accessory but outgunned by many in the ferociously competitive supermini arena. When will Rover stop practising this obvious and patronising tarting up?

Ratings

image	*Trite*
value	*Not bad*
quality	*Passable*
depreciation	*Predictable*
comfort	*Bijou*
resale	*Shouldn't hurt*
durability	*Questionable*
driving	*It's a Metro*

Best buys

111i 3 door
Low cost

114 SLi 5 door
Patriotic practicality

Star buy

114 GSi
Max speed 103
0–60 10.7
Mixed mpg 42.4

In a Word
Blue rinsers only

400

400 is a rebadged Honda Civic that blends Nipponese efficiency with British class

Ratings

image	*Respectable*
value	*Quite pricey*
quality	*Fine*
depreciation	*Average*
comfort	*Not brilliant*
resale	*Easy sellers*
durability	*Solid*
driving	*Up to scratch*

Star buy
416 Si
Max speed 118
0–60 10.0
Mixed mpg 29.9

For

Uptown ambience, sweet engines, practical diesels, responsive handling

Against

Not much rear head and leg room, jiggly ride and quite a bit of road racket

Overall

Commendable effort from Rover. Smart, able, well assembled family package. Drives nicely and likely to be a firm favourite with the fleets, but mean-spirited one-year-only warranty. Standard driver's airbag, side impact beams and alarm-immobiliser. Long-term ownership and depreciation costs look promisingly low. Another prime example of the contribution Honda made to Rover

In a Word
Better than Astra

600

600 is one of the best cars Rover make and the loony milers we've handled seem to wear it well

For

Restraint, build quality, image, resale, generous spec

Against

Some torque steer, fidgety ride, poor rear legroom and driver's headroom. Trim a bit disappointing

Overall

Clever package of engineering integrity and visual subtlety, the 600 is a credit to Rover (and Honda). Ride quality can be really awful and this is no luxury car, more a Mondeo and Cavalier alternative. Engines are excellent with the 620 Turbo best of bunch. Lower spec 620i provides a lot of image for Mondeo money. Not as versatile as Mondeo or Xantia hatches and all but base 620 have split fold-down rear seats. But why only a one year warranty?

Ratings

image	*Patriotic*
value	*Not bad*
quality	*So much better*
depreciation	*Average*
comfort	*So-so*
resale	*Likely to be decent*
durability	*Strong*
driving	*Reasonable*

Best buys

620i
Value package

620 SDi
Performance and economy

Star buy

620 Ti
Max speed 143
0–60 7.0
Mixed mpg 33.0

In a Word

A 3 Series it 'aint

800

Despite more facelifts than Michael Jackson, the 800 is no Peter Pan. If you want a luxury barge with clout, carry on looking

Ratings

image *Establishment*
value *Not bad*
quality *Pleasing*
depreciation *Heavy*
comfort *Yielding*
resale *Hard*
durability *Better*
driving *Faulted*

Best buys
820 SLi
Performance and economy
825 SLD
Credible and cost-effective

Star buy
Vitesse Sport
Max speed 143
0–60 7.3
Mixed mpg 34.2

For

Prestige appearance, traditional grille, comfortable cabins, safety features

Against

Woolly steering, noisy engines, unyielding ride, not much head or leg space, shiversome depreciation

Overall

Well past its sell-by date although heaps better built than they used to be. Quite well equipped and Vitesse Sport shares 620 Turbo engine, so a real blaster. 825 SD very parsimonious but feels and sounds like what it is. Don't buy without a hefty chunk of discount. Rover dealers know it's about to be pensioned off so will haggle. Sound barrier depreciation so best buys are nearly new 800s with tiny miles. Fine if you want to fly the flag but there are many that are better

In a Word
As old as the hills

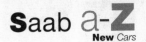

Saab a-z
New *Cars*

Service interval: *12,000*
Warranty: *36-months/ 60,000. 6-year anti-rust.*
105 dealers

900

900 looks rare and unusual and stands out among the Mondeos and Cavaliers. Distinctive choice

For
Everlasting build quality, heaps of safety features, stormtrooper tough, professional image

Against
Expensive parts and service, high first-year depreciation. Poor ride, not that economical

Overall
Although it shares the Vauxhall Cavalier floorpan, the 900 is every inch a Saab with the usual Swedish attention to detail. Life expectancy and integrity looking good. 2.0-litre models real value for money, 2.3 quite grunty but V6 a tad coarse. Vivid Turbo but all have a woolly gearchange and a tendency to lean strongly on corners. 2.0i three door is only £14.5k which for something this different sounds a bit of a bargain. Standard driver's air bag and ABS all models

Ratings
image	*Cerebral*
value	*Off the clock*
quality	*Bomb-proof*
depreciation	*Not the best*
comfort	*Pleasant*
resale	*Cult following*
durability	*Endless*
driving	*Fine*

Star buy
900 2.0i
Max speed 124
0–60 10.5
Mixed mpg 29.9

In a Word
Rock of ages

9000

9000 is built to last forever, looks unusual but price-wise doesn't compare too favourably with the competition

Ratings

image	*Well bred*
value	*So-so*
quality	*As you'd expect*
depreciation	*Hurtful*
comfort	*Among the best*
resale	*Not simple*
durability	*Resilient*
driving	*Supple*

Best **b**uys
CS 2.0i
Power and economy
CDE 2.0i
Big and posh

Star **b**uy
CSE 2.0 Ecopower
Max speed 131
0–60 9.5
Mixed mpg 30.1

For
Lusty and flexible with 2.3-litre engine, smooth styling, huge boot, limo-like ride, seats favoured by osteopaths, seriously crash-resistant

Against
Front-wheel scrambling from Turbo, high depreciation, baulky gear change, main dealer servicing bills

Overall
Solid, secure and sensible. Lots of room, comfort and mile-swallowing ability. Neat handling belies the car's bulk. Individual and separate executive car choice. Light pressure Turbo delivers considerable punch. 2.0-litre requires too much gear changing. V6 overpriced and underpowered. Ride loses composure on poor surfaces. CDs do not have split-fold rear seats. Standard airbag/ABS

In a **W**ord
Unbreakable

Seat a-Z
New *Cars*

Service interval: *10,000*
Warranty: *12 months/UL. 6-year anti-rust + 1-year paint.*
140 dealers

Ibiza

Looks good and VW build quality shines out. Generally quite able and not dear, but needs more safety features

For
Twinky looks, nicely screwed together, plenty of space, prices from £6,400

Against
Hard-riding, interior a bit plasticky, smaller-engined varieties don't have split rear seats

Overall
Seat's best car with the 1.4 CLS and 2.0-litre GTi real winners. Decent diesel too. Airbag and ABS only available on GTi and S models. Handles much better than most superminis but the 1.0-litre – which is actually quite good – really needs power steering. Smaller-engined variants and diesels will depreciate less and running costs won't be out of this world

Ratings
image	*18-30*
value	*Resounding*
quality	*Like a Beetle*
depreciation	*Pretty good*
comfort	*Not bad*
resale	*No worries*
durability	*Looks okay*
driving	*Surprisingly good*

Best buys
2.0 GTi
Cheap punch
1.0 CL
Bargain basement

Star buy
1.4 CLS
Max speed 98
0–60 12.9
Mixed mpg 39.0

In a Word
Almost as good as a Polo

Cordoba

Cordoba is set to be Seat's platform for a world car. Properly made, sensible prices, good equipment and reasonable abilities

Ratings

image	*Uncertain*
value	*Strong*
quality	*Improving*
depreciation	*Average*
comfort	*Not bad*
resale	*Pretty good*
durability	*VW*
driving	*Passable*

Star **b**uy
1.8 GLX
Max speed 130
0–60 10.9
Mixed mpg 37.0

For

Value, integrity, equipment, game engines, versatility

Against

Limited rear room, not that lively, ride can get crummy round town

Overall

Again VW have transformed a once appalling range of cars into something quite reasonable. Power steering, driver's air bag and remote locking standard across the range. ABS is a £610 cost option. 1.6 is decent rather than brilliant, and the 1.9 TD a little slow. 2.0-litre GT has guts and handles crisply although the ride is a touch firm. 1.6 CLX looks like an awful lot of car for under ten grand

In a **W**ord
Getting better all the time

Toledo

With prices starting at a little over £10,000 Toledo is great value, feels solid and drives and handles well

For

Competent, roomy, reliable, whopping boot, VW solidity, neutral handling. Good value

Against

Quirky dashboard, unyielding ride, quite a few squeaks and creaks

Overall

Big value five-seater, strong on sense and practicality. Not that refined and image won't impress but price tags will. I.9 TD GLX diesel worth looking at. Lots of spec, so plenty of car for the cash. Slightly smaller than a Mondeo but heaps cheaper and almost as much space inside. All but base model have ABS and driver's airbag as standard. Depreciation and resale not that bad so makes a shrewd alternative family buy

Ratings

image	*Plain*
value	*Keenly priced*
quality	*Not bad*
depreciation	*Reasonable*
comfort	*Plenty of space*
resale	*Not terrible*
durability	*Looks okay*
driving	*All right*

Best buys

1.6 CL
Priced to please

1.8 GLi
Value package

Star buy

1.6 GL
Max speed 103
0–60 13.3
Mixed mpg 37.9

In a Word

VW hits the mark

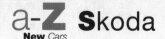

a-Z Skoda
New Cars

Service interval: *6,000*
Warranty: *24-months/UL. 6-year anti-rust. 230 dealers*

Felicia

A quantum leap for Skoda, the Felicia brings them into the 20th century.
Time to stop laughing now. Estate model planned

Ratings
image *Utilitarian*
value *Tremendous*
quality *Leagues better*
depreciation *Likely to be decent*
comfort *Improved*
resale *Surprisingly easy*
durability *Wait and see*
driving *Feels good*

Star *buy*
GLXi
Max speed 93
0–60 14.0
Mixed mpg 41.4

For
Astonishing price, workmanlike virtues, lots of space, surprisingly smooth-riding

Against
All those jokes, heavy steering, basic spec, crude 1.3 engine

Overall
VW has breathed new life into Skoda and the Felicia makes an intelligent budget buy with cheapest weighing in at £6,000. VW 1.6 petrol and 1.9 diesel engines ready later this year. Whole range needs power steering, which is not available. Better lines, better cabin and less noise make this a much improved motor car. Things start to lean badly round the bends but at these prices, what the hell

In a **W**ord
Cheaper than walking

168

Subaru a-Z
New *Cars*

Service interval: 15,000
Warranty: 36 months/60,000. 6-year anti-rust. 135 dealers

Vivio

Vivio is smallest 4x4 but doesn't really have much relevance or appeal. Not the quickest of sellers new or used either

For
Soft ride, thoughtful interior, four-wheel drive, park on a sixpence, quite roomy

Against
Slow, noisy, not much luggage space

Overall
Fine for Tokyo, but doesn't make much sense here. Solid build quality and the cheapest four-wheel drive you can buy. Too noisy and unsophisticated for anything but town toddling. They've never sold many, which isn't surprising, so secondhand resale is likely to be an uphill struggle. On the supermini role of honour the Vivio comes pretty near the bottom

Ratings
image	*Minimalist*
value	*Appreciable*
quality	*High*
depreciation	*Not good*
comfort	*Shoulder-rubbing*
resale	*Tough*
durability	*Low risk*
driving	*Eccentric*

Star buy
Vivio GLi 4WD
Max speed 83
0–60 17.8
Mixed mpg 44.4

In a Word
Buy a Fiesta

169

Impreza

Impreza is comfortable and hardy with a commendably long warranty but looks frumpy and has no image

Ratings

image	*None*
value	*Big*
quality	*Excellent*
depreciation	*Only average*
comfort	*Fine*
resale	*Dodgy*
durability	*Endless*
driving	*Engaging*

Star **b**uy
1.6 GL
Max speed 106
0–60 12.5
Mixed mpg 34.6

For

4x4 versatility, built forever, peace of mind warranty cover

Against

Plain, ugly estate, engines lack mid-range heave, resale hard because of ignorance

Overall

Too anodyne to woo most people and despite being driven at all four corners the Impreza's appeal is limited. Road behaviour is good, with a ride that soaks up every pimple and acclivity with aplomb. Brakes and gearchange are delightful but four-wheel drive needs the bigger 1.8 lump. Now winning rallys, the 4x4 might be okay in the Welsh hills but it's too expensive to be cost-effective for urban trundling. Makes a change from an Escort though

In a **W**ord
Not impressive enough

Legacy

2.2 Estate is one of the best hold-alls around with rock-solid used values
and tremendous fit and finish

For

Outstanding four-wheel drive, leech-like handling, versatile estates, excellent dynamics

Against

No image-builder, fast depreciators, drab-looking saloons, not many dealers, interior a bit plasticky

Overall

Better engineered than dressed. Tame-looking body hides one of the best built estates. Flat four 2.0 and 2.2 power plants are smooth and responsive with useful automatic option. Trim could be a little more inviting with less of a vista of grey plastic. Not quite as much room as a Peugeot 405 but pretty good nonetheless. Highly regarded but one-year-old tiny mileage used buy makes most sense

Ratings

image	*Droopy*
value	*Terrific*
quality	*Fine*
depreciation	*Highish*
comfort	*Friendly*
resale	*No picnic*
durability	*Solid*
driving	*Jolly good*

Star buy
2.0 GLS Estate
Max speed 114
0–60 10.5
Mixed mpg 30.2

In a Word
Looks aren't everything

171

SVX

Subaru SVX may look Thunderbird-weird but is individual, distinctive and loony quick

Ratings

image	*Odd*
value	*A bargain*
quality	*Impressive*
depreciation	*Uncertain*
comfort	*Fine*
resale	*Quite good*
durability	*Strong*
driving	*Interesting*

Star **b**uy
SVX
Max speed 145
0–60 8.1
Mixed mpg 27.1

For
Bold looks, class-beating price, refinement, technical excellence, dramatic performance

Against
Non-supercar image, few servicing dealers, quite heavy depreciation and less than easy resale

Overall
Serious performance, separate styling, heaps of equipment. Subaru's first venture into the performance market is a largely credible if off-focus one. In the shoulder-padded supercar market technical audacity is not enough and image always wins the day. If you want to impress the wannabes this may not be the one for you. But if you want to stand out from the herd, look no further

In a **W**ord
Restrained ferocity

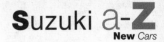

Suzuki a-Z
New Cars

Service interval: *6,000*
Warranty: *12-months/UL. 6-year anti-rust 134 dealers*

Swift

Swift is lively, fun and not that dear, but falls down when compared with class-leaders like the Polo and Punto

For
Dapper looks, taut handling, budget prices, fun GTi

Against
Maddening ride, motorway noise, anonymous image, rough 1.0-litre engine, feels a bit tinny

Overall
Not an obvious choice and no benchmark, but looks good for the money. 100 bhp 16v GTi goes well enough. 1.3 GLX big value at around £8,000. Built in Hungary, which explains the rummage sale prices. 1.3 the one to go for with power steering and lots of bits. Tight fit for four adults, with rough ride and heavy steering. Lots of competition from many better superminis and low street-cred mean used values are softish

Ratings
image	*Drab*
value	*Pleasing*
quality	*Strong*
depreciation	*Swift*
comfort	*Bouncy*
resale	*Hard work*
durability	*Good*
driving	*Not bad*

Star buy
1.3 GTi
Max speed 103
0–60 9.9
Mixed mpg 40.1

In a Word
Cheap but uncharismatic

173

Vitara

Vitara is fast becoming a happening car, which means depreciation is tiny, and resale guaranteed

Ratings

image	*Uptown*
value	*Worth it*
quality	*Rugged*
depreciation	*No regrets*
comfort	*Basic*
resale	*Immediate*
durability	*Solid*
driving	*Good enough*

Star buy
Vitara JLX SE 5 door
Max speed 90
0–60 14.3
Mixed mpg 29.2

For

Trenderama looks, car-like handling, lots of fun and space, inconsequential depreciation

Against

Token off-roader, Sloane Square image, nervous ride, quite thirsty, not many safety features, too slow

Overall

A Jeep in drag, the Vitara is a teenbeat Range Rover. Looks best in black, perked up with big wheels. Long chassis JLX SE Estate is best mix of all-round abilities. V6 engine promised soon, which is just as well as 1.6 performance too frenetic. Interior not the best and not that accommodating either, but all but base models have power steering. Five doors offer the best amalgam of fun and practicality. Fierce secondhand demand so buy with confidence

In a Word
More on-roader than off

Cappuccino

Pint-sized fun but a gallon-sized price – £12,000 – the Cappuccino isn't as good as an MX-5 or barchetta

For
Diminutive size, large helping of fun, rare and distinctive

Against
A real tight squeeze, blousy image, lacks serious cred, not fast at all

Overall
A charming little confection, Suzuki are to be congratulated for the Cappuccino's fizzy effervescence. Fine for a bit of urban posing but long-hauls up the motorway can get a mite wearisome. Everybody will approve of its dinkiness but this one is a bit too girlie-girlie to be taken seriously in the performance club. Well made, long warranty, and not many about, but can your image stand it?

Ratings

image	*Toytown*
value	*Lots better*
quality	*Excellent*
depreciation	*Pretty good*
comfort	*Two's company*
resale	*In demand*
durability	*No problems*
driving	*Smile-a-mile*

Star buy
Cappuccino
Max speed 82
0–60 13.8
Mixed mpg 41.9

In a Word
Noddy and Big Ears only

Toyota

Corolla

Corolla does everything well, except captivate. Well equipped and well made but modern cars shouldn't be this dull

Ratings

image *Inert*
value *Worth it*
quality *Impressive*
depreciation *Slow*
comfort *Okay*
resale *Easy*
durability *Hardy*
driving *Able*

Star *buy*

1.6 GLi 5-dr
Max speed 109
0—60 11.3
Mixed mpg 41.8

For
Solid, friendly, fluent, practical, reliable, long warranty, economy

Against
Tame lines, anaesthetised feel. Two-point-four children image, engines lack flexibility, noisy when pushed, only average handling

Overall
Competent in every department and not expensive either. Low ownership costs and utterly undemanding. Used values look pleasing too. Minimal fun factor though but runs like clockwork with standard driver's airbag and power steering. 1.3 engine is crap as is the 2.0 diesel. 1.6 is better but so it should be at £13,000. And at that money it's worth thinking about a Carina E instead

In a **W**ord
Safe

Carina

Carina is roomy, frugal, safe and as reliable as a microwave, but slightly less interesting than a tumble-dryer

For
Strong warranty, considerable equipment, total reliability, roomy and ruthlessly competent. Economical

Against
Getting expensive, uninvolving, steering lacks feel, body roll

Overall
Fine engines, huge accommodation, lots of spec, easy to drive. Hard to fault seriously, but too bland and faceless. GTi won't impress, XLi 2.0 Diesel thrifty but noisy. Lean burn 1.8 very parsimonious and all get driver's airbag and seat belt pretensioners. Despite tremendous room, the bucking bronco ride lets the whole plot down. Handling is not its best aspect and feels flabby when pushed to the limit

Ratings
image	*Predictable*
value	*Not cheap*
quality	*Excellent*
depreciation	*Not bad*
comfort	*Really good*
resale	*No problem*
durability	*Good*
driving	*Not much cop*

Best buys
Carina E GLi
Lots of kit
Carina 1.8 GLi
Low price

Star buy
Carina E 1.8 CDX
Max speed 118
0–60 11.9
Mixed mpg 42.7

In a Word
A domestic appliance

Camry

Camry is smooth, well specified, quite accommodating and carefully assembled, but as a luxury car it has no class

Ratings
image	*Sensible*
value	*Dear*
quality	*Excellent*
depreciation	*Not good*
comfort	*Fine*
resale	*No push-over*
durability	*It's a Toyota*
driving	*Surprising*

Star buy
V6 GX
Max speed 134
0–60 8.8
Mixed mpg 24.8

For
Peerless build, fine ride and handling, delightful V6, bags of equipment

Against
Not cheap, undiscriminating image, bit thirsty

Overall
Capable, well furnished and sweet to drive. Useful estates, built to last but unforgivably dreary. Unconvincing price tag means you'll probably buy something with a bit more personality. Mind you, the V6 is on the quick side and fit and finish is what you'd expect from the people who make the Lexus. The 2.2i 16 valve is £19,000 but the V6 is the one we'd buy for only £2,000 more

In a Word
No image-builder

Celica

Looks much better than it is, but Celica is expensive and has limited sporting appeal

For
Soft-riding, beautifully made, spacious for a coupe. Quick and utterly dependable

Against
Bulbous styling, gloomy interior, poor mid-range punch, oddly spaced gear ratios, little driver feedback

Overall
Some say it'll be a classic. We doubt it. Highly able but still without emotion. Four-wheel drive GT-Four hangs on to the road but it's not £9,000 quicker than the GT. Push it and it doesn't entertain like a sports car should, being set up more for boulevard cruising than hard charging. Relaxing to drive and commendably quiet though. Huge levels of equipment, but huge price too

Ratings
image	*Not there yet*
value	*Expensive*
quality	*Superior*
depreciation	*Tolerable*
comfort	*Good*
resale	*Easy*
durability	*Long-lived*
driving	*Disappointing*

Star **b**uy
Celica GT
Max speed 133
0–60 7.8
Mixed mpg 34.0

In a Word
More cruiser than bruiser

179

MR2

MR2 looks and handles well, feels special but gets vocal when pushed,
rides stiffly and isn't that cheap

Ratings
image	*Trendy*
value	*Pricey*
quality	*Special*
depreciation	*Limited*
comfort	*Tight*
resale	*Much loved*
durability	*Fine*
driving	*Sparkling*

Star **b**uy
MR2 GT
Max speed 137
0–60 7.7
Mixed mpg 34.2

For
High fun-to-money ratio, dinky looks, quick GTi, ultimate reliability, dependable resale

Against
Cramped, hard ride, needs more safety equipment, costs a lot

Overall
A Toyota with brio. Attractive, pliant and zesty. T-Top with removable panels gives alfresco charm and parking security. Fast too. Quick steering, tremendous brakes, accurate gear change and plenty of urge mean the MR2 is a beguiling bit of kit. Body control is commendable and chassis fine but engine isn't as good as the Honda Prelude V-Tec. Goes well enough but hasn't got that extra edge to set it apart. Solid long term-buy with containable depreciation and ownership costs

In a **W**ord
Sweet petite

Supra

Wild character and performance plus peerless handling make the Supra a bit of all right. Shame about the looks...

For

Six speeds, twin turbos, anti-establishment looks, awesome performance. Not bad at £41k

Against

Numb steering, too much plastic

Overall

One of the most interesting Toyotas money can buy, the Supra is a fully paid up member of the supercar set. Dynamically brilliant, indecently quick and incredibly stable. Much less money than a Honda NSX and almost as entertaining. Image not quite in the big boy league, for something that'll do over 150 mph and accelerate to 60 in six seconds, it's not bad value

Ratings

image	*Bit tacky*
value	*Cheap*
quality	*Wonderful*
depreciation	*Okay*
comfort	*Not bad*
resale	*Can be hard*
durability	*Bomb-proof*
driving	*Ab fab*

Star buy

Supra
Max speed 155
0–60 6.2
Mixed mpg 25.5

In a Word

Big grunt without tantrums

Previa

One of the only MPVs that takes seven people *and* their luggage.
Reasonable price, reasonable spec and huge on room

Ratings
image	*Private school*
value	*Big*
quality	*A Toyota*
depreciation	*Very low*
comfort	*Pretty good*
resale	*Brilliant*
durability	*Solid*
driving	*Not bad for a bus*

Star buy
2.4 GS
Max speed 111
0–60 11.3
Mixed mpg 25.5

For
Interesting looks, carrying capacity, tremendous secondhand values

Against
Hard to park, only four doors, dull trim, not as versatile as an Espace, not fast

Overall
Entry level at £19,000 means this one should be at the top of anybody's list of people-movers. Handles well with smooth, absorbent ride, but not having an off-side passenger door can be a pain, especially abroad when you deposit your passengers into oncoming traffic. Auto option and standard airbag, air conditioning and ABS on 2.4 GX. Sounds thrashy at high speed and not that thrifty. But as MPVs go, this is one of the best

In a Word
Middle class carry-all

RAV 4

Hugely impressive recreational runabout from Toyota that's likely to become
a fashion icon and give the Vitara an extremely hard time

For
Fun to drive, utterly able, nice detailing,
good safety, willing engine, iron-clad
secondhand values

Against
Not a real off-roader, a touch cramped

Overall
RAV 4 rewrites the suburban off-roader rule
book with class-leading ride, performance,
grip and handling. No roll-over antics like
some we could mention, plenty of power,
car-like handling, driving position and ride
sophistication usually absent in this type of
machine. RAV 4 is a real winner with usual
Toyota integrity, standard driver's airbag and
alarm, enjoyable interior and lots of space.
Future prospects are resoundingly promising
so buy with complete confidence

Ratings
image	*Cool*
value	*Stunning*
quality	*Serious*
depreciation	*Tiny*
comfort	*Surprising*
resale	*All day long*
durability	*Hard as nails*
driving	*Big fun*

Star buy
RAV GX
Max speed 105
0–60 9.9
Mixed mpg 30.8

In a Word
Little raver

Landcruiser II

Big, butch and brawny, the Landcruiser has acres of room, brilliant engine
and true gully-climbing ability. Vast size may put you off

Ratings

image	*Wannabe*
value	*Getting expensive*
quality	*Tremendous*
depreciation	*Not bad*
comfort	*Eight-seater*
resale	*Pretty good*
durability	*Made forever*
driving	*Surprising*

Star **b**uy
VX TD
Max speed 106
0–60 12.5
Mixed mpg 25.8

For
One of the most torquey diesels around,
huge accommodation, don't-mess-with-me
image and enticing specification. VX has
leather

Against
Big drinker, getting on for Range Rover
money, roly-poly handling, a bit too big for
its boots. Clonky manual gearbox

Overall
One of the more convincing off-roaders with
good on-road performance and enormous
tractability, quite smooth and quiet but new
massively powerful 4.5 petrol lump has a
voracious appetite for jungle juice. Not
something to be hurried round the corners,
although more composed on motorways.
Interior is on the tacky side and you could
never call it a lovely

In a **W**ord
Two tons of fun

Service interval: *6,000*
Warranty: *12 months/UL. 22 dealers*

Griffith - Chimera

TVR were one of the first to bring retro styling back to the sports car.
Glorious looks, soundtrack, urge - British too

For
Heavyweight straight line performance, handsome, thoroughbred interior, snug feel, retro charm

Against
Sometimes fragile build quality, interesting handling in the wet, not that many dealers

Overall
Muscle-bound macho slingshot that's evolved into a cult icon. Cerbera coupe is a honey, Griffith and Chimera are wonderful V8 bruisers. Raw and vital projectile that looks and feels every bit a true sports car. Image is separate, professional and intelligent, resale excellent and depreciation low. But do be very careful as build quality a bit cottage industry. We've heard some horror stories. Don't forget your steroids

Ratings

image	*Trad*
value	*Solid*
quality	*Iffy*
depreciation	*Low*
comfort	*Agreeable*
resale	*Promising*
durability	*Average*
driving	*Wow!*

Star buy
Griffith 500
Max speed 157
0–60 4.6
Mixed mpg 22.1

In a Word
Beefcake

a-Z Vauxhall

Service interval: *9,000 (Diesel 4,500)*
Warranty: *12 months/UL. 6-year anti-rust. 600 dealers*

Corsa

Corsa is no brainless bimbo but has bold looks, pleasing safety and light
and airy interior. Turbodiesel is the best in class

Ratings

image	*Dead trendy*
value	*Exceptional*
quality	*Fine*
depreciation	*Limited*
comfort	*Generous*
resale	*Certain*
durability	*Looks good*
driving	*Lively*

Best buys

1.4i Merit
Value

1.4i CDX 16v
Plush and nippy

1.5 TD LS
High resale

Star buy

1.4 GLS 16v
Max speed 112
0–60 10.5
Mixed mpg 40.0

For

Sizeable, 3-dr and 5-dr, class-leading safety
and security, broad range of engines, pretty
face, 4-speed auto, zesty 1.4 16-valve engine

Against

Bouncy handling, nasty gearchange, chassis
complains if pushed. All models need power
steering

Overall

Fetchingly cheeky Fiesta challenger with
optional ABS and airbag that majors on
safety. Youthful, practical and family-
orientated. Fine interiors and robust build
quality. A real winner and leagues better than
its Nova predecessor. Lots of neat interior
features, commodious cabin but choose the
1.4 over the 1.2 GLS and boomy SRi. Best
buying comes from 1.4 16-valve GLS with
standard PAS

In a Word

Right on course

Tigra

Tigra is brave, new and better than its Captain Scarlet looks might suggest.
Not huge and more a fun machine than a serious workhorse

For

Voguish, dinky cuteness, spry performance, exact handling, good value, lots of safety

Against

Nowhere to put tapes and chewies, confined and iffy rear visibility, nervous ride

Overall

Fizzy extrovert for children of all ages. Pert and showy supermini guaranteed to captivate anyone with soul. Practicality bows to the charm of driving with a decidedly cramped feel and claustrophobic cabin. Corners cheerily, hits sixty in eleven-and-a-bit and glides to a smudge under 120. 1.4 is sweeter than 1.6 but neither are quiet or particularly comfortable. Standard driver's airbag, low depreciation and a Vauxhall dealer on every High Street

Ratings

image	*Glossy*
value	*Yes*
quality	*Musn't grumble*
depreciation	*Not really*
comfort	*No*
resale	*Same day*
durability	*Tightly finished*
driving	*Zippy*

Star buy

Tigra 1.4i
Max speed 118
0–60 11.5
Mixed mpg 41.1

In a Word
Burning bright

Astra

Astra's ride and handling could be better but safety and security are class-leading and interior very welcoming

Ratings

i*mage*	*Reppy*
v*alue*	*Worth it*
q*uality*	*Good*
d*epreciation*	*Average*
c*omfort*	*No problems*
r*esale*	*Plenty of buyers*
d*urability*	*Solid*
d*riving*	*Able enough*

Star **b**uy

1.4i LS 5 door
Max speed 99
0–60 15.0
Mixed mpg 40.9

F*or*

Smooth lines, vast estates, quality build, heavy on safety, low fuel consumption and running costs, huge range of models, standard PAS and airbag

A*gainst*

Dumpy saloon, jiggly ride, inert handling, lumpy 1.7 diesel, noisy 1.6 petrol, sloppy gearchange

O*verall*

Miles better than its predecessor, now with a fine range of engines and not so rattly. Eager, crisp and keenly priced with spacious cabins. Cavernous estates need larger engines. Splendid GLS 1.4i makes most sense, 1.7 TD is quick and thrifty. 1.4i Merit 5-dr cheap and cheerful. SRi refreshingly insurable. Not nearly as interesting to drive as a Citroën ZX or Peugeot 306

I*n a* **W***ord*
Best Astra yet

Vectra

Cavalier replacement may look similar but hides an all-new car beneath

For
Cost, build, trim styling, fine engines, good equipment, plush interiors, lots of safety and security

Against
Wage-slave image, tame looks

Overall
Conservative General Motors have chosen not to be innovative with the Vectra's design, although it shares some family styling cues with the Omega. There's more room, more spec, standard power steering and an estate. Splendid V6 gets traction control and Ecotec 16-valve engines are ten per cent more frugal. New auto has coasting mode for more economy but entry level model still soldiers on with ancient 75bhp clunker.

Ratings

image	*Mainstream*
value	*Considerable*
quality	*Well tried*
depreciation	*No surprises*
comfort	*Good*
resale	*All day long*
durability	*Rep-proof*
driving	*Does its job well*

Star **b**uy
2.5 V6
Max speed 138
0–60 8.6
Mixed mpg 31.4

In a **W**ord
Cavalier returns from
finishing school

Calibra

Calibra is one of the best cars Vauxhall make. Swish, quick, practical,
inexpensive to own, looks and feels unusual

Ratings
image *Smooth*
value *Very good*
quality *No worries*
depreciation *Containable*
comfort *Okay*
resale *Well regarded*
durability *Reassuring*
driving *Captivating*

Star **b**uy
Calibra V6
Max speed 147
0–60 7.3
Mixed mpg 31.7

For
So pretty, four-seater, super-fast 4x4 Turbo
with 6-speed box, stonking V6, low
depreciation, pleasing thrift

Against
Low-rent interior, some handling histrionics,
fidgety ride, engines can get vocal when
pushed

Overall
The looks to stop a speeding train, but
practical, too. Only the 4x4 can put its power
down properly. Eight and 16-valve still
charm. Quiet, roomy, good value, stylish
with plenty of safety and spec. Hatchback
gives capacious boot with folding seats and a
genuine four-seater. V6 is unobtrusive and
mega-quick with leather and CD as standard.
Driver's airbag, ABS and PAS on all models

In a **W**ord
Much better than a Probe

Omega

Apart from the badge on the bonnet, the Omega is almost as good as a BMW 5 Series and Merc C Class

For

Plenty of equipment, lovely chassis, impeccable ride, reassuring safety, miles of cabin space, jolly good estate

Against

Annoying third rear headrest, loud 2.5 V6, dull facia, unrefined diesel

Overall

Carlton/Senator successor that's leagues ahead of either. 2.0 performance is spirited, while the 3.0 versions really shift. Space, equipment, controls, safety and security are first class, while handling never frightens and long-distance cruising positively delights. Estates are serious good news. Go for sybaritic CDX or Elite spec. 3.0 V6 is a real beaut as is 2.5 GLS. Endlessly practical, carefully detailed and a driver's delight

Ratings

image	*Getting reppy*
value	*Plenty*
quality	*High*
depreciation	*Low*
comfort	*Lots of it*
resale	*Piece of cake*
durability	*Rock solid*
driving	*A pleasure*

Best buys

2.5 GLS
Long legs

CDX 2.5 TD
Thrift and power

Star buy

3.0 V6 Elite
Max speed 136
0–60 9.8
Mixed mpg 28.9

In a Word
A barge with soul

Frontera

Frontera is better than it used to be, but still needs more safety and a much better dasboard

Ratings

image	*Recreational*
value	*Yes*
quality	*Not the best*
depreciation	*Average*
comfort	*Not bad*
resale	*Desirable*
durability	*Wait and see*
driving	*Like a car*

Star **b**uy
2.2 16-valve 5-door
Max speed 100
0–60 12.7
Mixed mpg 28.0

For
Chunky looks, young image, nice price, clever rear door, huge estate

Against
Crazy switchgear, some body roll, only occasional off-road ability, nasty diesel, sluggish 2.2, airbag and ABS optional

Overall
After major reworking the Frontera is improved but still not quite there yet. Ride is better but off-road abilities aren't among the best. Convertible gives fresh air off-roading and estate 5-dr carries everybody and their luggage. Image getting a little bit Essex of late and certainly not in the same class as the posh Discovery. Some shortcomings in the handling and braking departments too. We'd like to see standard airbags and seatbelt pretensioners

In a **W**ord
Buy a Jeep

Monterey

Monterey is a rebadged Isuzu Trooper but looks too clumsy to have much clout in the image stakes

For
Japanese build, gutsy power, lavish equipment, heaps of space

Against
Dated looks, drab interior, big drinker

Overall
Isuzu Trooper by another name. Commanding presence but struggling for style and bereft of vitality. 3.2 V6 is punchy, PAS surprisingly delicate at low speeds and spec bountiful. Off-road abilities fearsome, on-road drivability considerable. Takes those long motorway hikes in its stride. But it just isn't a Range Rover and never will be. Ugly fascia, limited safety features, high fuel consumption and a tendency to lean seriously on corners mean that Vauxhall has missed the mark by a yard on this one

Ratings

image	*Old hat*
value	*Sufficient*
quality	*Painstaking*
depreciation	*Par for the course*
comfort	*Inviting*
resale	*Has its admirers*
durability	*Undoubted*
driving	*Drama-free*

Star buy
3.2 V6 LTD
Max speed 106
0–60 11.5
Mixed mpg 19.3

In a Word
Yet another 4x4

Volkswagen

New *Cars*

Service interval: *10,000*
Warranty: *12 months/UL. 6-year anti-rust. 3-year paint.*
320 dealers.

Polo

Polo has raised the standards by which all other superminis are judged.
Nothing eclipses it for all-round confidence

Ratings

image *Discerning*
value *Loads*
quality *Superb*
depreciation *Negligible*
comfort *Relaxed*
resale *Certain*
durability *Assured*
driving *Gratifying*

Best buys
1.3 CL
Overall ability
1.9 D
Charming thrift

Star buy
1.3 CL
Max speed 97
0–60 16.3
Mixed mpg 42.7

For

Legendary build quality, lots of safety and security, upmarket feel

Against

Limited rear space, slow 1.0-litre

Overall

Not just another little car. Deceptively expansive, stable and solid feel combines with intelligent image to create one of the finest superminis around. Sober performance but safe-as-houses design and unflustered road manners make for totally stress-free driving. Forget it's a Polo and it could be many other larger machines costing considerably more. 1.3 is the ideal buy with sophisticated ride and engine refinement. CL has airbag, PAS, electric windows and central locking, which for under £9k is cool

In a Word
No holes in this one

Golf

Tough, endlessly efficient and long-lasting, the Golf has class, practicality and low costs. We like it very much indeed

For

Comfort, refinement, engineering integrity, resale, aspirant image, mile-consuming ability. Class-leading VR6

Against

Austere cockpit, lowish spec, hard ride, flabby handling at the limit

Overall

Still Britain's best used car. Pretty good new, too. Definitive small hatchback with mature style. Fight buyers off when you come to sell. 100,000 miles a breeze. Still a touch on the pricey side. GTi 16V and VR6 major league performers. All have power steering and driver's airbag but 1.4, 1.6 and 1.8 engines can't cut it. GTi has put on middle-aged spread. TDi gives oustanding economy with a decent clip of speed. But the build quality of the Golf really sets it apart

Ratings

image	*Adult*
value	*Pricey*
quality	*Outstanding*
depreciation	*Slow*
comfort	*Low standard spec*
resale	*Guaranteed*
durability	*It's a VW*
driving	*A bit tepid*

Best **b**uy

1.8 Driver
Value and style

Star **b**uy

VR6 3-dr
Max speed 137
0–60 7.6
Mixed mpg 28.9

In a **W**ord
No handicaps

Vento

Vento looks bland and boxy but is as big as a Cavalier and as well screwed together

Ratings

image	*Conservative*
value	*Pricey*
quality	*High*
depreciation	*Uncertain*
comfort	*Loads of room*
resale	*No big deal*
durability	*Excellent*
driving	*Dull*

Star **b**uy
VR6
Max speed 140
0–60 7.6
Mixed mpg 28.8

For

Volkswagen integrity, plenty of leg and headroom, standard airbag and PAS, VR6 is a gem, economical TDi

Against

Not cheap, stodgy looks, questionable depreciation, bouncy ride, soggy handling

Overall

Limited standard spec, hard seats and stiff springing don't help the Vento's case much. 1.8 doesn't have much urge so go for the 2.0 GL at under £15k. Boot is voluminous but the downside is you trade the Golf's looks for the Vento's accommodation. No one could call it pretty. VR6 makes a mighty saloon with understated looks but a sting in the tail. Credible 405/Primera competitor but needs more sparkle and a lower price tag

In a **W**ord
Practical but staid

Passat

Passat is sensible, safe, secure and solid but lacks serious dynamism and image. Doesn't feel like a big car though

For
Voluminous, relaxing, solid, lasts for ever, safe handling, vast passenger space, all but two lowest models have driver and passenger airbags as standard

Against
Not cheap, little standard kit, passé image, uncertain resale, 1.8 a bit turgid

Overall
Frightfully sensible, big on room, comfort and quality. Loves clocking up the miles, not a squeak anywhere but fails to captivate, except for bracing VR6. Estates and diesels sell better used. Best buys are 2.0 16-valver – good for 132 mph – or 1.9 TDi which will do 50 mpg. Generally very able with decent performance, incredible solidity but not much to make you enjoy yourself

Ratings
image	*Middle class*
value	*Not cheap*
quality	*Brilliant*
depreciation	*High*
comfort	*Austere*
resale	*Estates best*
durability	*Excellent*
driving	*Competent*

Best **b**uy
CD TDi Estate
Room and resale

Star **b**uy
VR6
Max speed 132
0–60 10.7
Mixed mpg 27.9

In a **W**ord
A practical asset

Corrado

By the time you read this the Corrado will be deleted, which is a terrible
shame as it was one of the best handling front-wheel drive cars ever

Ratings

image	*Different*
value	*Not bad*
quality	*Peerless*
depreciation	*Improving*
comfort	*It's a coupe*
resale	*Not bad*
durability	*Eternal*
driving	*Yes please...*

Star **b**uy
VR6
Max speed 141
0–60 7.3
Mixed mpg 28.3

For

Handling, bomb-proof build, glam looks,
VR6 was best sports coupe money could buy

Against

Expensive, hard ride, not much in the safety
department, cramped rear

Overall

Saturday night Scirocco, but prettier and
more accomplished. Hard to fault as a
package of styling, practicality, performance
and engineering. Accurate steering and a
lovely chassis make up for most deficiencies.
2.0 is fine but VR6 is a belter. Might not be
too late to pick up one of the last 500 limited
edition Storms which will become certain
classics. We're very sorry to see this one go

In a **W**ord
Cocky coupe

Volvo a-z
New *Cars*

Service interval: *10,000*
Warranty: *36-months/60,000. 3-year paint, 6-year anti rust. 220 dealers*

440/460

Supposed to take on Mondeo, Cavalier and Primera but fails hopelessly. The Parker Knoll of family cars. New 540 model replaces it soon. Hooray...

For

Comfortable, reasonably priced, squeaky clean respectability, big on safety

Against

Late perpendicular styling, anorak image, not outstanding in any department, dated looks

Overall

Dynamically flawed, the 440/460 already looks old. No competition for Rover 400 or Cavalier. How Volvo can ignore the 440's dowdy image problem beats us. Practical, tough, with ample equipment levels but really a bit too dull for our tastes. Avoid CVT auto like the plague as it sounds like a bison with a migraine. For all those actively seeking a low profile, queue here

Ratings

image	*Confused*
value	*Can do better*
quality	*Passable*
depreciation	*Average*
comfort	*Not bad*
resale	*Okay*
durability	*Solid*
driving	*Predictable*

Best buy
460 Si
Equipment

Star buy
460 CD
Max speed 109
0–60 11.8
Mixed mpg 36.3

In a Word
Not in the least bit spontaneous

850

850 has transformed Volvo's image. Quick, interesting, lively and practical, it's a beguiling all-rounder. 850 T5 is wicked

Ratings
image *New age nineties*
value *Solid*
quality *Impressive*
depreciation *Low*
comfort *Very big*
resale *Dead easy*
durability *Hard as nails*
driving *Big fun*

Best buys
GLT 2.0 10-valve
Ability
850S T5
Urge

Star buy
850 T-5R
Max speed 149
0–60 6.8
Mixed mpg 29.4

For
Goes like no Volvo you've ever seen, front-wheel drive, crisp handling, smooth ride, very safe, silky 5-cylinder engine

Against
Looks like every Volvo you've ever seen. Uninspiring cabin

Overall
The best Volvo so far. Pleasing to drive. Solid, secure and crash-resistant. Used values mega-strong. Estates are favourite with 2.5 10-valve best all-round engine. Seats are firm, plenty of safety and one of the biggest cargo areas in its class. Perhaps the chassis isn't as refined as a BMW but the image certainly is. In estate form there are few that can hold a candle to the 850's poise and panache. We'd be proud to drive one every day

In a Word
A Volvo with cred

940/960

Huge capacity and optional seven-seater payload make the 9 series a
serious load-lugger. All those antique dealers can't be wrong

For

Polished, predictable, very safe, vast space,
huge dependability, smooth engines, tidy
handling

Against

No flair, slab-sided looks, choppy ride, ugly
fascia, quite thirsty

Overall

Built to last a millennium, reassuringly
protective with steady middle class image.
Estates carry everything. Top of the range
saloons quite pampering but no road-
burners. Impressive flexible option selection
means you can pick and mix your spec. Base
960 is a bargain with ABS and standard
airbag. Low-loading sill and wide floor
swallows wardrobes. The whole plot feels
surprisingly agile and nimble. 2.5 straight six
is the best engine choice

Ratings

image	*Improving*
value	*Costly*
quality	*Impressive*
depreciation	*Average*
comfort	*Cosseting*
resale	*Not a disaster*
durability	*Robust*
driving	*Sparkling*

Best buys

960S 2.5
Cheap muscle
960 CD 2.5
Plush muscle

Star buy

960 2.5 GLE manual
Max speed 130
0–60 9.9
Mixed mpg 25.8

In a Word
Rock solid

Buying a **used car**

Where to buy

There are three routine sources of used cars: dealers, private sales and auctions. And there are other marginal, unorthodox outlets like bankruptcy sales, liquidations or company fleets. Such sources can be cheap but they're risky and not recommended for the private buyer. But every source has its dangers. Here are some of the more obvious.

Buying from **dealers**

Depending on your budget, you'll choose either a large franchised dealership with a used car operation selling late low-mileage cars, or a smaller non-franchised independent dealer specialising in older vehicles up to 10 years old. At the bottom of the used car hierarchy are the bombsite dealers. You've seen them – low-rent open air operations with a garden shed for an office and indifferent cars poorly presented at rock bottom prices. We'll ignore these here because the banger type of car is better bought privately through the classified ads.

> At the bottom of the used car hierarchy are the bomb-site dealers with indifferent cars poorly presented at rock bottom prices

Franchised dealers

FOR:

Usually honest, anxious to safeguard their reputation and don't indulge in sharp practice intentionally

AGAINST:

Expensive

Generally, dealers are a good bet because their reputation is at stake. They may appear to be in the business of selling only new cars, but a large proportion of their profits will come from used sales. Volume dealerships – outfits that can shift perhaps 1,000 cars a year – try to sell one used for every new car. At specialist franchises like BMW or Jaguar, the ratio is usually a bit higher.

You're likely to have to pay top money for a used car from a franchised dealer. In return you'll be offered a choice of carefully prepared vehicles with genuine mileages and service history, efficient after-sales service and a no-quibble warranty, adding up to complete peace of mind. But security costs money and, if you're buying a one-year-old 1.6 L Cavalier, reckon on giving the dealer up to £1,500 profit for his trouble. If time and convenience are important, this is the easiest and most secure route. You simply walk in, pick your car, give the salesman your old model and pay the balance. In an ideal world the process would be smooth and trauma-free, but in reality the quality of used dealers varies wildly. At this level it's not sharp practice you need to watch for so much as overpricing and human error.

Car dealers make mistakes like everyone else. Selling used cars is all about detail and, unless the dealership works to high standards and realises that preparation is all, the odd mistake will slip through the net. I've watched buyers for big franchises sit at auctions bidding for cars they've only glanced at. I've come across dealers getting the date of first registration wrong, missing serious accident damage, inadvertently buying and selling clocked cars and paying far too much for indifferent vehicles in the heat of the moment.

Often the fault lies with the salesman. Staff turnover in large garages is huge and young commission-hungry salesmen are frequently found to be selling a range of cars they know very little about and haven't personally inspected. They're no more than items on a stock list to be shifted as quickly as possible. If the salesman hasn't even driven the car he's about to show you, how can he sell it with any conviction?

There are three stages your used car goes through before it reaches the showroom or forecourt and, if any link in the chain is broken, the customer invariably inherits the mistake. First, the buyer for the dealership must buy or take in part-exchange a good car. If he misses a serious fault, or pays too much, the error can be passed down the line. Next, the preparation stage: the car is put through the workshops and prepared for sale. If the mechanic also misses a fault or skimps on servicing and repairs, more mistakes are carried down the line. At the last stage, the sales manager and salesmen get together and set the screen prices. If the buyer has paid over the odds, or the car has fallen in value significantly in the monthly price guides, they're unlikely to make an allowance. The sales manager wants as much as he can get and he wants you to pay his price. That's one reason some forecourts seem to be lined with very expensive cars.

If you're buying a nearly new, one-year-old car from a respectable large garage, it isn't that difficult to protect yourself against someone else's mistake, but you need to know what you're doing. You must know how much the car is really worth by comparing prices with other dealers', watching the classified ads and consulting your price guide. You must make sure the car has been fully serviced before you take collection. That means checking the oil on the dipstick – is it fresh? – ensuring there's a new oil filter and a set of new spark plugs.

> In an ideal world you simply walk in, choose your car, give the salesman your old model, pay the balance and drive away

Nobody will mind if you ask to see a list of what's been done during the car's preparation. Check that the service history is stamped up-to-date as well. Get the garage to warrant the car's mileage in writing – that way, if they have mistakenly bought a clocked car and passed it on to you, you'll have some comeback. Ask them to guarantee that the car's had no serious accident damage in its life and have that put in writing on the receipt.

If you do end up buying someone else's error, a franchised dealer should be happy to rectify the fault or change the car. This is the justification for buying from a large dealership in the first place – their commitment to keeping you, the customer, satisfied. In my experience, few volume dealerships engage in dodgy dealing – they have too much to lose – and most will aim to do fair and honest business. So, apart from having to pick your way past some creative pricing, your level of risk should be limited to making sure that the job of selecting and preparing your chosen car has been done properly.

*Here are the **checks** you **should make***

✓ Make sure the price is fair. Compare it with other similar cars. If you think it's too much, tell the salesman and, if he won't soften, walk away

✓ Ask to see a preparation report which lists reconditioning work that has been done to the car prior to sale. If you're paying retail money, you want a car in retail condition. Insist on a full service according to the manufacturer's schedule and that any paintwork problems, broken trim or detail faults are rectified before you take delivery

✓ Make sure the mileage is warranted in writing on the receipt and that a full service history comes with the car

✓ Insist that the garage provides a written declaration that the car you're buying has never sustained serious accident damage

✓ Make sure you get a minimum 12-month parts and labour warranty

✓ Offers of a 14-day money-back guarantee, or 'we'll change the car if you're not 100 per cent happy' are encouraging signs

Non-franchised dealers

FOR:

A more interesting selection of makes, models and ages for buyers who can't afford later, higher-priced cars

AGAINST:

Not always competitively priced, variable product quality, limited after-sales service, not so concerned about reputation

These are altogether different animals. While they're usually based in one place with, theoretically, a reputation to protect, some don't always operate to the same high standards as franchised dealers. Their selection process can be price-led – buying the cheapest rather than the best. Some aren't as scrupulous about mileages either, and don't put their cars through the same rigorous pre-sale checks as a larger garage.

In general terms, the moral code of the non-franchised dealer is different too. The lower you go down the motor trade ladder, the more elastic the code becomes. Larger dealers don't have a great deal of contact with the bottom end of the motor trade, but some smaller dealers do. Often they'll buy cars from the less reputable auction sites or from one-man-band traders. In effect, they're buying the cars the franchised boys don't want. They're also exposed to elements the franchised dealer seldom sees and in some cases their standards are necessarily compromised.

With smaller dealers, mileage inaccuracy is far too common, reconditioning can be cosmetic rather than mechanical, and the less reputable approach after-sales service on a let's-get-away-with-it-if-we-can basis. I've seen non-franchised dealers cut corners, skimp repairs, zero or wind back mileages and use facile excuses to wear down unhappy customers seeking redress to such a degree that the poor buyer eventually gives up.

I once sold a Sierra Ghia estate with a whopping 139,000 miles to one such dealer who, after vigorous application of the usual beauty products, proceeded to sell the car as a 39,000-miler. Fords have five-digit mileometers, so the extra 100,000 miles wasn't registered. Although this guy knew that the Sierra had covered all those miles, he didn't bother to tell the customer.

I have also watched the same dealer handle an after-sales problem. A woman who had bought a Rover 800, which had been persistently troublesome, gave it back to the dealer with a list of faults to be fixed. My man made all the right noises and was suitably unctuous, reassuring the customer they would do everything they could to put the problems right. But all he did was shove the car to the back of the workshop for three days, claiming he'd been over it with a fine tooth-comb, and that Rovers like this one 'all do that and they're impossible to get absolutely right'. The technique is to grind the customer down so that he or she either doesn't bother or takes the car somewhere else.

This isn't to say that every non-franchised dealer runs his business in this way. But some do. This is how to spot the less scrupulous operators:

✓ Are their advertisements truthful and honest? Are mileages unashamedly declared along with a clear mention of the date of first registration? Garages who never declare mileages in ads, or describe cars as '90 Model' etc, instead of giving the exact year, are being economical with the truth.

✓ How are you treated on the phone? Are they courteous, eager to volunteer information and sound like they know what they're doing? A salesman who offers his name without being asked has nothing to hide.

✓ Look for a clean, orderly sales site or showroom, and signs of organisation and efficiency.

✓ Ask yourself if it looks like there's any money behind the operation. Dealers who don't have much capital often cut corners and tend to sell much older and cheaper cars, usually A, B and C platers in the sub-£3,000 bracket.

Buying a **used car**

✓ Are the cars well prepared? Does it look like someone cares about detail? There's nothing worse than a line of hastily prepared cars with interiors misted up by condensation, missing hubcaps, flat tyres and shabby paintwork

✓ Are the cars festooned with meaningless blandishments? Are the windscreens covered with stickers like 'very economical', 'five-speed gearbox', 'long MoT', 'lady owner', 'good runner', or roof signs proclaiming 'This Week's Star Buy'? This type of simplistic marketing speaks volumes about the dealer's patronising attitude to the customer

✓ How quickly does the salesman or dealer approach you? You want time to relax and look round at your own pace. If you're pounced on the moment you cross the threshold, you'll feel hassled. If a salesman instinctively recognises the moment you'd welcome his involvement, you know you're in the right place.

Buying **privately**

FOR:
Cheaper than dealers, you're eye to eye with the car's owner and there's no high-pressure selling

AGAINST:
You don't get a warranty, your legal rights are limited, there are no finance or part-exchange facilities

Buying privately means you'll make a solid saving over a dealer price, you'll be buying directly from the owner, but you won't get a warranty. Forty per cent of all used cars sold in this country are sold privately and for many car buyers this route is the cheapest and most comfortable.

Your first contact with the private seller will normally be through a classified ad. So before you even leave your home it's important to read between the lines and judge whether a particular car is worth bothering with. Sit most people down and ask them to write a lineage ad for their car and they might as well be writing a fairy tale. Truth and accuracy are buried beneath gilded description and imaginative flourishes. By definition, a used car is a flawed product, so the more superlatives there are, the more each devalues the next. Read carefully and you'll spot the advertisers who are trying too hard or telling fibs.

The first major problem is trying to decide if the seller is a genuine private man, or a dealer or trader in disguise. One local authority estimated that almost eight per cent of advertisements peddling used cars are placed by undisclosed car traders. The law requires anybody who sells cars for a living to declare the fact by putting a 'T' (for Trade) at the end of an advertisement. Generally speaking, most traders' cars should be avoided as they're unlikely to be as cheap or as genuine as privately owned cars. The worst offender is the trader masquerading as a private seller. He's bad news because he wants to avoid his legal obligations while trying to earn his week's wages from you. But the more blatant examples are fairly easy to spot.

Private sale or **trader in disguise**?

First, the terminology used in the ad will sound too slick, too dealer-like. Phrases such as 'clean and straight', 'first to see will buy', 'part-exchange considered' always give the game away. This is a sort of street-wise tradespeak. Genuine private ads are much more naïve and often give irrelevant information – 'new battery' or 'radio cassette' – because they're written by inexperienced private sellers without a profit motive.

You can pick up clues from the phone call too. When you ring up say 'I've rung about the car', rather than 'I've rung about the Cavalier'. That way, if the bloke's a trader with more than one car to sell, he's likely to say, 'Which one?' If, when you arrive at the seller's address, his driveway is cluttered with cars, or there are bits of engines and gearboxes littering his back garden, it's a fair bet he's selling motors on the side.

Honest *private sale*

Buying privately, you're more likely to encounter cluelessness than outright deception. The more cynical elements of the motor trade claim that private punters are some of the worst car sellers, merrily clocking their Metros on a Sunday afternoon and stripping out radios, spare wheels and wing mirrors before they sell. I've never come across a privately clocked car or been met with anything but charming naïveté. Nobody minds a bit of dizziness. Often the more out of touch the seller is, the cheaper the car will be.

Reading **between the lines**

Always ring up about cars that are clearly priced first. Don't bother with anything that says 'offers'. If the seller can't be bothered to put the price in his advert, more often than not it'll be expensive. Look for encouraging signs like the mention of a service history, few owners, low mileage, always garaged, just serviced, fresh MoT. Avoid anything that sounds remotely lukewarm such as 'average condition', 'good condition for the year', 'reasonable body', 'fair runner'. If the seller can't think of anything more positive to say, chances are the car's a dog.

Ask only **direct questions**

To save time and annoyance looking at cars that aren't truthfully described, make sure your questions on the phone are as searching as possible. It's no good asking, 'Is the car in good condition?' Any owner trying to sell his car will inevitably say 'Yes'. Far better to be more direct.

Questions like, 'Are there any dents, scratches or marks on the body?' can't easily be dodged. If the seller's honest, he'll give you a list of any body defects. If he's not, he'll be evasive and sound uneasy – then it's time to put the phone down. The same direct technique applies to questions about the interior, mechanics and service history. Asking 'Are there any burns, tears or holes in the interior?' will tell you far more than simply asking 'Is the interior in good nick?'.

This way, you build up a factual picture from the phone call and make an informed judgement about whether it's worth going to see the car or not. Here are some things to watch when looking at private ads:

- ✓ Is it a genuine private ad or a trader in disguise?
- ✓ Read between the lines of the ad.
- ✓ Look for signs of careful maintenance, service history, garaging etc.
- ✓ Ask only specific, searching questions. You want to know what's wrong with the car, not what's right.
- ✓ Ads with 'T' at the end mean dealer or trader.
- ✓ Beware of 0836, 0831, 0850 numbers – these are prefixes for mobile phones and could be traders or dealers.

For inspecting a used car see 'How to check a car's condition' on page 227

Buying from **auctions**

FOR:
The cheapest place to buy a secondhand car
AGAINST:
Risky if you don't know what you're doing, limited legal protection, no warranty, no part-exchange or finance facilities, no contact with the seller

Car auctions are minefields. For the private buyer they're certainly the cheapest place but also the most dangerous. Venture onto the auction circuit with your eyes shut and you'll wish you'd gone to a dealer. And don't assume that if you buy a dud you can always put it through the next auction and get your money back. It doesn't work like that. You'll probably lose money instead because, through inexperience, you'll have paid more than the car's worth.

Know the system well enough, on the other hand, and you won't buy a car anywhere else. But to win at auctions you must know exactly what you're doing. Spend some time at a few sales before you buy. Know your prices and models well and learn to recognise a genuine car.

> **Car auctions are minefields. They might be the cheapest place to buy, but without doubt the most dangerous**

Choosing your auction

There are about 60 car auction sites, so there's plenty of choice. The market is dominated by the big three, ADT, National Car Auctions and Central Motor Auctions, and all have branches nationwide. Stick to these because the quality and range of cars offered is of a high standard.

One of the most important skills you need is an ability to identify cars that have come from non-profit-making sources like major plcs or rental and leasing companies. If no middleman is involved and you buy direct, it's bound to cost you less.

Fleet auctions

It's worth finding out which auction companies regularly hold fleet sales. If you're looking for an ordinary family car like an Astra, Cavalier, Sierra or Escort, these sales are your best bet. Direct, unmolested company cars make a lot of sense. All mileages will be genuine, most cars will have a service history and are usually realistically priced.

Manufacturers' sales

These aren't open to the general public, only bona fide motor dealers. Cars offered will be only a few months old, have very low mileages and come direct from Ford, Vauxhall, VAG, Rover etc. Although you won't be able to attend these sales, there's always some overspill of unsold cars into the regular sales. Cars that are unsold at manufacturers' sales are re-entered in general auctions and can be excellent buys. Listen for the auctioneer to declare 'direct from Ford' or 'direct from Vauxhall'. If you can afford the higher price, you can virtually buy one of these tiny-mileage-as-new cars with your eyes shut. Most will have the balance of their manufacturer's warranty to run, so if anything does go wrong you're covered. This type of car involves very little risk.

General auctions

Car auctions which include cars from a wide variety of sources involve far more risk. Some of the sources are none too reputable, either. Sellers can hide behind the anonymity of an auction, so it's difficult to distinguish between a genuine car that's offered for sale for the first time and one that's done the rounds of every auction site in the area. Some cars spend more time at auction sites than they do on the road. They're known in the trade as 'landmarks'. Learn to recognise them.

In a general sale you'll find cars from fleet users, rental companies, part-exchanges from garages and traders' cars. Entries come from all over the place, so great care must be taken not to buy something that's unsaleable anywhere else. Since cars at auction can't be driven beforehand, it's an ideal place to unload a car with a serious mechanical fault that would show up on a test drive. That's why it's so important to find out if a car has come from a non-profit-making source rather than from someone looking for a fast buck.

Traders' cars

Cars entered by motor traders can be a dubious proposition because they're entered specifically to make a profit. Some traders do nothing else but inter-auction trading. That means buying from one auction and selling at another. They work on small margins, sometimes only a couple of hundred pounds a car. And low margins mean they'll spend as little as they can on reconditioning.

From the trader's point of view, cosmetics are more important than mechanical integrity. Cars at auction are sold on appearance, so it's unlikely they'll even change the oil on a car bound for 'the ring'. All a car has to do at an auction is limp from the compound to the auction hall – all of several hundred feet. Even if it's sold with an 'end-of-sale trial' or 'warranty', this expires just an hour after the sale. If the gearbox seizes solid in a week's time it will be your problem.

How car auctions work

A car is auctioned for many reasons. It's not necessarily true that cars are at auction because nobody wants them. Companies and car hire firms use auctions because they're the easiest and fastest way of selling. Part-exchanges from garages or franchised dealers are normally entered because they're not considered retail propositions. The mileages are too high or they've been stocking them for too long and want their money back.

The **entry form**

The seller must complete an auction entry form giving details of his vehicle – make, model, year, MoT, whether the mileage is guaranteed or not and whether the vehicle has sustained serious accident damage or even been written off. He must then declare if the car's being sold 'all good' or 'as seen'. If 'all good' he must say if there's anything wrong with the mechanical condition. Only major things are relevant, like engine, gearbox, clutch, brakes and steering and not minor stuff like electrical or trim problems.

With *or* **without** *warranty*

If a car is sound, it's sold 'with warranty'. This means you get one hour after the sale to reject the car if you find anything seriously wrong. The auction company would then refund your money or negotiate a lower figure with the seller. A one-hour warranty sounds a bit of a joke but the thinking behind it is that any catastrophic problems should show up immediately. This isn't always the case, so a 'with warranty' car isn't infallible. The car can very easily disgrace itself days, weeks or even months later, so do make sure that you, or someone else, checks it very thoroughly before you start to bid.

If the car is sold 'as seen' or 'without warranty', you're stuck with any problems. Some fleet users don't warrant cars as a matter of company policy, but this doesn't mean there's anything wrong with them – it's just the way large companies work. Leave the stuff that's sold 'as seen' to the dealers. There should be plenty of 'with warranty' cars to choose from.

The **Engineer's** *report*

Some auctions sell cars with an engineer's report. This means the auction engineer has inspected the car and noted any faults before the sale. This is a good idea, but these reports aren't definitive by any means. There are so many cars to be inspected that they can only really get a general impression of the car's condition. So then the engineer sticks to safe remarks like 'engine serviceable for mileage', 'no undue wear' etc. which could mean anything

ADT *Auctions*

ENGINEERS' REPORT

Branch LEIGHTON BUZZARD

This report has been prepared as the result of a road test only, carried out by one of the Company's engineers and is, in the opinion of the engineer, a fair report for the age of the vehicle.

Lot No:	144	Engine	SOUND
		Gearbox	SOUND
Date:	22 05 90	Clutch	SERVICEABLE
Examined by	S MULLINS	Brakes:	GOOD
Reg. No:	G268 BNO	Steering:	NO UNDUE WEAR
Chassis No:	N/A	Transmission:	NO MAJOR FAULTS
Make	VAUXHALL	Electrics:	ALL WORKING
Model:	CAVALIER	Chassis:	AS SEEN
Rating:		Tyres:	AS SEEN
Year:		Body and Interior:	AS SEEN
First Reg'd:	16 01 90	Remarks:	
Equipment	Spare wheel YES		Odometer Reading
	Jack & w/ brace YES		8,042
	Radio/Cassette YES		
	Other		75 0389

The **reserve** price

The seller must also give his 'reserve price'. This is the lowest price he'll take for the car. This doesn't automatically mean it's worth that amount. Some sellers just try it on, hoping that a private bidder might get carried away and pay the optimistic reserve. The only defence is to know your prices.

Windscreen **information sheets**

Not all auction companies have these. Some simply attach a lot number to the screen and you must wait for the auctioneer to read out the details over the microphone. It isn't easy to take in the vital statistics when they're being read out by an auctioneer at a demented derby gallop. If there is a windscreen information sheet, read it carefully. Check:

- ✓ The car hasn't been a write-off
- ✓ There's no mention of serious accident damage
- ✓ The mileage is warranted
- ✓ The car is sold 'all good' or 'with warranty'

And don't forget the obvious things – date of first registration, exact model specification (L, GL, Ghia etc) and check that the speedometer reading actually agrees with the mileage written on the information sheet.

Into **the ring**

When the car is driven into the 'ring', as it's known, the auctioneer will read out the details. Don't be fooled by weary-looking traders who don't look interested. They won't want to attract attention to themselves or the car they want to bid for, in case it generates unwelcome competition. As soon as the bidding begins, they'll make their discreet signals to the auctioneer.

Bidding sequence

The auctioneer will then look for opening bids. A lot of the time there won't be any at all, so he'll have to

start with an imaginary bid. This will be based on the reserve price. If the reserve is £4,000, he may kick off at £3,300 to get people going, hoping he might get a bid of £3,400 from the floor. If the bidding doesn't reach the reserve, the car will be sold to the highest bidder 'provisionally'. This means the auction will contact the seller and ask if he'll let the car go for a figure that's lower than his reserve. If he agrees, the highest bidder buys the car. If he doesn't, it's entered again or withdrawn.

If **you bid**

The trade buyers use signals to bid. The slightest twitch of an eyebrow is enough. Make sure the auctioneer can see you and your bids clearly, so keep him in eye contact all the time. Remember the maximum figure you want to pay and don't go over it. It's easy to become possessive about a car you want and tussle with other bidders for the sake of it. Don't be pressured by the auction atmosphere or by the auctioneer. Ignore remarks like 'don't miss it for a hundred pounds', 'fill it up', 'cheapest in history' and so on.

Trotting

Not all auctions do this. 'Trotting' means chasing a single bidder up to the reserve price by pretending there's someone bidding against him. It's difficult to spot when this is happening, so join the bidding sequence as late as possible to ensure you're not competing with the Invisible Man.

The **highest bid**

If you buy the car 'outright' and not 'provisionally', you must go to the auctioneer's clerk and give your name, address and a cash deposit. If you don't have a cash deposit, don't bid. You can pay for the car in cash, with a banker's draft or building society cheque. There's no VAT on cars, just commercial vehicles.

You could pay by personal cheque but you'll have to wait until it's cleared before you can take the car away. Drafts and building society cheques are the safest form of payment. Don't walk round auction sites with large amounts of cash. Car auctions don't take credit cards.

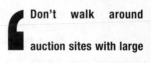

> Don't walk around auction sites with large amounts of cash. Drafts and Building Society cheques are best. Car auctions don't take credit cards

The trial

Once you've paid your deposit you can try the car, accompanied by a member of the auction staff. Get this sorted out as soon as you can – anything serious will have to come to light within the one hour warranty period. Test the brakes. Turn the steering from lock to lock. Select all the gears, including reverse. See that the clutch doesn't slip and listen to the engine. Rev it hard, look for blue smoke from the exhaust, and give the

Buying a **used car**

engine time to warm up properly. Some engine faults will show up only when the car reaches full operating temperature. Bodywork and trim faults aren't covered by the warranty, they're your problem.

Check the *mileage*

Once you're happy with the mechanical condition, ask for the name and address of the last keeper as it appears on the V5. There's no reason why they shouldn't give you this
information. Ask Directory Enquiries for the last owner's telephone number. Phone him or her and ask what the mileage was when the car was sold. If it's consistent with the odometer reading, that's fine. If there's a discrepancy, go back to the auction, tell them you think the mileage is false and they'll investigate.

Indemnity

When you finally pay for your car, there's an indemnity fee included in the price. This gives you protection against the more serious risks:

✓ If the car is sold to you with a warranted mileage that turns out to be false, you should get your money back.

✓ If the car turns out to be stolen, you'll get a refund.

✓ If it has been seriously damaged and this isn't declared, you'll get your money back.

✓ If the car is still the property of a hire purchase company because a loan hasn't been paid off, the finance company has no claim on you. They have to chase the seller who doesn't get paid the proceeds.

Indemnities are compulsory and very sensible.

Don't get carried away at **auction**

Follow these simple **guidelines** and you'll come away with a sound car. There's nothing complicated or mysterious about car auctions – you just need to know what you're doing. Here's a set of **basic** rules. *Stick to them*:

1 It's not a day out for the family, so don't bring the children or they'll distract you, and that's when mistakes are made

2 Look, listen and learn. Find out as much as you can before you bid. This means going to the auction at least a couple of hours before it starts and allowing plenty of time for your inspection. Go the day before, when you won't be under any pressure. Listen to every single word the auctioneer says and read all the notices on display. If you don't understand anything, don't be afraid to ask the staff for help or advice

3 Never buy on your first visit. Return to your chosen auction site several times before you try bidding, so you understand the system

4 Don't go looking for a bargain or a cheap set of wheels. Choose models that you know something about. Most of the really disastrous mistakes at auction are made on impulse. When you've decided on a price ceiling, stick to it

217

There are different categories of auction cars. Some you should buy, some you shouldn't. Find out where it has come from by **listening** to, or **asking,** the auctioneer.

Direct *fleet and* **ex-lease** *cars*
Good buy. Make sure they've got the service history and warranted mileage.

Finance *company* **repossessions**
Don't bid for these. If an owner couldn't afford the repayments he won't have splashed out on servicing. Often repossessions are wrecks: locks get forced, windows smashed, keys and documents are lost and so on. Leave them to the trade.

Manufacturers' *cars*
If you've got the money, these are the best of the lot. They're genuine, virtually risk-free buys.

Traders' *cars*
No bargains to be had here. They know exactly what they're doing and hope you don't.

Cars to **buy** and cars to **avoid** at **auction**

Cars from **official bodies**
Ex-police, local council and health authority cars often lead hard lives as pool vehicles driven by many drivers. Police cars are superbly maintained but are usually painted in flat colours such as white and navy, have basic specifications, tatty interiors and holes in the roof from lights and sirens.

*Ex-***rentals**
Okay, if reasonably low mileage and not too ancient. Anything over 30,000 miles is a risk as they're subjected to a wide range of driving styles.

Auction nasties

These days there is less sharp practice at auction than there used to be. **But here are a few favourites.**

1 **Immobilising** or **sabotaging** cars so they run badly or have to be pushed into the auction hall. Ignition leads are mixed up or removed by people hoping to land a bargain. Go **early** and you'll have a better chance of hearing it running properly.

2 **Unchecked mileages** are unchecked for a reason – there's usually some doubt. So don't be taken in. If the trade knows a mileage to be correct, they get the megaphones out.

3 **Traders bidding** for their own cars to drive up prices. Always done visibly.

4 Ignore **Man A** who pronounces from under the bonnet in a loud voice 'This one's had it', and **Man B** who says with bell-like clarity 'Never seen one so good'. Man A doesn't want you to bid for the car because he wants it, and Man B does want you to bid because he's selling it.

5 Make sure you don't buy a **base** specification car with an **'L' badge** stuck on the boot. Know your specifications.

6 Broken bonnet release **cables** can mean that someone doesn't want you to open the bonnet and see the worst. If you can't open the bonnet, don't buy it.

7 Be suspicious of a car that's **locked** until the last moment – the owner may not want anybody to inspect it too closely. Its useful life may not extend beyond the other end of the auction hall.

8 If you can't find the **service book** in the glove box, try looking under the seats. A full service history is good news and scoundrels who want the car will hide the book from other bidders.

9 It has been known for less than honest sellers to put a five-speed **gear knob** on a four speed gearbox. Check there's a fifth gear there.

When to buy a **Used Car**

JanFeb Buy ex-company part-exchanges now. This is when the big companies change most of their cars and supply is plentyful. Consumer gloom continues with the bad weather.

March Insurance rates change – a good time to buy sports and performance cars – GTis, Cosworths etc. Generally, the used market picks up at this time and prices firm up as dealers start looking for stock to meet demand. Clever time to part-exchange.

AprilMay Market picking up well – good time to sell privately. Demand for soft-tops increases and prices rally.

JuneJuly Demand lessens as private buyers think about holidays. Traditionally an expensive time for estates and caravan-towing cars.

July Buy 4x4s out of season – when the sun's shining. The price you pay out of season can be as much as 10–15 per cent less.

AugSep Buy used cars after the rush of new registrations and trade-ins. Supply of used cars is at its highest, so prices soften. Choice is wider, too.

OctNov Buy sports, convertibles and classic cars when the season's fading into winter. Soft-tops aren't much fun when it's raining. Good time to sell your 4x4.

The big hire companies de-fleet, sending hundreds of nearly new low-mileage cars onto the market – the right time to buy nearly new. Used car sales in the dumps.

Dec Private buyer's bonanza time. The motor trade machinery stops, showroom traffic reduces to a trickle and dealers are keen to make some Christmas profit. Private sellers can be desperate to sell too. No-one wants to tramp round car lots in the cold.

A **strategy**
for **buying**

Limit your choice to a couple of models at most. Don't approach the market looking for anything that's cheap. Get to know your chosen models and their faults. With so much information available, there's no excuse for not knowing what you're doing. Good sources are the magazines such as *The Top Gear Magazine, What Car?, Which Car?, Autocar,* and *Car.*

Decide how much you can afford and stick to it. All used cars have teething troubles when you buy them, so make sure you've got enough money left to maintain and service them. Don't forget tax and insurance as well.

Learn market values. To get the best deal, learn how much your chosen models are fetching at any given time. There are no fewer than four consumer price guides available at newsagents. The best are *Parker's Guide* and *Motorist's Guide.* There are also used price guides in the back of some car magazines.

Shop around and try at least half-a-dozen cars. Only by repeated viewing, inspecting and test driving will you get a feel for the wear patterns and expected condition of your particular model. Never buy the first car you see. Comparing different cars will teach you all you need to know. The more you see, the more you'll learn.

If you're not confident of your ability to inspect, call in someone who is. There's no dishonour in enlisting the help of a specialist examiner such as the AA, RAC or National Breakdown. Shrewd buyers ask the seller to put the car through another MoT before sale. That way, if there's anything seriously wrong, the MoT inspector will pick it up.

Don't rush. The world is full of used cars. Always be prepared to turn on your heel and walk away. The golden rule is – if in doubt, don't.

Used car **scams** to **watch** for

Secondhand car dealers are the least trusted businessmen in the UK. In a recent survey, four out of 10 people singled out the motor trade as dishonest. Car buyers fear they'll be treated badly in the showroom and end up with a sub-standard car.

It might not be so bad if this was some cottage industry or black economy. But no, a great deal of money is involved. To be exact, some £20 billion turnover from the 3.5 million used cars sold in the UK every year. Despite the size of this market, legislation to protect the consumer is woefully inadequate. Trading Standards officers estimate that every year 1.5 million used car buyers are dissatisfied. So nearly half the used cars sold in Britain are in some way faulty.

> **Nearly half the cars sold in Britain each year are in some way faultly, costing consumers billions of pounds**

Here's some of the more common trickery.

Clocking

Government statistics show that nearly one million secondhand cars are clocked each year. In any other business such wholesale deception would prompt outcry headlines and urgent investigations. But we just accept it as a risk you run when buying a used car.

Write-offs

Over 120,000 write-offs are rebuilt and sold every year. There's a thriving trade in damaged repairables – cars that have been written off and rebuilt. Some find their way undeclared onto dealers' forecourts. This is hardly surprising, as there's no official inspection procedure to check that a car's been properly repaired and isn't dangerous. Amazingly, it isn't illegal to sell a write-off either. Dealers don't even have to tell you they're selling a car that's been seriously damaged.

Ringing

Stolen cars are given new identities by swapping number plates and chassis numbers from crashed cars. It works like this. Steal a red F-registration Sierra, find an identical one that's been crashed and 'buy' the registration document and chassis number and put them on the hot car. Some stolen cars are advertised in classified advertisements. Look for desperate phrases like 'must sell this week', or 'emigrating, quick sale required'. If you buy a stolen car through a classified advertisement, even in good faith, the owner or insurance company still has legal title, which could leave you high and dry.

Zeroing

This is winding back a speedometer to 000,000. Dealers do this to confuse buyers. A car sells better if you don't say it's done 99,000 miles. In a recent survey of 199 zeroed cars 110 had covered high mileages. Who zeros a low-mileage car?

Switching

If a car is obviously going to fail its MoT some dealers switch the number plates to a car of the same make and model but in much better condition. The dummy car's chassis number is altered as well and a wreck can then have what appears to be a nice new MoT certificate.

Forged **service books**

A full service history adds a considerable amount to the price of a secondhand car – as much as £1,000 on a Jaguar or BMW. Some sellers will forge service histories to support a suspiciously low mileage. They buy a blank book from the main agent parts department and stamp it up with one of those kiddies' printing sets. Watch out, too, for clocked cars with pages of a genuine history substituted and altered to correspond with the lower false mileage.

Disclaimer stickers

These are stuck to the speedometer glass and say something like 'we don't guarantee the accuracy of this car's mileage'. This really means the dealer doesn't wish to check a mileage with previous owners, but does suspect it's inaccurate. It also gives him some protection if he's bought a clocked car from someone else.

'Pendle' price system

This is a calculated way of baffling customers when advertising cars. It becomes impossible to compare prices of cars from dealer to dealer because the only price shown is the difference between the trade-in price for the old car and the new one. 'Your car plus £1,500, £2,000 etc' the ad might say. This way nobody knows whether they're getting a good deal or not – except the dealer.

Minimum **part-exchange** allowance

This is to attract people who can't afford a deposit to finance a newer model. Dealers offer a high minimum trade-in price for any car, even scrappers without an MoT, offering up to £1,500. This makes the buyer think he's getting such a good deal on his old car that he really can't lose. It also neatly sidesteps the legal requirement for a deposit on a credit deal. Rest assured that whatever car the punter ends up with will be at least £1,500 more expensive than anywhere else.

Misrepresenting a car's **age**

It's routine, even for large dealers, to advertise cars as '87 Model' or '87 Series', even though they were actually registered the year before i.e. 1986. The newer the car, the more it's worth. The dealer's trying to suggest it's a 1987 specification and charging an 87 price for an 86 car. Always ask for the exact date of registration. If in doubt, the DVLA's Enquiry Unit will be happy to tell you on 0839 858585.

The **registration** *document's at* **Swansea**

Sometimes this is a genuine excuse – the V5 may still be at DVLA after an ownership change. But the unscrupulous seller can blame DVLA when he doesn't want the buyer to see the registration document. This could be for various reasons – a lot of former keepers, a colour change, or even differing engine and chassis numbers. He holds back the V5 and sends it to the buyer long after the deal is completed, or not at all. So one Monday morning you could find out your car's had 12 owners and used to be a taxi. Don't buy without seeing the V5.

> **One Monday morning you could find out your car's had 12 owners and used to be a taxi**

Trade sale

If you've managed to negotiate a hefty discount on your car, some dealers will slip in 'trade sale' on the receipt. They're working on a smaller profit margin and trying to sell you the car on a trader-to-trader basis so there can't be any warranty claims. Trade sale means no guarantee.

Selling **unroadworthy** cars

Some dealers in older cars often sell vehicles that are unroadworthy. DoT examiners recently inspected a number of cars on garage forecourts. An incredible 70 per cent weren't fit to be used on the road even though they had valid MoTs.

Dodgy MoTs

The lower elements of the motor trade have a special talent for seeking out myopic MoT inspectors. It's not unknown for money to change hands between dealer and tester to ensure a pass certificate on a sub-standard or dangerous car.

Badges

A wide and colourful range of badges and stickers are available. Most of them mean zilch. Ignore non-manufacturer model descriptions such as 'special edition', 'limited edition', 'executive' etc. 'L' models can suddenly become 'GLs' by sticking a badge on the back. Check the registration document for the exact model designation before you buy.

Rubber mats and seat covers

A set of mats and seat covers are the easiest and cheapest way to hide a worn out interior. Dim dealers use them to make a tatty car appear nice and neat inside. Remove them and see what delights lurk beneath.

Reconditioned engines and gearboxes

On older cars a reconditioned engine or gearbox is a strong selling point. Dealers have been known to steam clean engines, paint them up and claim they've been rebuilt. If a reconditioned engine has been fitted, ask to see the bill or guarantee.

Disconnected **warning lights**

If an engine is worn or on its last legs, the oil pressure warning light on the dashboard will usually start winking. It's quite easy to disconnect this light either at the engine or behind the dashboard. Switch on the ignition but don't start the engine. If there's no oil pressure warning light, don't buy.

Filler

The trader's friend. It's like a putty that sets hard and is then smoothed, not always very well, to conform to the car's body shape. Commonly used to fill dents and camouflage rust holes. It's a bodge and only lasts a few weeks when determined rust bubbles will reappear. Older cars are often riddled with it. Affectionately known by the motor trade as 'gob'. Some devotees use it whenever they can, even on load-bearing parts like suspension turrets.

Vinyl roofs

Once fashionable but now tasteless, these cover up a damaged car's rippled roof very neatly, or can hide the fitment drill holes on ex-police cars.

Beauty products

There's a huge range of products, most in aerosol form, designed to give tired cars a temporary face-lift. You name it – there's a cosmetic to do the job. Lacquer for engines, rubber dressing for tyres, silicone gloss for dashboards, door panels and bumpers. A few hours or a shower of rain and it's worn off. This is why your showroom car looks very shiny, but get it home and it quickly goes dull. Ideal for auctions to give cars a quick shine.

Schutz

This is a spray-on underseal, originally intended to protect metal from moisture. The trade uses it to cover up rusting sills and front valances – out of sight is out of mind. Also found in engine compartments to hide accident-damaged inner wings.

Coachlines and **stripes**

Buy them by the roll. Coachlines along a car's flank visually break the area up, distracting the eye from differences in paint match after poor accident repairs. Designer graphic stripes are commonly used to help cars in unattractive colours like beige and grey. They're useful for covering up dents and rust too.

Part-worn **tyres** and welding **exhausts**

Many fringe traders will fit secondhand tyres to get cars through MoTs. At a few quid a wheel they make a considerable saving on a new set. Often these tyres are perished, have cracked sidewalls and little usable life left. It's also standard practice to weld up rusty or holed exhausts rather than replace them. A month or so later and the holes are back.

Overfilling automatic *gearboxes*

Automatic gearboxes that are slipping or have slurring changes because of low pressure can be improved until the seals burst by overfilling. You can even buy additives to pour into the gearbox to harden perished seals for the duration of a test drive.

Thick **oil**

Noisy engines are quietened down by using thicker oil. Works well with an engine that's clattery when cold. You can also buy special oil additives to minimise engine rumbles. Another ploy is to retard the ignition timing to cover up knocking big ends.

As seen

Avoids any legal responsibility for selling rubbish. 'Sold as spares' is another favourite. Be careful if this is on your receipt. It assumes you're completely familiar with all the car's faults and accept them.

Copy and **substandard parts**

Dodgy cars rarely go near a main agent. If any pre-sale servicing does take place, corners are cut at a back street garage using cheaper non-standard parts. These can cost as little as half the genuine article. Copy brake pads and shoes are often fitted – they don't last any time and can fade alarmingly in extreme situations. Then there are oil filters that don't filter properly, body panels in wafer thin steel that fit badly and exhaust parts that last only 12 months. You'll also find reconditioned alternators and starter motors that have just been cleaned and repainted. Bodgers also like the cheapest engine oil with the viscosity of washing-up liquid.

Clocking

One in four cars sold in the UK is clocked. That means a quarter of the secondhand cars for sale in this country have wafty mileages. Hair-raising though this statistic is, the clocking problem, like some incurable disease, resolutely refuses to go away. The Government seems oblivious to the persistent and sometimes hysterical advice of underfunded and frustrated Trading Standards officers. A long overdue Motor Trade Act is badly needed to clean up the business.

'**One in four cars sold in the UK is clocked. That means that a quarter of secondhand cars have had wafty mileages**'

Tamper-proof odometers are still some way off because insufficient resources have been devoted to their research and development. Given today's technological sophistication, these can't be impossible to produce and could be fitted to every new car in five years. In the days of the ever-capable microchip it's just a matter of application.

Some elements of the motor trade buy high milers specifically to wind back odometers. They're then put through auctions under false selling names or sold to unwitting private buyers. The clocker's aim is simple. Clock the lot. As many as he can. This way, if the Trading Standards boys do catch up, he's made more than enough to pay the fine.

The best defence against buying a clocked car is to wise up:

✓ Be more suspicious and fussy about documentation.

✓ Speak to the previous owner. Check the service book and any old MoTs for mileage discrepancies.

✓ Assume mileages to be incorrect unless the seller can produce proof that they aren't.

✓ Ignore ads that say the odometer is 'showing', or so many miles are 'recorded'. These are carefully chosen weasel words.

✓ 'Guaranteed' and 'warranted' mileage cars make most sense.

✓ Pressure the seller to declare in writing that the mileage of the car is 100 per cent genuine.

How to **check** a car's **condition**

Paperwork

This is an area most private buyers blindly ignore. Yet past maintenance history and signs of conscientious ownership can tell you just as much about a car as a physical inspection. Documentation and service history are vital when you come to sell. Dealers and informed private buyers know the extra value a full service record can add to a secondhand car. Don't buy without one and make sure yours is kept up-to-date. It can add hundreds to the price. Here's what to look for:

✓ Look at the registration document or V5. Check the name and address are the same as the one the seller has given you. If not, be suspicious and ask why it's different. The car could be stolen, being sold without the owner's permission or someone could be trying to cover their tracks.

✓ See how long the seller has owned the car. If it's only for a few months, ask why they're selling it so soon.

✓ Take a note of the previous owner's name and address, so you can ring up later to verify the mileage.

✓ Check the date of first registration, the precise model designation and whether the car's been previously registered abroad.

✓ Old MoTs, bills in the seller's name and past insurance cover notes are a sure sign of long-term ownership.

Buying a **used car**

✓ Spend at least a couple of minutes looking at the V5 to satisfy yourself all is well.

✓ Ask to see any service history, leaf through the booklet and check that servicing has been carried out at regular intervals and been stamped up-to-date. This means the car's been well maintained and gives you a valuable aid when selling.

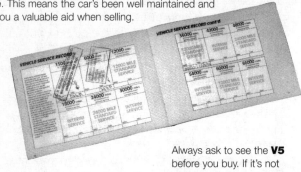

Always ask to see the **V5** before you buy. If it's not available, **be suspicious.**

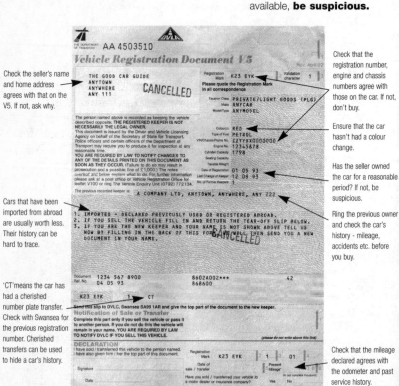

Check the seller's name and home address agrees with that on the V5. If not, ask why.

Cars that have been imported from abroad are usually worth less. Their history can be hard to trace.

'CT' means the car has had a cherished number plate transfer. Check with Swansea for the previous registration number. Cherished transfers can be used to hide a car's history.

Check that the registration number, engine and chassis numbers agree with those on the car. If not, don't buy.

Ensure that the car hasn't had a colour change.

Has the seller owned the car for a reasonable period? If not, be suspicious.

Ring the previous owner and check the car's history - mileage, accidents etc. before you buy.

Check that the mileage declared agrees with the odometer and past service history.

Quick **checks**

Inspecting a used car is easy. If I can do it, anybody can. Very few car dealers I've ever met have any technical expertise. It's all a question of keeping your senses peeled and looking for clues at the scene of the crime. Take all the time you want to look over your prospective purchase, because it'll be the only chance you get. Make sure you open all the doors, bonnet and boot, lift up the carpets and look in as many crevices as you can.

Be fussy, ask as many questions as you can and make sure you go for a minimum 20 minute test drive, so the engine warms up properly. Don't be embarrassed to make lots of notes, and be sure you have all the important facts before you make your final decision. Better still, leave it till the day after, so you can sleep on it and talk to the previous owner.

Taking a friend along is a clever move too. Two sets of eyes are better than one, and it's useful to have a witness around if anything does go wrong. Don't feel pressurised and don't believe the old one about 12 other blokes coming to look at it this afternoon. If you rush your inspection, you'll only regret it later.

Make the following simple, mechanical, interior and bodywork checks on every car you look at.

Roof check
Make sure there is no evidence of filler or repairs in the roof. This usually indicates serious accident damage.

Flank test
Look along each side of the car for ripples or uneven surfaces suggesting accident damage that's been repaired.

Paintwork mismatch
In daylight, look for signs of paintwork repairs. Concentrate hard on both sides of the car and check for colour differences between adjacent panels. This can be particularly noticeable on metallics, which are harder to match. Colour differences show up particularly well under street lights at dusk.

Buying a **used car**

Overspray check
Examine all the sealing rubbers around the front and rear screens and side windows for a build up of excess paint. Look at badges, door handles and light units for any tell-tale signs of overspray. You're looking for paint that shouldn't be there. Any overspray in the engine compartment means that the car has seen front-end damage.

Oil filler check
Open the oil filler cap and look for white mayonnaise deposits – a mixture of oil and water – suggesting a blown head gasket.

Chassis check
Open the bonnet and look at the area around the front headlamps and inner wings. Check for flaking paint, distorted metal and filler. Check the chassis rails that run parallel to the engine for signs of damage or distortion.

Clutch test
Try to make the clutch slip. Put the handbrake on, select first gear and bring up the revs. If you can feel the clutch slipping or smell burning, the clutch is likely to be down to the rivets and on its last legs. It can often be made to slip on fast gear changes or up hills.

Boot floor check
Open the boot and lift up the rear mat for signs of overspray or accident damage. Remember to take out the spare wheel as well.

Dipstick check
Pull out the dipstick and see how much oil is in the sump. Low level is a sign of neglect and future engine problems. Black and dirty oil suggests poor maintenance, infrequent oil changes and advanced engine wear.

Radiator check

Open the radiator cap (with the engine cool) and make sure the water is clean and free from oil droplets or excessive rust. Anti-freeze is a sign of careful maintenance and acts as a corrosion inhibitor.

Crankshaft rumble test

Start the engine from cold and listen carefully for the first few seconds for any metallic rumbling or knocking noises. Walk away if you hear anything you don't like.

Gearbox test

With the engine idling in neutral, depress the clutch and listen. Then bring the clutch up and listen again. Any gearbox bearing noise will be easy to hear. On automatics select 'D' and 'R' checking that there isn't a long delay before either engages. More than a couple of seconds mean the auto box is worn. Make sure the handbrake is on when you do this test.

Blue smoke test

With someone else watching the exhaust pipe if possible, rev the engine hard and lift off looking for excessive discharge of acrid blue smoke – a sure sign of a worn engine.

Gravel rash

Look at the windscreen. If it's peppered with tiny stone chips, the car's been around. Often means 80,000 miles plus.

Gearbox synchromesh check

On the test drive with the gearbox oil still cold, try and beat the synchromesh by fast changes down the box. Changing down quickly from third to second often shows worn gear clusters. Any graunching or baulking from the box can mean an impending and expensive overhaul or replacement. Check the reverse synchro, as well.

Shiny steering wheels and gearknobs

A sure sign that many hands have steered the car many miles and inconsistent with a low recorded mileage. This sort of wear is usually evident above 70,000 miles.

Interior check

Check the driver's seat for frays, tears and sagging. Also headlining for cuts and tears especially around boot area on hatchbacks. Trim problems can be costly to put right.

Speedo binnacle check

Look carefully at the digits in the odometer. Are they level or uneven? Examine the screws that hold the instrument binnacle in place. Do they look as if they've been removed and have burr marks and scratches from a screwdriver? Does the steering wheel look centred when the front wheels are straight? Often clockers have to take the steering wheel off to withdraw the binnacle, and refit it badly. Look also for scratches and marks suggesting the speedo's been out.

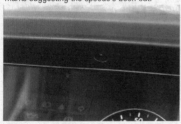

Oil pressure warning light

Before you start the car, turn the ignition on and check that the oil pressure warning light is working. If it's not, the bulb's either been disconnected or it's blown. Walk away. If it does light up, watch it very carefully on the test drive, especially when the car's fully warmed up. If it glows, flickers or lights continuously, the engine has serious problems and needs a rebuild. Leave that car alone.

Service books

Usually found in the glovebox or a small pocket in the footwell. Pay close attention to these. Check the mileage at the last service isn't more than the indicated mileage on the speedo. Don't buy a car that doesn't have some sort of service history.

Inertia reel seat belts

Pull out the seat belt and let it go. If it ravels up quickly, the mechanism's not worn. If it takes an age to gather itself up, it's seen a lot of action and the car's mileage may be high. Check that the belt is not excessively worn or frayed.

The **test drive**

If you've inspected the car and are happy all's well, it's time to take a spin. Ideally, test drives should be in a cold car. If the engine hasn't been started for several hours, the oil won't have circulated and metallic noises are more audible. The first few seconds after start-up are always the most revealing, so listen closely. The drive should last 20 minutes minimum in all sorts of driving conditions. It's important to get the engine up to normal operating temperature.

Some dealers may let you out on your own, but private sellers often won't. Some may not want to let you drive at all. You can't assess a car as a passenger, so ask to drive yourself. If the seller's not keen, find one who is.

Make sure the legalities – insurance, MoT and road tax – are valid. Don't let the seller distract you with conversation, concentrate hard and keep listening and looking.

Warning lights

Check that the oil pressure warning light is both working and goes out after no longer than a split second. If it doesn't go out immediately, the oil pump or engine could be worn. Watch the light for the entire duration of the drive, especially at idle. If it comes on at any stage, the engine's suspect.

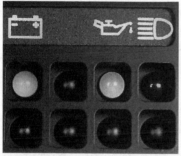

Slow to turn

An engine that's slow to turn means either a duff battery or lazy starter motor. Neither are that serious, but a tired starter motor could be £100 territory.

Slow to fire

Repeated churning before the engine fires isn't a good sign. It could be anything from a blocked carburettor jet or injectors, poor automatic choke to a badly worn engine with low compression. Ask the owner to get the car tuned before you go any further.

Start it from cold

Cold starting is most revealing. Listen for camshaft ticking from the top of the engine and big end rumble from the bottom. Both mean big bills. All metallic noises on start-up mean plenty of miles.

Exhaust blowing

Nasal or growling noises from under the car often mean a blown exhaust. Not the end of the world but work on a minimum of £50 to fix.

Clutch take-up

A clutch should bite promptly. The higher you have to lift the clutch before it engages, the greater the friction plate wear. If it bites near the top of the pedal travel, judders or feels sloppy, it hasn't got long. Squeaking or whirring from the clutch between changes could be a signal from the release bearing. Reckon on at least £100 to replace clutch and bearing.

Temperature gauge

Watch the engine temperature as it rises. If the gauge hasn't moved much after a few minutes, the thermostat may have been removed to hide a faulty head gasket. If the gauge shoots up too quickly and the engine cooling fan cuts in, there could be an overheating problem. Might be anything from £200 to £500 to fix.

Turbos

On turbocharged cars a whistling noise means the turbo's on the way out. A discharge of white smoke when you boot the throttle points to the same thing. Excessive lag before the turbo cuts in after you accelerate is another sign of wear.

Diff whine

A whining from the back of the car could be a worn differential or back axle. Costly.

First gear

First gear should engage smoothly and not have to be forced. There's often more resistance from a cold gearbox than a hot one, but if you have to use undue force the gearbox is on the way out. Expensive.

Lock to lock

Turn the steering both ways from lock to lock while moving slowly. Listen for any clicking noises. On front-wheel drive cars this could be worn CV joints, and on rear-drive cars a duff steering rack. Anything between £100–£200. On cars with power steering, squealing on full lock could be a slipping power steering belt or worn pump.

The high mileage ride

On a smooth surface decide if the car shakes, rattles and rolls too much. A racket from the rear means weak shock absorbers, clonking from the front means tired suspension struts. If the car can't seem to cope with anything but billiard table surfaces, chances are it's done a big mileage and the suspension and steering components are shot. Avoid.

Watch that mirror

Keep an eye on what's happening behind you. Oil-burning blue smoke is the easiest way of detecting a worn engine. If you see a discharge of blue smoke from the back of the car, especially when you accelerate hard or lift off the throttle between changes, the engine may need major work – £500 upwards upwards. White steam-like smoke and drops of water from the exhaust pipe while the engine is warming up are just condensation and quite normal. Black smoke means an over-rich fuel/air mixture and can be easily adjusted.

Brake test

If the car almost changes lane when you brake, there could be a seized brake caliper or serious brake imbalance. Get it checked. If the car is fitted with anti-lock brakes (ABS), check there's no-one behind, then stamp on the pedal. The car should stop without the wheels locking up and the ABS light on the dash should illuminate. ABS problems can be expensive.

Hands off

On a flat surface of road without camber, like a dual carriageway, *carefully* take your hands off the wheel. If the car doesn't stay in a straight line, the front wheel tracking could be out, the tyres could be worn or the car could have had serious frontal accident damage. Make sure you get it checked out.

Wheel judder

A juddering steering wheel between 50–60 mph could be as simple as wheel balancing. If it continues throughout the speed range, there's something more serious amiss such as bent suspension or steering. Get it checked.

Drive belt squeal

A high-pitched squealing on acceleration could just be a slipping or overtight drive belt, worn alternator bearing, or, in cold weather, a water pump about to pack up. Get it checked.

How to **spot** a **clocked car**

Assume all mileages are false until proven otherwise. Get the recorded mileage put on the receipt and make the seller guarantee it in writing.

Look at the instrument binnacle. Check for uneven odometer digits, scratches and marks in the surrounding area suggesting the binnacle's been removed. Check, also, that the screws holding the binnacle to the dashboard haven't been burred by a screwdriver.

Speedometers that have been tampered with often don't work properly. Make sure the needle moves smoothly up its arc and doesn't jerk or stick.

Examine all documentation – service books, past MoTs and garage bills to establish a consistent mileage pattern – going up rather than down.

Satisfy yourself that the overall condition is consistent with the recorded mileage. If you're not sure, go to a large franchised dealer and find out what a genuine low mileage car looks like. Then compare the two.

Tired-looking engines, shabby underbonnet areas, rusty or missing jacks and wheelbraces and bald spare tyres are other signs of high mileage.

Note the name of the previous recorded keeper on the registration document, ring up and ask what the mileage was when the car was last sold. Do this before you hand over any money.

A car's interior holds the most obvious clues to clocking. Look for smooth pedal rubbers, sagging or frayed seats, scuffed driver's door sill, slow to return inertia seat belts, floppy window winders, hesitant electric windows, worn or broken switches, discoloured driver's headlining, worn carpets and heel mats.

Examine the outside of the car for scratches around the driver's door lock and handle and stone chips on the bonnet and front valance. Peppered windscreens and stonechips on the roof are common on high mileage cars.

Cars that
hold their **value**

There are a handful of cars that depreciate like a 747 running on empty. Yet there are others that shed their value at a more glacial pace, returning high resale prices to their grateful owners. Spotting which ones do and which ones don't is the tricky bit, and no salesman in his right mind will tell you that 12 months down the line his shiny offering will be worth £3,000 less than you've just scribbled on the cheque. Here are seven cars that hold their value longer than most.

VW Golf

(from £1,000)

Britain's best used car. Much admired by private buyers and trade alike. Mechanical resilience and rust-resistance spell high used values. Mk II and III models sell well, Mk I is fading now. GTis depreciate most. Five doors most popular. Metallics at a premium. Usually more expensive to buy than Escort or Astra but holds value longest.

Mitsubishi Shogun

(from £3,500)

The only 4x4 with the cachet (almost) of a Range Rover, but holds its value better. Very reliable, well built with used values ahead of competitors. The model that put Mitsubishi on the map in the UK. Dealers love them, so trade-in values are strong, but most are snapped up by eager private buyers. Diamond Option Pack essential.

Fiesta Diesel

(new shape - from £3,000)

Accomplished all-rounder. Much favoured by private and fleet buyers. Fast (for a diesel), reasonably refined, well built, cheap to run; 1.8 DL 5-dr most popular. Long-term used value prospects very sound.

Mercedes 190E

(from £5000)

Cheapest late Merc and most popular. Smooth, compact, reliable and not that expensive to live with. Neatly under the 2000cc tax threshold. Best in automatic guise with alloys, sunroof and electric windows. New model means 190E prices easing slightly. 200,000 miles likely. Service history essential. Much loved by dealers. Colour choice very important.

Land Rover Discovery TDi

(from £9500)

Not as expensive as a Range Rover but just as fashionable. Diesel can be noisy and a bit slow, but they're very frugal. Very difficult to find any bargains here – most sold by Land Rover dealers or switched-on private sellers. Immensely practical with reasonable ownership costs.

Mercedes 300SL 24v

(from £27,000)

Not a car but an icon. Smooth shape and usual Mercedes solidity mean big money. After halcyon period of premium prices, values have settled. Major depreciation in the first two years then levels off. Three-to four-year-olds hold their value best. Chic image, titanium build quality and very safe. Long term prospects good.

BMW 3 series

(new shape – from £9,500)

Seriously trendy so much in demand. BMW dealers pay the most money and sell for highest prices. 316i/318i best bets. 325i coupe good news, too. Alloys and sunroof help values. Probably the slowest depreciating sports saloon there is.

Best **bangers**

Not everybody squanders money on cars. To some people cheerily writing off thousands in yearly depreciation and signing three figure cheques for bowel-shattering servicing bills is unthinkable. Shoestring motoring is in, practised by a thrifty band of minimalist motorists who wouldn't give you tuppence for style, image or the latest year letter.

There's a hidden world of sensible, pragmatic types who drive around in simple, straightforward cars designed and bought to perform a single function - covering the greatest distance at the lowest cost. We may have laughed at their tawdry transport, mocked their mouldy motors, even glanced over at the traffic lights and shivered at the sight of their lacklustre Ladas. But they're laughing all the way to the bank. Here are half a dozen cheerful cheapies.

Ford Granada 2.3 GL Mk II

(from £500)

Built in Germany, so reliability and build quality high. 2.3 V6 engine lasts and lasts. Very low prices. Available everywhere. Some have sunroof and electric windows. All cover big mileages without serious problems.

Mazda 626

(from £800)

Solid Japanese-built family saloon that's barely fashionable but cheap. Hatches best. Avoid early rear-wheel drive saloons. Well equipped, smooth-running and easy to fix.

Buying a **used car**

Ford Sierra
(from £400)

Strong, reliable, predictable resale. Mend them anywhere. Avoid 3-dr versions, 1.3s and ex-taxis. 1.8 CVH engine variants best. Roomy hatchback with simple mechanics. Go for post-'85 facelift cars. 150 000 miles quite normal.

Ford Cortina Mk IV
(from £200)

Very cheap. Under £500. Last of the 1.6 Y platers make fine budget family runabouts. Plentiful cheap spares and an expert in every garage. DIY repairs easy. Good ones always find homes.

Audi 80
(from £900)

Drab image so low prices. Well built but spares and repairs can be expensive. Audi 80 Sport and CL make interesting transport. Avoid thirsty autos and coupes. Renowned for high mileage ability.

Saab 900
(from £800)

Solid old bus. Five doors best. Avoid turbos. Plenty of genuine low mileage examples around for not much money. A touch steady but practically bomb-proof. Spares can be pricey but non-franchised specialists abound. 250,000 miles not unknown.

Cheap **fast** cars

Fast cars have never been cheaper. 1994 saw prices of prime performers plummet because of huge hikes in insurance premiums. The GTi, a victim of its own tremendous success, is still sometimes cheaper than its slower and much less interesting standard counterpart. For some, getting a cover note for an Escort Cosworth is as easy as insuring a burning building. But this market malaise won't last forever. The rest of the used car buying public may be running away from heavy metal, but really canny buyers are realising that this is a market sector strewn with bargains. Buy your fast car now before the word gets out.

Porsche 944
(from £2,500)

Much cheaper than you'd think. Early Y plate cars down to £2500. Very rust-resistant and hardy. Avoid old big mileage turbos which can cost loads to fix. Still some nice genuine cars lurking about. Insurance high.

VW Golf 16v
(from £2,000)

Probably the most reliable hot hatch. Cheapest D platers down to £2000. Thirty mpg and 130 mph mean great value. Interior spartan but durable. Mechanics well up to usual VAG standard. Main agent parts and service very expensive, so find a tame expert.

Peugeot 205 1.9
(from £2,500)

Porsche-chaser. Very rapid but handling can feel frenzied at the top end. Gets rattly with miles but is quite reliable. Hard to insure so prices depressed. Accident damage and abuse a major worry.

Ford Sierra Cosworth
(from £3,500)

150 mph bargain. Sometimes rough, raucous and unrefined but always blisteringly quick. Four-door Sapphire makes most sense. Three-door cars rattle a lot. Sure-footed 4x4 the real steal. Loads of dealers, easy parts and service. Look out for smash damage, clocking and signs of life in the fast lane.

Vauxhall Astra 16v
(from £3,500)

Good for 135 mph and thrifty with it. Off-the-clock insurance depressing prices. Can be very skittish at the limit; lots of front-wheel drive wheel scrabble. Fit and finish flimsy, too, but quick in a straight line. Look out for stolen recovered, smashed and thrashed stuff.

Jaguar XJS 3.6
(from £4,500)

Remarkable value if well bought. Straight-6 XK engine less ruinous than V12. Feels more agile, too. Fluent manual Getrag gearbox. Servicing expensive but most non-franchise specialists can cope. Sumptuous cabin and big feel appeal. History crucial; watch for body rot.

Best **value**
luxury cars

Cuff-link carriages are in. The market for used luxury cars has improved dramatically over the last year or so. As we move out of the recession, clued-up private buyers have realised what wonderful value well-kept used examples of BMW 7 Series, Jaguar XJ6s and big Mercs actually are. For the price of a one-year-old Cavalier you could be driving round in a three-year-old Mercedes 190E or BMW 525.

Remember though to be much more fussy when buying luxury cars - a main agent service history is essential, buy the highest specification possible and, in most cases, automatic transmission will ensure that you'll get a larger chunk of your investment back when you come to sell. These days luxury cars can be complicated machines, so condition is all. You might not be so fussy about the odd scratch or cigarette burn, but the next purchaser certainly will be. Be extra vigilant in your inspection.

Vauxhall Senator 3.0 CDi
(from £4,000)

Incredible level of standard equipment and build quality. Very solid, rewarding and reliable. Vauxhall badge puts image-conscious buyers off, but it's just as well screwed together as a BMW. 24v versions very quick. All come with leather, air con, heated seats and power everything. Avoid 2.5s, manuals and Senators with velour trim.

BMW 525iSE
(new shape, from £5000)

Graceful, strong and big-money image. Fast depreciators, so plenty about for less than £10,000. Some starship mileage E-platers down to £5,000. Auto preferred. SE spec with alloys and sunroof best. Beautifully built, plush and long-lived.

Mercedes 420 SE
(from £8000)

Expansive opulence. Usual peerless M-B craftsmanship. Not the last word in technical refinement but very smooth, cossetting and impressive. Mileages up to 300,000. Best in black. Leather, air con and cruise control add value. History important. Buy a minter for £10,000.

Range Rover Vogue SE
(from £10,000)

Up-market mountain climber. Tough, versatile and very socially acceptable. SE has leather, air conditioning and all the toys. Depreciation heavy in first couple of years, so three-year-old makes good buying sense. Autos preferred. They look well in Beluga Black.

Lexus 400
(from £14,500)

Whispering technocrat. Bristling with all the essentials of gracious living - fast, too. Most end up with Toyota dealers. Image not the finest, but sells on engineering excellence and unrivalled reliability.

Ford Granada Scorpio 2.9i
(from £3,000)

So cheap it's criminal. May be a rough diamond, but tremendous value. Most have leather trim, cruise control, ABS, power everything, trip computer and heated seats. Autos best. Saloons preferred to hatches. Dark metallics lend gravitas. Buy a proper one for £4,000.

Best **value**
family cars

Thanks to the phenomenon of the company car, family saloons have evolved into tough, capable and long-lived machines. Cars like the Mondeo, Cavalier and Rover 400 not only make cost-efficient corporate cruisers but risk-free family buys as well. A legitimate mileage expectation for something like a Citroen Xantia is well past 100,000. Many a Sierra has romped past the 200,000 mile mark without too much drama. We can thank the fleet buyer for increasing the specification of family cars too. Most have electric windows, central locking, PAS and sunroofs, some have ABS, with more and more boasting standard airbags. Servicing is likely to be moderate and routine, and economy pleasing. So if you're looking for no-frills, low-cost and practical motoring, the family saloon is hard to beat.

Peugeot 405 1.9/1.6 GR

(from £2,000)

Crisp handling, lithe styling, economical. The 405 has much more élan than Cavalier/Sierra alternatives. Build quality not as bad as they say. Very rewarding to drive and live with. Diesels and estates best in class. Depreciation moderate. Something for everybody with prices from £2,000. Service history essential.

Sierra 1.8 LX

(from £2,500)

Last of the Sierras were the best. Cars from 1990 on with dark rear lights and standard electric windows make sensible cost-conscious transport with a smudge of style. Proven reliability, 30 mpg plus sunroof, central locking and remote boot and fuel filler release. Usual Dagenham toughness and simplicity. Can't go wrong.

Vauxhall Cavalier 1.6 L
(from £2,000)

All those reps can't be wrong. Sturdy, economical, spacious with rewarding front-wheel drive handling. Carefully built, solid resale and pleasing ownership costs. '91-on cars have power steering. All have sunroofs. Capable of massive mileages with well-proven strengths.

Rover 216 GSi
(from £2,500)

Up-market cabin, much improved assembly processes and lively engines make the 216 a safe bet. Resale strong, long-term durability promising, sparing with the gas. Lots about so finding a decent one shouldn't be a problem.

Nissan Primera 1.6 LX
(from £3,500)

Excellence from all directions. Comfortable seats, friendly interior, huge cabin. Five-door hatch best. 16v engine torquey yet economical. Standard power steering, central locking electric windows, sunroof and three-year 60,000 mile warranty. British made too.

Best **value** **small** cars

The British love small cars. Look at the success of the Micra, Clio, Corsa and Citröen ZX. In fact we're spoilt for choice, with the Town Tiny segment of the market bristling with able and rewarding candidates. While economy is a major factor in most people's buying decision, don't take it to extremes and go for too small an engine size. Buy a 950 Fiesta or 1050 Polo and you'll be overtaken on hills by people on bicycles - much better to go for the 1100 and 1300. The same rule applies to doors and gearboxes. The five-door, five-speed always sells better than the 3 door 4 speeder. An automatic gearbox isn't so popular on a Cavalier or Sierra, but is a definite plus on something like a 205 or Renault 5. Watch those mileages though, since most small car buyers won't entertain the higher mileages clocked up on some family saloons. Small cars with big mileages take ages to sell.

Citroën ZX
(from £3,000)

Endearing alliance of space, cheeky styling, simplicity and sophistication. Easy controls, durable trim and firm build. Reliability now established and used values looking very firm indeed. One of the best small cars you can buy.

Fiat Uno 45
(from £1,200)

Ageing but still holding its own. Strong, punchy engines, galvanised bodies and much-improved quality control. Practical five-door hatchback, very parsimonious and cheap to buy.

Colt 1.6 GLXi

(from £4,500)

Happy Japanese blend of zip and practicality. Limited by import quotas so not too many about. Used values should stay high, as with most Mitsubishis. Well equipped with auto option and standard electric windows. Three-year unlimited mileage warranty.

Peugeot 106

(from £3,500)

Superior, capacious, competent little car. Handles deftly, so engaging to drive. Build quality better than 205 and secondhand values among the most robust. Suburban style.

VW Polo

(from £1,000)

Tough and long-lasting. Not the most refined in its class but built for keeps. Vague steering and woolly brakes, but outlives virtually everything. Usually owned by conscientious middle-class types who service regularly. Easy to sell all year round.

Used **cars** to **avoid**

In the mid-80s the Germans pioneered car assembly technology with millimetric efficiency, but not everybody followed. For the used buyer the early to middle 80s are the dark ages of car quality – remember British Leyland. Here are some of the used car dinosaurs which are unreliable, often worthless and always money-pits. Avoid them all.

Alfa Romeo Alfasud/75

Appalling reputation for rot, unreliability and hopeless resale. Don't even think about it.

Austin Maestro/Montego

84–86 cars badly built. Some with problems impossible to eradicate. Body rust, electrical, engine and gearbox faults. Often exorbitantly priced on forecourts – you can lose fortunes.

Buying a **used car**

Austin Princess/Ambassador

Woefully inadequate in every department. Rusty, unreliable and collapsing suspension, has engine and gearbox gremlins too. Valueless now.

Austin Metro (old shape)

Some good, some bad. Earliest 81–85 cars worst. Body rust, crumbling trim and suspension, gearbox and engine faults, fast deterioration with age. Often repairs won't be economically viable.

Austin Allegro

One of Leyland's worst. Cheaply made, rust-prone and ugly. Worth less than a tank of unleaded, which it can't use.

BMW 5/7 Series

Oldest 77–80 cars worst. High parts and service mean that any reconditioning costs will usually exceed the value of the car; 7 Series particularly complicated. Buy a Granada instead.

Ford Escort Mk III

Avoid 80–86 examples as most disintegrating with loads of electrical, carb, engine and gearbox faults. Pre-86 XR3s duds as well. Buy a Golf.

Citroën GS/CX

Serious corrosion, complicated and awkward to mend, villainous ownership costs, expensive parts and service.

Fiat Strada/127/ Regata/Croma

Too rusty to contemplate. Very poor trim and finish. You'll have to pay someone to take them away.

Ford Fiesta Mk I

Consider only latest 86-on cars. Some early '80s cars are up at silly money. Can be very troublesome and very rusty. Hard-driven XR2 Mk I is horrible, too. Buy a VW Polo.

Lancia (all pre-88 models)

Huge depreciation, expensive complex to maintain, rusty. Walk – it'll be cheaper.

Morris Marina/Ital

Most going through their death throes now. Vast investment required for every MoT. Too old, too flawed to be viable.

Nissan Cherry Europe

Unholy alliance between Alfa and Nissan. Alfa supplied the rust, Nissan the tedium. No-one's ever heard of them so zero demand.

Nissan Silvia Turbo

Medallion man image and a propensity for blowing turbos. Tacky, rusty, expensive to run. Disinclined to start. No resale future.

Peugeot 104

Nasty little buzz box. Engine and gearbox problems, plenty of terminal corrosion. Crusher material.

Peugeot 604

Vast leviathan with no redeeming virtues. Complicated, shortage of parts, thirsty, unreliable and rusty. Worth only the value of mixed metals.

Renault Fuego/20/30

Dire. Fuego Turbo the most awful. All thirsty, rust-prone, unreliable and pricey to maintain. Parts a problem, too. See the scrap man.

Rover SD1 2000/2300/2600

Litany of problems a mile long. Can look deceptively attractive on the dealer's lot. Just walk away.

Talbot Samba/Horizon/ Alpine/Rapier/Minx/ Solara/Tagora

Leave them all alone – they're junk. From gear levers that come off in your hands to engines that sound like a machine gun fired from a concrete pill-box. Sad banger auction specials.

Triumph Toledo/Dolomite
Another Leyland folly. Leave them to the classic boys.

Yugo (all models)
Tragic build quality and warp-drive depreciation.

A-z
of used
cars

A-Z Alfa Romeo
Used *Cars*

Alfa Romeo 33 *(84A–95M)*

Latest cars best buys. Decent enough transport if bought cheaply. Don't pay top money – you'll regret it later when dealers bid low

For
Budget brio, gorgeous engines, grippy handling, alternative looks

Against
Iffy used values, fragile trim, terrible at trade-in. Early cars are rust-raisers

Best **b**uys
1.5 IE, 1.7 16v Cloverleaf, 1.7 Veloce Cloverleaf

Avoid
Slow-selling Sportwagon, earliest A and B platers, all 1.3s and high-mileage cars

Over**all**
1.5 and 1.7 best. Cloverleaf desirable. Facelifted 33 90-on, with standard power steering, makes good buy. Boxer 16v very urgent. Permanent 4 and Sportwagon not strong sellers. Dealer prices too high. Pay less than book or nothing. High mileage cars bad news, start to look ragged at 70,000. Not many servicing dealers about.

What to *look for*
Service history, few owners, frayed seats, broken trim, front tyre wear, stone chipping, oil leaks, wayward electrics. Later H, J and K cars best. Cheapest cars privately sold in classifieds. Leather trim, metallic paint, alloy wheels and sunroofs desirable

Alfa Romeo 164 *(88F–95M)*

Really a splendid car and fast becoming quite desirable. Alfa dealers likely to be expensive, but plenty in classifieds. High spec 164s most wanted

For
Handling, looks, quality finish, proven reliability, pleasing alternative big car choice

Against
Not too many dealers, 3.0 used values wilting, high mileage cars unloved

Best **b**uys
164 Twin Spark, 3.0 V6 Lusso, Cloverleaf, 24 valvers

Avoid
Very high mileage cars, anything without a service history, over-priced dealer examples. White not a strong seller

Over**all**
Good steady demand for most models. Twin Spark best seller, no auto/manual price penalty, Lusso spec means ABS, sunroof and alloys; very fast Cloverleaf worth having. Best colours red or dark metallics. Leather and air add £750. Ownership costs highish on 3.0-litre cars. Impressive high mileage strengths. 100,000 miles a breeze

What to *look for*
Service history, assertive colours, Lusso spec. Watch gear-selector linkage, front tyre wear, bonnet stone chipping, electrical gremlins (especially with air-conditioning motors). Rear suspension bushes need replacement every 30,000. ZF auto gearbox needs careful checking. Clocking prevalent, so look for worn seats and shiny steering wheels. N.B. Recent recall for front suspension mount rust!!

Audi 80/90 *(86D–91J)*

Drives well, looks good, lasts for ages. Fine value if bought well. VAG dealers price them high – so private buying best course

For
German build quality, middle-class image, squeakless ride, lively handling, low fuel thirst, galvanised bodies, hard-wearing interiors

Against
Small boot, gloomy cabin, softish used values. Quattros depreciate fast. Overpriced 90 a slow seller

Best **b**uys
1.8S, 1.8E, 2.0E, Sport 16v, Turbo D, 20v

Avoid
1.6 autos, overpriced or high mileage Quattro models. Drab colours and solid blue and primer grey. Cars without service history. Value least popular 90 models with care and buy at less than book

Overall
Sound, medium-sized buy with proven reliability. Parts expensive, main agent dealer pricing exorbitant. Autos unloved, high milers wear it well, precise front-wheel drive handling pleases. Bright colours sell best. 89-on have standard power steering. Sport 16v fun. Turbo

D drives and sells convincingly. 2.0E makes best overall buy

What to *look for*
Bonnet stone chipping, leaking power steering racks, wheel bearings, clocking, parking dents on doors, chipped windscreens. Ragged interior means very high miles. Big mileage Quattros mean heart-stopping bills. Boot spoilers and Speedline alloys desirable. Must have sunroof, power steering and power windows

Audi 100 *(83Y–91H)*

Value with care as used values crumbling. Don't pay dealer prices. All 100s need to be cheap

For
Space, economy, handling, reliability, excellent diesels, capacious Avant estate

Against
Fast-fading used values, expensive parts and service, big bills at high mileage

Best **b**uys
2.3E, 2.0 Turbo Diesel, 2.0E , Avant CD, Avant 2.3E

Avoid
4-cylinder cars, high milers, anything without service history, Quattro saloons, boring colours like navy blue, grey and green, ex-taxis

Overall
Huge value saloon with galvanised body and reasonable fuel appetite. Tremendous long distance cruising ability but poor low-speed take-up. Well built and finished. High mileage examples unwanted. Avants sell well but rest of range had it now. Diesels are good news. High-spec CD models value for money. 2.3E auto strong seller. Quattro saloons complicated and undesirable

What to *look for*
Slipping auto boxes, groaning wheel bearings, leaking steering racks, warped brake discs, worn injectors. Slab-sided doors attract parking dents, rear valances vulnerable. Many tatty clocked cars about. No auto-manual price penalty. The more options, the better. Value with care as prices on the skids. Avoid main agent cars - cheapest are in the classifieds

Audi 100 *new shape (91H–94L)*

Second generation 100 is smooth, refined and understated, not bad value either

For
Galvanised body, vast estates, impressive looks, roomy cabin

Against
Heavyish depreciation, not as desirable as a BMW 5 Series, parts and service not cheap

Best **b**uys
2.0E, TDi Estate

Avoid
Non-metallic colours, high mileage Quattros, cars without service history. Value with care as some franchised dealer prices are over-the-top

Overall
Almost there but not quite. Fine car in many ways but no match for BMWs and Mercs. Diesels and Estates hold value longest. 2.0E best seller. Higher spec 2.6, 2.8 and Quattro can be hard to sell. S4 Estate rare and valuable

What to **look for**
Main dealer history, stone chipping, steering rack leaks, slurred changes on automatics, parking dents, grumbling wheel bearings, clocking on diesels. Alloys and sunroof add desirability

Bentley T2 *(77R–81W)*

Still acres of presence and dignity and heaps rarer than a Roller. Ten grand buys a honey

For
Huge value, huge fun, huge image

Against
Watch it on the corners, biggish bills, nice ones getting rare

Best **b**uy
1980 T2

Avoid
Ex-wedding jobs, anything without history, white ones, pre-77 cars and overpriced skinny-tyred T1s

Overall
Still an uplifting conveyance and not as ruinous as you might think with plenty of clever specialists to ease the pain. Decent ones easily bought for under £10k. Gloriously hand-crafted and cosseting. Service history is all – don't buy without. Dark colours best – Masons Black at a premium. Much rarer than Silver Shadows with only 500-odd made. Mechanicals utterly bomb-proof but twiddly bits can be pricey. Careful selection means everything, so be pernickety

What to **look for**
Tired interiors, sagging headlinings, lifting veneer, rust on arches, sills, holed quarter bumpers, leaking suspension accumulators, corrosion on top hat wishbones, ticking hydraulic tappets, duff electric seat and window motors, leaking PAS pump

BMW 3 series *old shape (83Y-91H)*

Sturdy and not bad value. Bigger-engined 3-series hard to sell. Avoid cars with non-BMW body kits and big wheels. Not many nice ones left now

For
Image, high mileage abilities, smooth 6-cylinder engine, dependable resale. Myriad non-dealer copy parts available

Against
Tail-happy handling, cramped rear space, clumsy gear shift, fading image

Best **b**uys
316i, 318i, Touring models (except 325i), 318i convertible, high spec 320s

Avoid
2-door models, earliest 83-84 examples, cars with after-market body kits, tired mileagey 325s, anything with accident damage, Bauer convertibles

Over**all**
Spent force now - convertibles and 325i hardest hit. 318i and 320i best for resale. Take 100,000 miles in their stride. Options critical – all need alloys, sunroof, power steering and electric windows. Much clocked and mediocre scrap about, so buy with care. Touring estates very good news. Autos desirable, 2-dr models unwanted. Thrifty 316i a strong seller. Colour crucial – reds, blacks or metallics

What to *look* **for**
Signs of conscientious ownership such as fully stamped service booklets, full tool kits and torch still in the glovebox. Clocked in abundance, so check for worn interiors. Many accident damaged cars about as well. Whining gearboxes, smoky engines, ticking camshafts. BMW dealer prices often hair-raising – best deals in *Exchange & Mart* and *Auto Trader*. Value carefully as plenty about

BMW 3 series *new shape (91J–95M)*

Epic used prices across the range, so don't expect any bargains. Beware snail-slow 316 auto and don't buy without dealer history

For
Grace, kudos, aspirant image, handling, brilliant resale

Against
Everybody wants one, lethargic 1.6, expensive parts

Best **b**uys
318i/S, 320i/Coupe, 325i Coupe

Avoid
Cars without history, solid colours, 1.6 auto, high priced high milers

Over**all**
Design and marketing tour de force and a vast improvement on its forebear. Evergreen resale. Painless second and third year depreciation. Coupe a fashion accessory. Convertible the knees of the bee. 318i and 320i best for resale. ABS standard after 92. Metallics preferred. Alloys nice to have. Service history crucial. 318i S Coupe overall best retail bet. Digital odometer hard to clock. SE models add £1000 for retail

What to *look* **for**
Bonnet stone chipping, damaged wheel rims, mangled dashes from phone removal, flogged 325is, tasteless big wheel bodykit conversions, cam ticking on cold start-up. Some very early J-platers had quality control problems, mainly in the trim department. Leaking radiators. Some worrying reports of cam failure on four cylinder cars. Main agent service history essential for resale

BMW 5 series *old shape (81X–88E)*

Falling in value now. Image evaporated long ago and now driven by people you wouldn't want to have round for tea

For
Value, poise, build quality, solidity

Against
Ageing now with heavy ownership costs. Image and values fading. Big-engined variants thirsty. 518i unloved

Best **b**uys
520i, 525 auto, 525e, 528i SE, M5

Avoid
518, non-metallic colours, cars with few options, high milers, manual gearboxes on bigger-engined variants

Overall
520i and 525i most practical. Long-stroke 525e economical, but don't expect to impress anybody. Dealer parts and service very expensive. Non-franchise specialists best bet. Later cars make most sense. Options are all for resale. Air, sunroof, power windows, TRX allows, and metallic paint desirable. Switchable autos good news. Avoid million milers – they're pricey to fix. 528i SE and 535i very fast and make fine budget rocketships

What to *look for*
Stamped up service booklets, full tool kits, mint few-owner cars. Check for smoking engines, ticking camshafts, whining manual gearboxes, past accident damage, clocking, mismatched panels on metallic paint, soft shock absorbers, overheating on 528i, stone chips, broken headlights, rusty quarter bumpers, faded interiors

BMW 5 series *new shape (88E–95M)*

Tremendous value for money. Plenty for sale so take your time. Some dodgy stuff on the market so be fussy. M5 fast becoming a cult car. Estates very good news too

For
Style, performance, ride, handling, build quality, space, high mileage abilities

Against
Heavy depreciation, expensive parts and service, pre-24v 520s slow

Best **b**uys
520i, 525i auto, 535i SE auto, M5

Avoid
518i, few-option cars, very high milers unless ridiculously cheap, manual 530i and 535i, asthmatic auto 520, staid colours

Overall
Big-value quality saloon with shoulder-padded image. 520i and 525i best sellers. Assertive colours sell best. Larger-engined cars harder to sell. Options vital. Sunroof, power windows, ABS and alloys make all the difference. SE spec preferable. 518i gets driven like 520, so avoid. Digital odometer deters clockers. SE and Sport models add £750. Leather and aircon add £1,000

What to *look for*
Stone chipping around bonnet and front wings, bullet holes in windscreen, non-functioning digital odometers, worn driver's seat, frayed seat belts, whining manual gearboxes, past accident damage. Service history essential – don't buy without. Image beginning to wane now and not the force they were

For
Silky 6-cylinder engines, top-notch build quality, plutocrat image, olympian value if bought well

Against
Hurtful depreciation and running costs, high envy factor, pricey main agent parts and service

Best buys
730i SE auto, 735i SE auto

Avoid
Manuals, no-cost option velour trim, very high mileage or tatty cars, anything without a service history, overpriced BMW dealer examples, V12 750s

BMW 7 series (86D–94M)

Hard to value, so don't pay top whack. Usually well cared for by company types. Marvellous transport but expensive to live with

Overall
Endearing big car choice that's bullet-proof and built to last. 730 SE best seller, 735i SE good value, 750i unloved. Steer clear of manual gearbox and cars without air con and leather. Earliest cars can have electrical problems. Look best in dark metallics. Some now down to under £5k and fast becoming a villain's motor

What to look for
Only few owner, reasonable mileage mint cars worth buying. Look for vandal damage and heavy stone chipping. Creased leather on driver's seat means big mileage. Service history crucial. Check all electrics as problems can be expensive to fix. Some average and shabby 86/89 cars about now. No shortage of sensibly priced examples in the small ads

For
Fun factor, thrift, individuality, practicality

Against
What other people think

Best buys
Special, Dolly

Avoid
Scrappy Charlestons with torn seats and hoods, pre-81 drum-brake cars, cars covered in politically outspoken stickers, anything with signs of past frontal accident damage, abused and heavily dented examples

Citroen 2CV (81X–90H)

Fun on a shoestring. But make sure you have a tame Citröen mechanic

Overall
Much, much, better than they say. Cheap, charming and very cheerful. More expensive to walk. 50 mpg and loose change insurance. Special models best value. Dolly, Charleston and Bamboo add £200. Optional rear-opening hatchback worth finding. Easy DIY prospect, and there are scores of independent repairers. Deceptively sensible budget shuttle. Not classic material so don't pay silly money for the last of the H-platers.

What to look for
Rusty floorpans, ripped hoods, noisy engines and gearboxes, blown exhausts, front tyre wear. Service history desirable but not a must. Evidence of Dinitrol rust treatment is good news. Loose cardboard heater pipes can cause engine fires. Damp starting problems. Corrosion around bonnet hinge and fresh air dashboard flap

Citroen AX (85B–95M)

AX are good cars and cheap to buy but there are so many special editions that it does your head in. Bit more interesting than a Fiesta though, and cheaper

For
Economy, style, affordability, reliability. Plenty in the classifieds and usually owned by nice middle-class types. Never a fleet car, so mileage usually low

Against
Early cars flimsy, used values shaky. Not what you'd call a fast seller

Best **b**uys
11 TRS, 1.4 TZX, 1.4 DTR

Avoid
1.0 models, rattly high mileage stuff, GT as it can't take the strain

Over**all**
Useful and sensibly priced bargain shuttle. Able, roomy and very parsimonious. Later cars better built. AX GT insurance still earth-bound. Diesels excellent sellers. Plethora of special editions, but worth little more than standard item

What to **look for**
Post-88E models best, have superior seats and sound-proofing. Well worn interiors can be expensive to rejuvenate. Blue smoke and start-up chatter mean engine wear. Thin steel body susceptible to dents

Citroen BX (83A–93K)

Latest BXs make the best buys, as early cars shedding value fast and becoming banger auction material. Pricey to fix in their middle age

For
Gallic panache, taut handling, comfortable ride, superb diesels, vast estates

Against
Soft used values, quirky mechanicals, highish main agent parts and service costs

Best **b**uys
1.9 RD, 1.7 TZD Turbo Estate, 1.6 RS Estate

Avoid
Base spec and special edition models, dull colours, high mileage ex-fleet cars, battered GTis

Over**all**
Stylish Cavalier/Sierra alternative with proven reliability. Avoid poverty spec 1.4 and Leader models. Early cars very cheap and mostly tatty. Diesel and estate values very strong. GTi prices collapsed long ago. 4x4 GTi unwanted. Value high milers with care. For all special editions add £200

What to **look for**
Clutch cables, rattly and smoky engines, collapsing and torn seats, rust, cracked headlamps, broken trim, worn carbs, broken cam belts, sheared brake pedal mountings on early cars. Service history vital

Citroen ZX *(91H–95M)*

For
Breezy performance, calm ride, game handling, Gallic flair

Against
Over-sensitive ABS, some transmission snatch, needs PAS, fierce used prices

Best **b**uys
1.4 Advantage, 1.8 Furio, 2.0i Volcane, 1.9D Advantage Turbo

Avoid
Mileagey petrol cars, expensive Special Editions, base spec

One of Citroen's finest and solid value. Dealer Hallmark cars perfectly prepared but pricey. Watch expensive Elect finance schemes too

Over*all*
Resounding budget buy that's widely revered by informed private buyers. Advantage spec popular package. Furio and Volcane exceedingly rapid but nasty insurance. Non-turbo diesels a touch lethargic but still prime buying stock. Plenty around so don't pay outlandish main agent money. Parts and servicing can be traumatic – it'll pay to shop around for a competent independant specialist. One of the most gifted small hatches around

What to *look for*
Faulty brake pad and handbrake warning lights, dodgy electric window switches, waterlogged rear wash/wipe motor, poor hot starting, blown turbos, clocking, accident damage, myopic paint matches, missing or hiccupping from worn fuel injection

Citroen XM *(90G–95M)*

For
Ride, handling, comfort, space, styling, entertaining interior

Against
Heavy depreciators particularly 3.0 V6. 2.0 not that quick. Not good at trade-in time. Early G and Hs had plenty of problems. Silly handbrake

Best **b**uys
2.0 SEi, 2.0 SED, SD Turbo, All estate models

Avoid
Very high mileage cars without service history, base spec 2.0

Interesting big car choice with plenty of panache. Values very jittery so don't go overboard. Dealer prices high so buy privately. Can be hard to sell later on

Over*all*
Smooth magic carpet, big car choice, but more expensive to run than a Granada. Diesels and estates in fierce demand. Some cheap ex-company high milers about. Servicing not ruinous but V6 cars thirsty. Fast V6 24v is slow seller. Diesel SD estate most desirable. Watch those early models, and if you can afford it, refined 94 models are much better, especially 2.5 TD

What to *look for*
Lack of maintenance on complex V6 models, front tyre wear, slipping auto boxes, broken electric window lifts, parking dents, heavy oil consumption. Massive electrical malfunction. Knackered suspension

Daihatsu Applause *(90G–95M)*

Competent but desperately worthy. Non-existent street cred and precious little in the excitement department

For
Distinctive, reliable, holds value well, practical

Against
A touch pedestrian, not that many dealers, expensive parts. Absolutely no image whatsoever, and who on earth thought of that daft name

Best *buys*
1.6 Xi Notchback, 1.6 GSi Notchback

Avoid
1.6L carburettor, anything high mileage

*Over**all***
Not a bad buy. Much more exclusive than a Nissan or a Toyota. 1.6 Xi best seller with fuel injection. Used prices steady with no low points. Usually sympathetically driven and maintained, but mainly for town runabout work – watch for parking wounds. Not that many in the classifieds, so Daihatsu dealer may be your only recourse

What to ***look for***
Service history, weak second gear synchro, worn camshaft belt on 1.6L, rattly engines, blue smoke on start-up, poor paint repairs on metallics. Low milers may not necessarily be best as they never warm up on the way to the hip replacement specialist. All in all a seriously dull car

Fiat Panda *(81W–95M)*

Not bad for the money. Most Pandas are second cars and carefully driven. Buy newest and best you can afford. Avoid scruffy examples

For
Frugality, cult charm, reliable mechanicals, reasonable used values

Against
Hard seats and ride, early cars rusters, don't hold value that well. Often bought by people who can't afford the bus fare and never get them serviced

Best *buys*
1000S, 1000CL

Avoid
Pre-88 cars and ragged examples, all 750s and 4x4s. Anything without some form of maintenance history

*Over**all***
Able Italian shopping basket. Later models sell best. 750 underpowered, 1000cc sells fastest. Trade prefer low milers. Tatty big mileage Pandas worthless. 4x4 and Sisley unpopular. Dance and Tacchini special editions add £100

What to ***look for***
Rust on early cars. Look at bonnet, sills, doors and floorpans. Engine oil leaks, noise and smoke, worn interiors with broken seats and trim. Gearboxes can be shot at high mileage. Worth checking for unpaid finance as many were sold with the help of the Pound of Flesh Finance Company, with hair-raising APRs. Lots of sob stories about people who couldn't pay for their Panda that stood them at £10k

For
Zippy, commodious town performer.
Budget prices. Later cars much improved
build quality. Very economical to own
and run

Against
Weak used values. Early cars attract
serious rust

Best **b**uys
45 Fire, 60 Selecta, 60S, 60DS

Avoid
Pre-86 cars, overpriced dealer special
editions, any high mileage car, Turbo
models

Fiat Uno (83Y–95M)

All those Italians can't be wrong. Uno is bright, breezy and
cheerful and doesn't cost much to live with

Over**a**ll
Spacious and economical. Fire and 60S
versions sell well. Selecta (with continuously
variable automatic transmission) in demand.
60DS rare and expensive. Jan 90-on models
have restyled front. Multitude of special
editions only worth £100–£150 extra. Uno
Turbo values on the linoleum. Good small car
bet if bought well

What to **look for**
Electrical problems, rust on older models,
worn interiors, tired 1.1 and 1.3 engines,
battered bodies, kerbed wheels, front tyre wear,
broken switchgear, abused and never serviced
finance company repossessions. Unos come in
two conditions – quite nice or quite terrible.
Don't pay book as depreciation swift when
they come of age

For
Galvanised body, huge room, lovely
chassis, excellent turbodiesel. Much
underrated

Against
Poor trade-in values, some electrical
naughtiness

Best **b**uys
1.6 DGT, 1.9 Turbo D, 1.4 S

Avoid
High mileage examples, ex-rentals,
finance company repossessions, over-
priced dealer special editions, 1.4 base
spec, some early 88 cars with build
quality problems

Fiat Tipo (88F–95M)

Bigger and better than an Escort, cheaper too. Well worth a
long hard look. Strong on value, size and driver appeal.
We like them a lot

Over**a**ll
Capacious, compact and cheap. Just as able as
comparable Fords and Vauxhalls - sensible
family buy. 1.4 sells best, 1.6 surprisingly fast,
1.9 turbodiesel highly regarded. Cheerful
colour choice important. Reasonable parts and
service costs, vast dealer network. Best bought
privately. One owner low mileage cars best bet

What to **look for**
Rattling and squeaking trim, broken interior
parts, lack of service history and signs of
cheapskate ownership, persistent blowing of
bulbs and fuses, pronounced front tyre wear
on larger–engined variants. Watch low mileage
suburban shuttles – they trundle round Tescos
and never warm up

Fiat Tempra *(90H–95M)*

Adequate transport if cheap enough. Never pay anything
like retail otherwise you'll do your brains when you sell.
Estates more desirable than saloons

For
Cheap, roomy, competent, mega-thrifty
diesels, capacious estates, much less to
buy than mainstream equivalents

Against
Inert image, dodgy resale, eye-watering
depreciation, a feeling of all-round
flimsiness

Best buys
1.6 S, 1.8 ieS, 1.9 TDS

Avoid
1.4, high mileage saloons, finance repos,
ex-taxi diesels, some dire colours.
Anything used as a company car

Overall
Fiat's fleet car that didn't. Reasonable
capabilities but much buyer resistance. 1.6 S
and ieS most popular. Diesels much admired
but rare sight. Station wagons worth much
more than saloons. 1.9 TDS makes best
buying sense. 1.4 slow with no PAS. Autos
worth less. Need to be chosen carefully and
bought well behind trade book. Fiat dealers
will deal. Galvanised bodies now, so rust not
the problem it was

What to **look for**
Collapsing trim, electrical waywardness, valve
guide smoke, panel damage, sketchy history,
front tyre wear, persistent bulb and fuse
blowing, worn gearbox linkage

Ford Fiesta *old shape* (77R–89F)

Some very tatty Fiestas about. Best buys are C and
D-platers from middle class mummies. No longer the brilliant
second hand car it used to be

For
Easy to fix, easy to sell. Undemanding
budget runabout

Against
Hard ride, small boot, only two doors,
getting on in years

Best buys
1.4 Ghia, 1.4 GL, 1.3 L, 1.6 LD

Avoid
All 950 variants, base spec 1.1, crashed
and thrashed XR2s, driving school cars,
earliest pre-84 models. Poor colours like
ivory, mistral, beige and galaxy blue

Overall
Dating fiercely and no longer the peppermint
cream of used cars. High milers difficult to
move. Popular and 1.1 L too basic and slow.
GL and Ghia still desirable. Steady demand
for clean few-owner cars. XR2 loathed and
unwanted, so don't get involved. 950 cc
variants will be overtaken by bicycles on hills

What to **look for**
Rattly and smoky high mileage engines,
especially XR2 1.6 CVH, hard driven 950
engines, worn carbs, rigid rear shockers,
uneven front tyre wear, damaged load areas,
stolen recovered XR2s with broken locks,
bonnet stone chipping, front valance damage.
Prime candidate for clocking, so check for
shiny steering wheels and gear knobs and
frayed driver's seat. XR2 is lowest form of
motoring life

Ford A-z
Used Cars

Ford Fiesta *new shape (89F–95M)*

For
Able, tight little car that's well equipped and quite refined

Against
High prices, dreary to drive, small boot, dull steering

Best **b**uys
1.1 LX 5-dr, 1.8 LD, 1.4 Ghia

Avoid
1.0 models, base and Pop spec, driving school cars, 3-dr variants. XR2is having a serious image problem with jittery prices, villainous insurance and you'll wait an epoch to sell one

Cheap drama-free transport from Ford's best seller. 5-doors, diesels and latest injection models hold value longest, sound buy and lasts well

Over**all**
Accomplished sellers, 1.1 LX 5-dr best package. Ghias, autos and splendid 1.8 Diesel in fierce demand. Low spec Pop Plus too spartan. Special edition Bonus models same price as Popular. 1.6S, XR2i and RS Turbo prices fading fast. Metallics good news. Small mileage Channel Island ex-rentals make shrewd buying sense. Shortage of H, J and K platers. Plenty of dealers, cheap to mend. Highly regarded

What to *look for*
Stone chipping, signs of clocking, missing service histories, hard driven XR2is and RS Turbos, accident damage, flimsy trim, tappet and camshaft wear, brake and tyre wear on 1.8 models, leaking or inoperative sunroofs, gear linkage wear, kerbed wheels. Prices always on the high side, so negotiate hard

Ford Escort/Orion *old shape (80W/84A–90H)*

For
Ease of maintenance, cheap parts and service, strong resale

Against
XR3i is awful. Hard ride, rough engines, jerky automatics, fragile 1.6 CVH engine. Bad rusters

Best **b**uys
1.4 LX, Orion 1.6 LD, 1.3 5-dr Estate

Avoid
3-dr, 1.1 and base spec models, overpriced Ghias, smoky 1.4 and 1.6 CVHs, pre-86 cars. XR3is now driven by people in shell suits. Care also with Cabriolets – don't pay collector prices for RS 1600i and often dodgy Turbo. Very high mileage ex-taxi Orion Diesels. Overworked and under-serviced Estates.

Decent Escorts getting hard to find now as most of them have been worn smooth

Over**all**
Long in the tooth now. Consider only 86-on facelift cars. Five-door GL, Ghia and estates sell best. Few owner service historied cars safest course. Late G and H plate LX cars clever buys. Orion 1.6i Ghia usually more responsibly maintained than XR3i. Cabriolet

has severe scuttle shake and is joyrider's favourite. Orion Diesel best of bunch for reliability and ownership costs

What to *look for*
Rust on doors, boot, bonnet, sills, wings and especially battery tray, signs of clocking and abuse, scrappy load area on estates, accident damage on XR3i and Convertible, worn carbs, duff auto chokes, worn gearboxes and selector linkage, uneven front tyre wear, poor paint match on metallics, seized sunroof mechanisms, oil-burning 1.4 and 1.6 CVH engines, warped brake discs

A-Z Ford
Used Cars

Escort/Orion *new shape (90H–95M)*

Useful if unexciting, but proven longevity and strong resale.
Later, oval-bonnet cars best buys

Overall
Strong cost-effective family buy. 1.4 LX perkiest seller. Auto Ghias unpopular. Orion Ghias and Cabriolets suffering. Estates very popular. 1.8 Diesel values very firm. 3-dr and base models difficult to sell. 1.3 and 1.4 engines lack urgency. RS 2000 unexpectedly rewarding. 1.8 Zeta engine worth finding. Metallic paint preferred. Early H and J platers unrefined and not much cop. Ford have had three goes at getting the Escort right, so buy the latest you can afford

For
Low ownership costs, massive dealer network, easy resale, practical and reliable

Against
Uncomfortable seats, ragged handling, excessive front tyre wear

Best buys
1.4 LX, 1.6 GLX Estate, 1.8 LD Estate, 1.8i LX, 16v Estate

Avoid
3-dr models, 1.3 base, 4-speed gearbox, Ghia Auto, high mileage company cars without service history, insipid colours

What to look for
Uneven front tyre wear, stone chipping on bonnet and front wings, mismatched metallic paint, worn rear shockers, smoky engines, collapsing trim on early cars, tappet and cam noise, clocking. Service history advisable. Safe auction purchase; ex-rental Channel Island cars make good buys. Plenty about so shop carefully. Private sales can be expensive. Radiant Red best colour

Ford Sierra *(82Y–93K)*

One of the most uncomplicated used cars you can buy.
Cheap, dependable and thrifty. Plenty about too

Overall
Excellent dependable workhorse with proven strengths. Sapphire saloon looks more modern than hatch. 4x4 Cosworth is bargain slingshot. 2.9 XR4x4 good all-rounder. Capacious estates. Useful 1.8 turbodiesel. 1.8 LX finest package with sunroof and electric windows. Leave rattly Y to D cars alone, 90G darkened rear light models onwards best buys. Auto Ghia values shaky. 1.6 Pinto engine less able than 1.8 CVH. Terrific high mileage abilities. GLS surprisingly swift. 2.0 ohc engines prone to wear at mileage. Clocked in quantity

For
Value, reliability, ease of maintenance, resale, build quality, practicality

Against
Rough engines, dated to drive, image getting tacky now

Best buys
1.8 L, 1.8 LX, 2.0 GLS, XR4x4, 1.8 LX TD Estate

Avoid
3-dr models, 1.6 engines, thirsty 2.3 V6, Ghia 4x4, Ghia Auto, overpriced RS 500s, damaged, stolen recovered or mileagey Cosworths, pricey Ghias, all 1.3 models, high mileage 2.0 variants. Flat colours

What to look for
Camshaft noise, engine smoke, weak gearbox synchromesh, accident damage, stone chipping, cracked headlamps, rust on early cars round rear wheelarches, front wings and door bottoms, broken parcel shelves, frayed driver's seat, worn carpets, warped brake discs, clocked ex-company cars, broken locks and lack of service history on Cosworth. Thousands available, so take your time

Ford Mondeo (93K–95M)

One of the best family cars money can buy. Makes even more sense used

For
Refined and intelligent with affordable ownership, practicality, clever design, fix it anywhere

Against
Novelty gone now and already got a fleet car image, no crowd-puller either. Beginning to depreciate quickly

Best buys
1.8i LX, 1.8 LX TD Estate

Avoid
Base models, weary ex-rentals, cars without history

Overall
Outstanding family or fleet buy with routine Ford reliability and easy maintenance. Heaps better than the Sierra and a class-leader in the company car stakes. Hatches much more desirable than saloons. Estates stylish. 1.8 LX and GLX best for retail. Diesels lowest depreciators. Along with the Xantia and the 405, the Mondeo is a fine all-rounder

What to look for
Accident damage, clocking, interior cigarette burns, stone chipping, cam noise on 1.8, blue smoke on 2.0, warped discs, tatty load areas, rumbling wheel bearings, vandal damage, infrequent oil changes. Quite a few ex-daily rental cars in the system now so ask to see the V5 before you buy

Ford Granada (85B–95M)

Granada is Ford's big car bargain. Easy to fix and built to last but becoming council estate fodder now

For
Space, high mileage strengths, versatility, tough as nails

Against
Heavy depreciation, V6 cars thirsty, middle-aged image

Best buys
2.0i Ghia, 2.9 V6 auto, All estate models

Avoid
All 1.8 and 2.0 L models, 4x4, ex-taxis, ex-police cars, manual V6, 2.4 variants, older B and C plate cars unless mint, Scorpios with cloth trim, non-metallics

Overall
Motorised sofa. Fast, cosy and reliable with bomb-proof V6 engine. ABS standard. 2.0i Ghia preferred. Lusty but juicy 2.8/2.9 values on the wane. Scruffy B and C platers down to £1,500. V6 needs auto, 2.0 should be manual. Estates very sought after. 4x4 unwanted. Booted models less practical than 5-dr but look more modern. Scorpio with leather and air con pleasing way to get about. Diesels good for 200,000 miles. 24v models exceedingly quick. Clocking rife. Missing service histories and worn interiors tell all

What to look for
Fuel injection problems, warped brake discs and heavier than usual appetite for pads, drive line vibration, signs of paintwork repairs on doors, broken interior trim, slipping auto boxes, tired and smoky 2.0 engines, ABS problems, inoperative electric windows, stone chipping on bonnet, paint differences on metallics. Wear their miles well – 100,000 easy – so many clocked cars around

Honda Civic *(87E–91J)*

Civic is strong, reliable and holds its value. Can be expensive and hard to find

For
Solid build quality, high resale values, zesty engines, perennial demand

Against
Difficult to find, elderly image, high parts and service costs

Best **b**uys
1.4 GL, Shuttle GL, CRX

Avoid
Any high mileage car unless dirt cheap, Civics without service history, thrashed CRXs

Over*all*
Fine family car loved by private buyers. Condition is all, so avoid high mileage cars. Auto and CRX very sought after. Tremendous reliability and mechanical integrity. Most owners part-exchange so dealer purchase usually the only option. Shuttle good news, too. GL most popular for retail sale. All models always in short supply.

What to *look for*
Overpriced dealer cars, clocking, accident damage from elderly drivers, lack of servicing, manual gearbox whine, hard-driven 1.4s, slipping auto boxes, uneven front tyre wear

Honda Accord *(85C–93K)*

Find a good Accord and you won't regret it

For
Specification, refinement, good resale

Against
Expensive, staid image, high insurance, parts and servicing

Best **b**uys
2.0i

Avoid
Anything tatty, non-historied or very high mileage

Over*all*
Solid and accomplished performer. Built for keeps, lots of standard kit. Most privately owned and carefully driven. Rough ones rare. Seldom seen outside franchised dealer network. Autos desirable. 2.0 best seller. Thirsty 2.2 not so favoured. High mileage severely affects prices. Resale values very strong

What to *look for*
Slipping auto boxes, power steering leaks, front tyre wear, clicking CV joints, overheating, incomplete histories. But that's about it – it really is true what they say about Hondas – you'll only ever open the bonnet twice a year when you change the oil

Honda Prelude (87E–95M)

Prelude makes a fine used buy with the usual trauma-free Honda ownership. New shape cars seriously flash

For
Slow depreciation, punchy engine, nimble handling, sporting road manners. Latest shape Prelude a really happening car with iron-clad residuals and endless demand to prove it

Against
Bit cramped, old shape Prelude looks a bit bland, thirsty when driven hard

Best **b**uys
2.0 EXi

Avoid
Overpriced 4WS cars

Over**all**
Lively engines, surprisingly fast, sleek lines and no shortage of eager buyers. Always pricey, very few cheap cars about. 4-wheel steer expensive gimmick. 2.0 EXi best for value. Prelude 2.2i VTEC a real burster but surprisingly not well loved by retail buyers or the trade

What to **look for**
Paintwork problems on early cars, high mileage examples can be smoky, front accident damage, cars without service history are worth significantly less, air conditioning can malfunction. Check insurance before you buy. Very few cars in the classifieds, but efficient well organised dealer network

Honda Legend *new shape (91H–95M)*

One of the great unsung luxury car bargains. Understated, plush, formidably fast and endlessly reliable. We've got one

For
Slumberland ride, wall-to-wall luxury, epic performance, build quality, hi-tech equipment, unimpeachable reliability

Against
Dull steering, not as interesting or involving as a Jaguar, heavy thirst

Best **b**uys
All of them

Avoid
Unless it's been on its roof, even an intergalactic mileage Legend makes a marvellous motor

Over**all**
Much underrated effortless express. Hardly an image-builder but exudes an aura of restrained and mature excellence. Rare sight too, so some individuality. 3.2 V6 silky smooth and very quick. Utterly dependable with painstakingly efficient and willing dealer network. First year depreciation heavy but levels off thereafter

What to **look for**
Main agent service history crucial. Engine oil leaks, slipping auto box, electrical malfunctions, parking dents, spongy brakes, warped brake discs. Coupes sell better than saloons. Darker metallics good news. Black with magnolia leather looks the part

Isuzu Trooper (87D–94M)

Trooper is big on value but short on image. New ones now called Vauxhall Monteray so watch depreciation

For
Tough as old boots, separate, some cachet, super-frugal diesels

Against
Vastness can intimidate, rare and desirable, you'll need a big garage

Best buys
2.8 Citation Turbo Diesel 5 door, 3.1 Citation Turbo Diesel 5 door

Avoid
Short wheelbase 3 door, tired early 2.3/2.6, cars showing signs of heavy off-road use

Overall
Rugged off-roader with more than a smudge of style. Revised Feb 92 with new engines and facelift. 3.1 Turbo Diesel Citation is the one to go for. Rare sight in the small ads. Isuzu dealers buy up all the best stuff. Petrol models less favoured than diesel. Long wheelbase are most popular

What to look for
Worn engines on 87–88 examples, whistling turbos, wheel umbrella handbrakes, leaking shockers and differentials, brittle trim. Missing service histories, hard driven diesels, noisy gearboxes from towing-tired Troopers. Be concerned that the long-term future of second-hand 4x4 values looks a touch uncertain

Jaguar XJ6 old shape (79T–86D)

Last of the Sir William Lyons Jags. Good ones are delightful, bad ones a nightmare. Take your time to find a minter and you'll enjoy every mile. Still cuts a mild suburban dash as well

For
Poise, space, elegant lines, enormous character, magic carpet ride

Against
Prodigious thirst, rust-prone, expensively complex

Best buys
Sovereign 4.2

Avoid
Manuals, 3.4s, cars with cloth trim or vinyl roofs, worn out £1,500 specials, anything requiring major work. Projects won't pay. Poor colours (yellow, beige, white)

Overall
Still disarming after all these years; classic bloodline. 4.2 variants best. Later 85-on cars make most sense. Leather and air very desirable. Sovereign a classy package. Metallics and pepperpot alloys look the part. 3.4 cars with cloth trim worth much less. Manuals despised. Service history essential, and only mint warranted mileage cars worth the trouble. Tidy well-kept examples are great value though

What to look for
Service history makes an enormous difference. Check head gaskets, low oil pressure, unreliable fuel injection systems, timing chain rattle, blue smoke from exhaust, overheating, failed air conditioning and window lifts. Look for rust in wings, sills, doors, back valance, discoloured headlinings, slipping auto boxes, heavy tyre wear, pitted chromework, blown exhausts, tired leather interiors

Jaguar A-z

For
Image, value, breeding, style, silence, ride

Against
Heavy depreciation, early quality control problems, expensive whole life costs

Best buys
3.6 auto, 4.0 Sovereign

Avoid
Non-metallic paint, tweed trim, manuals, ex-police cars, tatty high milers, overpriced Sovereigns

Jaguar XJ6 *new shape (86D–95M)*

Digital dashboard makes them virtually impossible to clock. Beware forged service histories though. Buy best spec you can, with leather, air and auto

Overall
Graceful uptown transport with big money image. 2.9 bit basic and not popular. 3.6 auto best seller. 4.0 desirable. Sovereign tends to be pricey. Lots of retail demand for nice cars with history. Manuals unwanted. Tweed trim ruins the ambience. All need sunroofs, leather, alloys and strong colours. High mileage cars without history very difficult to sell. Entry level down to £3,000. Will run forever if sympathetically maintained

What to look for
Stone chipping, rattling or leaking shock absorbers, rear axle whine, worn front discs, handbrake shoes, electrical problems, air conditioning and engine management computer malfunction. Service history of paramount importance. Main agent prices often high. Plenty in the classifieds, though. Be pernickety and buy with extreme caution. Only pukka examples worth taking on

For
Class, magnificence, finish, performance, pedigree

Against
Huge thirst, heavy maintenance costs, fast depreciation, wicked insurance

Best buys
3.6 manual, 3.6 Cabrio, V12 Convertible, 4.0 Convertible

Avoid
Bargain-sounding £2,000 pre-80 cars, high-mileage V12s, anything tatty without service history

Jaguar XJS *(75P–95M)*

XJS is still a supercar. Looks, performance, silence and breeding. Running costs off the clock. Warranty advisable and Jaguar dealers have all the best – at a price…

Overall
Still one of the best grand tourers in the world and relatively cheap. V12 models cost big money to own. 6-cylinder 3.6 more containable. Manual 3.6 quite fun. Glam convertibles excellent value. Consider only post-81 HE cars. ABS after 88. Le Mans special edition add £500. XJR-S needs specialist valuation. 3.6 Cabrio and very early manual cars could be future classic contenders. Historied low-mileage examples worth buying but dodgy projects likely to be ruinous

What to look for
Rust in footwells, sills, wings and wheel-arches, wayward electrics, overheating, misfires, expensive trim faults, tyre wear, power steering rack leaks, signs of infrequent servicing, low oil pressure, rattly timing chains, leaking water pumps, no kick-down on auto box, suspension clonking, scored brake discs, oil-burning blue smoke from exhaust on acceleration. Best in metallics, Sebring Red or black

Kia Pride *(91H–95M)*

Korean-built Pride is cheap, charming, and sturdy. Not the usual Far Eastern budget lash-up. You could do worse

For
Mammoth value, lively engines, decent build quality, generous room

Against
Wallowy ride, intrusive wind noise, tasteless whitewalls

Best **b**uys
1.3 LX 5 door

Avoid
Ex-driving school stuff, finance repos, seldom serviced and never warmed up town shuttles

Over*all*
Credible small car choice that's much better than you'd think. Good re-sale as long as sensibly priced and a nice bright colour like red. 1.3 5-dr a firm retail favourite. Big cabins and willing engines. It may be a rebadged Mazda 121 but at under four grand you can't grumble. Sensible budget choice

What to *look for*
Parking scars, kerbed wheels, collapsing trim, child-devastated interiors. As with all these budget shuttles, most are bought on finance and some are never serviced. Check that it doesn't owe a fortune on HP, and insist on a service history or deduct £300. Generally a lot tougher than you'd think they are

Lada Riva *(84A–95M)*

Riva estates make a rummage-sale priced carry-all, but don't expect the last word in build quality and refinement

For
Cheaper than walking, anti-style image, makes cost-effective transport if looked after

Against
Crudeness, high first year depreciation, generally iffy build quality

Best **b**uys
1300/1500 Estates, 1600 SLX

Avoid
Never serviced finance company repossessions, anything over 50,000 miles, ancient B, C and D plate examples, hard worked estates. Dreary colours (hearing aid beige, pond green, pavement grey, varicose vein blue)

Over*all*
Not bad value budget runabout. Estates sell well. 1500 models best. 1600 SLX is as good as it gets. Hard ride and vintage handling, but cheap servicing and parts. Buy latest year possible with very low mileage. Easy DIY maintenance but worth only a pocket-full of change when five years old. Buy a Skoda

What to *look for*
Rust on older cars, tired interiors, rattly engines, big end clonk, excessive oil consumption, whining gearboxes, poor fitting panels, indifferent paint quality, damp interiors and boots, soggy brakes

Lada Samara *(91H–95M)*

For
Reasonable performance and handling, economy, value

Against
Bumpy ride, heavy steering, high whole life depreciation

Best buys
1300/1500 GL

Avoid
Finance company repos, seldom serviced wrecks, anything over 60,000 miles

Ladas may be crude, but for this money you get what you pay for, and it's not much…

Overall
Cheap and cheerful shuttle for those who don't care. Estates sought after. Rust not a headache yet. All engines sound rough but last the course. Pre-90 cars have assembly problems. Later examples improved. Interior ugly – cheap finish lets the car down. Both hatchback and saloon variants available. Drive line is tough and easy to maintain. Lada dealers have all the best examples

What to **look for**
Signs of poor driving – parking dents, kerbed wheels, collapsing trim, smoky engines, slipping clutches, overheating, surface rust, cars with outstanding HP owing, unsupported mileages – Ladas get clocked like everything else. Ever so tricky come part-exchange time and not what you'd call an instant seller

Lancia Delta Integrale *(88E–95M)*

For
Tenacious grip and fine handling balance, grunt, major street cred, pleasantly economical

Against
Left hand drive only, punitive insurance, some silly retail prices, constant theft target

Best buy
Integrale 16v 210 bhp

Avoid
Cars with rallying backgrounds or modified stuff, rough rhd conversions, electrical problems

Integrale has banshee performance and cult looks. Rare and special too, particularly now Lancia isn't importing them any more

Overall
Enormous fun with four wheel drive and turbo. 210 bhp after 92. Post-89 16v preferred. Very quick, very exciting and very exclusive. The best car Lancia make. Evolution models highly prized and likely to assume neo-classic status in the not too distant future. Prices might even rise. Definitely worth buying

What to **look for**
Wayward electrics, cambelt change at 36,000, crankshaft wear, brake fluid leaks, stone chipping, gimcrack interior trim. Service history a must. Remember this is no comfortable cruiser with its wash-board ride, wailing engine and left-hand drive. Great fun but hugely tiring

A-z Land Rover
Used *Cars*

Land Rover Discovery *(89G–95M)*

Discovery, is tough, trendy and holds its value well. Diesels best for resale. Much lower depreciation than a Range Rover

For
It's not Japanese, brilliant diesel, space, off-road abilities, green wellie image

Against
V8 thirst, early build problems, high used prices

Best *buys*
V8 5-dr, TDi 5-dr 7-seat

Avoid
High-mileage V8s, battered examples. Don't look their best in white

Overall
Cheaper but not down-market Range Rover alternative. Stylish, hardy mechanicals but interior trim tacky. TDi best seller, V8 values weaker. High-mileage V8s difficult to sell. Special Value Option Pack desirable. Always in demand so few cheap ones about. Metallics and 5-dr best bet. Good long-term used values. Seven-seaters worth finding. Injected V8 uses less fuel than carb unit

What to *look for*
Body prone to dents and rust in seams, broken handles and switchgear. Dirty engine oil on V8 spells infrequent servicing and trouble ahead. Broken springs and shock absorbers, tailgate problems, torn or frayed seats, clonking suspension, ticking tappets, corroded alloy wheels

Range Rover *(70H–95M)*

Range Rover is handsome and desirable. Early build quality not much cop. C-platers onwards make most sense

For
Slick style, off-road abilities, refinement, county image

Against
Heavy thirst, expensive maintenance, early build quality, high depreciation

Best *buys*
Vogue 5-dr, Diesel, Vogue SE, the first 1970 ones good for investment

Avoid
Early cars without power steering, non-standard engine transplants, badly rusted examples, 3-dr variants

Overall
Still a market force after 24 years. Ageing design doesn't look it. One of the best hill-climbers. Oldest ropey now, Vogue/SE models and diesels sell best. Late examples currently hard to sell, but D, E and F plate Vogues in demand. Rare diesel rough and underpowered but depreciates much more slowly. Autos preferred, service history vital. Air con and leather add £1,000. Cheap interior fittings and some body rust. Irksome transmission backlash on pre-88s. 3.9 variants much smoother and more refined. LSE 4.2 still making big money. Fuel injection after 89

What to *look for*
Ragged interiors, rusty tailgates, broken springs, smoking V8, dented wheels, knocking half-shafts, whining diffs, broken switches, dented and filled aluminium panels, rust in body seams, dented roofs, rattling engines, overheating, lack of anti-freeze, sloppy gearboxes, soft shock absorbers, worn steering ball joints, steering rack fluid loss, faulty handbrake, damaged headlining

Lexus LS 400 (90G–95M)

One of the best cars in the world. Hard to buy used at sensible money, but well worth the few quid extra

For
Oriental efficiency, so quiet, insatiable secondhand demand, benign depreciation, discreet affluence

Against
Touch too insulating, not the prettiest face, easy to sell but expensive to buy

Best **b**uy
LS 400

Avoid
Ridiculous retail prices, tatty high milers that will be hard to sell, anything carrying outstanding finance

Over**all**
Widely admired and now firmly on a par with BMW and Mercedes. Built for ever with one of the quietest drive trains we know. Endless entertainment from all the gadgets, unbelievably relaxing and one of the slowest depreciating luxury cars you can buy. We have a 100,000 miler that's still the dog's twitcher

What to **look for**
Scrupulous maintenance history, accident damage, don't look very nice at all in white. Anything with gold badges and wheels! To make its money, a Lexus does need to be mint, so don't be drawn towards cars in average condition unless cheap. The only problem with the second-hand Lexus is finding it

Lotus Elan (89G–93K)

Classic alfresco fun but not hugely practical. If you're spending this sort of money, buy an MX5 or better still a TVR. Image a bit girlie too. Bring back the old one...

For
Handling, individuality, Turbo on SE, period charm

Against
Wee bit toy-like, values unpredictable, MX-5 is cheaper, not many servicing dealers

Best **b**uy
Elan SE

Avoid
Anything tatty with star-cracked body or tired trim. Service history essential, some horrid exhibitionist colours which decimate the car's value and appeal

Over**all**
A brave effort but Lotus lost money on every Elan they sold. Cute, fine handling and patriotic choice, though, with few downsides. Some nonsense talked about rising prices since production stopped, so don't pay silly money. 165 bhp SE with blower good news, but be fussy about colour. Green looks the part, yellow doesn't. Main dealer history makes all the difference. Still some market uncertainty with retail buyers going for more orthodox confections

What to **look for**
Clonking from front CV joints, front tyre wear, worn suspension ball joints, ripped or slashed hoods, kerbed or corroded alloy wheels. Fibreglass body hard to repair if well stuffed

A-Z Lotus - Mazda

Used Cars

Lotus Esprit (81W–95M)

Bit of an 80s throwback, looking its age and outgunned by many other more serious coupes

For
Heady performance, fluent handling, sensuous lines, supercar image

Against
Some brittleness on early cars, over-the-top insurance

Best buy
Turbo SE

Avoid
Tired pre-'84 tackle, cars without history, accident damage

Overall
Mid-engined fibreglass concoction that looks pretty and goes well. Turbo SE preferred. Early cars have anti-social driving position and poor visibility. Used prices capricious as majority of decent examples in specialist hands. Values wholly dependent on history and condition. Early cars can be a handful and difficult to sell so don't pay mad classic car money

What to look for
Vocal engines, rattly timing gear, turbo whistle, oil leaks, engine fires, failed electrics, broken heaters, star-cracked fibreglass bodies, accident damage. Esprits don't react to well to life in the fast lane so always get a professional inspection before you buy. Nice ones can be fun, horrid ones a pain in the proverbial. Have you thought about a Nissan 300 ZX instead?

Mazda 323 (85C–94L)

Mazda's 323 may be light on excitement but lasts well and won't break the bank. Simple dependable cars

For
Efficient, reliable, solid, high resale

Against
Soulless, unremarkable, lacklustre image

Best buys
1.3 5-dr, 1.5 GLX Estate, 1.8 GT

Avoid
4x4s, 1600 Turbos, SEs, 1.1 and 1.5 models

Overall
Tough, workmanlike, easy to drive. Painless ownership with low servicing and repair costs and minimal depreciation. Hatches more saleable than saloons. 1.3 and 1.6 best. 1.1 and 1.5 less desirable. Used prices on the high side. Not many about so dealer purchase the usual course. 1.5 GLX good news. 1600 Turbo not wanted. SE Exec Estate difficult to sell. Turbo 4x4 unloved. 1.8 GT quick

What to look for
Pre-'86 models rusting now, turbos unreliable, hard driven 1.3s, high-mileage cars difficult to sell, heavy steering automatics not favoured. The 323 came very high in the *Top Gear – JD Power Car Customer Satisfaction Survey* for its reliability, ease of maintenance and low depeciation. An all-round good buy if a touch on the steady side

Mazda A-Z
Used Cars

Mazda MX5 *(90G–95M)*

Sixties looks with ninties reliability. A sensible sportscar and instant seller. Best buys around in winter, but you still won't find many under eight grand

For
Retro charm, alfresco fun, affordable prices, minimal depreciation, fine build quality

Against
Over-sensitive steering, dainty image

Best buy
MX-5 SE

Avoid
Tarted up tat, poorly camouflaged accident grief, ripped hoods, shagged interiors

Overall
Rides and handles predictably. One-shot seller. Not blisteringly quick but looks the business. Perfect summertime poser. Used prices rock steady. Red best colour. MX-5 SE add £700. Desirable hard top add £350

What to look for
Vandal and envy damage, kerbed wheels, parking dings, bent chassis, smoky engines, clocking, ringing, unpaid HP. Watch paying silly summer-time prices for used ones as a brand new 1.8i is only fifteen grand. Generally a brilliant second-hand buy

Mazda 626 *(87E–95M)*

626 goes and lasts well but looks like so many other Jappo cars. Even new shape ones don't have any street prescence

For
Reliability, ease of maintenance, low cost, reasonable depreciation

Against
Bit bland, 4WD versions tumble in value heavily, no head-turner

Best buys
1.8 GLX, 2.0 GLX

Avoid
Saloons, 4WD and 4WS, ex-taxis, clocked starship milers, special editions with no extra value

Overall
Sturdy with predictable ownership costs, the 626 is sensible if undramatic. A bit dated with larger-engined and higher specification variants not so desirable as 1.8 Hatchback. GLX 5-door good news. Saloons generally worth less. Autos worth more. Painless and cost-efficient transport. New shape models depreciate slowest

What to look for
Timing chain rattle, camshaft failure on 2.0i, cambelts need regular replacement, advanced tyre wear on 4WS cars, shagged estates, rusting round bonnet and tailgate. Unlike the majority of Japanese cars, the 626 has patchy secondhand demand, so don't assume it'll depreciate as slowly as a Toyota Corolla

Mercedes Benz 190 *(83A–94M)*

190E is the accountant's choice. Slow depreciation and reasonable running costs make it the affordable prestige car. Looks and feels good too

For
Low depreciation, efficient image, bomb-proof build quality, last forever

Against
Traditionally high prices, parts/service, cramped rear, options up the price

Best **b**uys
190E 2.0 auto, 190E 2.6 auto, 2.5 16v, 190D 2.5

Avoid
Bog standard 190s, without a sunroof, manuals, tacky after-market bodykits, clocked A, B and C platers, high-mileage ex-London cars without service history, ex-taxis, left-hand drive

Over**all**
Compact and disarming baby Benz. Recession-proof depreciation. Supple chassis but slow steering and ponderous manual gearbox. Only buy automatics – manuals worth much less. 190E auto fastest seller. Options make all the difference. Sunroof, electric windows and alloys desirable. Diesels held in fierce esteem. 1.8 under-powered. 2.0 good news. 2.6 rapid. 2.3/2.5 with 16v Cosworth head the business. ABS after 91. Restyle after 88. Service history essential. Only warranted mileage cars worth paying for. Dealer purchase pricey but worth it

What to **look for**
Faulty clutches, alternators, starter motors, power steering rack. Ragged engines, low oil pressure, camshaft ticking, clattery timing gear, crankshaft rumble, rear axle whine. All 190s do 100,000 in their stride, so many are clocked. Full service history and contact with last owner is your only defence

Mercedes Benz W123
200/230/250/280/300 *(76R–85C)*

Benz W123 lasts forever, image failing now but they just go on and on and on...

For
Grace, comfort, performance, long life

Against
Highish running costs, stodgy handling, clumsy manual gearbox

Best **b**uys
230E auto, 280TE estate auto

Avoid
Ex-taxis, 200, 250, 200D, 200TE, over-priced and supposedly classic 230/280CEs, all left-hand drive, manuals, non-power steering models, few option cars

Over**all**
Germany's second best-seller. W123 range is hewn from granite. 200D slow. 280E quite fast, 230/280CE ugly, 7-seat estates and diesels highly regarded. 230E good value package. 240D best diesel. 250 gutless. 200,000 miles not unheard of, so clocking widespread. Some rough ex-taxis about. Warranted mileage for buying sense. All petrol cars should be auto. ABS and power steering valuable options, 5-speed gearbox standard after 85. Four-speed auto, alloys, sunroof and metallic paint sell best

What to **look for**
Rattling timing chains, evidence of non-Mercedes pattern parts being fitted, low oil pressure, slipping or jerky auto boxes, whining differentials, head gasket failure, overheating, valve guide wear, sloppy power steering, blue smoke indicating advanced engine wear, rear shockers and broken tailgate hinges on estates, rust beneath exterior trim, on sills, wings and wheel-arches, corroded and dented bumpers. Worn interior means round-the-world mileage

Mercedes Benz A-**z**

Mercedes Benz W124
200/230/250/260/300 *(85C–94M)*

Excellent package of strength, longevity and image. Prices are always high but worth paying the extra for

For
Low depreciation, tremendous solidity, high used values, upper crust image

Against
Costly servicing, expensive to buy

Best **b**uys
230E, 260E, 300TE

Avoid
Few option cars, ex-taxis, cars with bodykits, non-metallics, manuals, left-hand drive, non-historied examples, basic 200 without spec

Over**all**
Worry-free investment, built for keeps. Racks up vast mileages with aplomb. 230E auto strongest seller. 260E goes well. 300E and 300TE reasonably quick. Estates serious good news especially full-house gentleman's express 300 TE. 4-MATIC overpriced. All petrol cars should be auto. Metallic with dealer history, sunroof and electric windows preferred spec. Alloys, leather, air con the options to go for. Don't pay extra for trivial options such as outside temperature gauges, centre armrests and ski bags

What to *look for*
Vandal and accident damage, worn smooth interiors, clocked ex-company cars, tired estates, whining differentials, leaking water pumps, fuel injection problems, soft shock absorbers, scored brake discs, prop shaft rumble, smoky engines. Big mileage capability means scores are clocked, so verify mileage with previous owner before you buy

Mercedes Benz S class W126
280/300/380/420/500/560 *(81W–91J)*

We have a 100,000 mile 500 SE which is a constant source of undiluted joy. We like them a lot

For
Plutocrat image, adamantine build quality, space, comfort, authority

Against
Anaesthetised feel, expensive to keep, depreciation becoming heavy

Best **b**uys
300 SE, 420SE, 380SE, 500SEC

Avoid
Earliest W, X and Y platers unless mint, 280/300 manuals, 500SECs with darkened windows and pimpy bodykits, early '80s colours: thistle green, petrol blue, white, metallic brown, ivory

Over**all**
Plenty of street presence despite new model. Wonderful value and still a class act. A big impressive motor. Early SE saloons buyable for £4000ish. SEC coupes look very sexy. Replacement megabuck models beyond purchase, so W126 values likely to stay firm. Look best in blue-black or other dark metallics. Leather and air con add extra desirability. 380/420/500SEC premium sellers. Superb value if well bought

What to *look for*
Timing chain rattle, valve guide wear, distorted alloy wheels, low oil pressure, overheating on V8s, signs of skimped servicing, jerky auto gearboxes, soggy shockers, scored brake discs, power steering leaks, frontal accident damage, cracked windscreens, clocked high mileage ex-company cars. Dealer service history exerts a huge effect on used values – don't buy without

A-Z Mercedes Benz
Used Cars

Mercedes Benz SL *(71J–89G)*

Merc SL makes entertaining buy with certain resale future.
V8s thirsty though. 300SL more economical

For
Cool, glam, indestructible, virtually depreciation-proof

Against
Not cheap to run

Best **b**uys
280SL, 300SL, 380SL

Avoid
Indeterminate mileage '70s cars with ripply paintwork and chrome arches, anything with a bodykit, manuals, weak colours such as green and yellow

Overall
Merc sports a synonym for style. Not really fast or taut but so beautifully made. Seventies and eighties 350/450 still look as chic as later cars but a fraction of the price. six-cylinder 300SL favourite. V8 380SL fun, 500 SL twitchy at the limit and thirsty. Stuffy cabin, so air con is a help. Leather, ABS and cruise control useful options. Can be cheaply up-specced with flat-face alloys and front chin spoiler. Rare manuals and tin-top SLC worth much less

What to *look for*
Rust in sills, doors, wheel-arches, wings. Timing chain rattle, blue smoke from V8s, overheating on 300, camshaft ticking on 280, broken or weak engine mountings, suspension clonking, woolly steering, jerky auto box, noisy tappets, groaning differential, torn hoods with discoloured windows, scruffy interiors, Usual service history caveats apply

Mercedes Benz G Wagen *(83A–95M)*

G Wagen is exclusive but too agricultural. Lasts forever but not that easy to sell

For
Better made than a Range Rover, prestigious bonnet badge, toughness

Against
Drives like a Land Rover, disappointing resale

Best **b**uy
300 GE

Avoid
The early stuff with skinny wheels and dreary colours, all soft-tops, 230 is too slow, 300 GD not that quick either

Overall
There are better 4x4s but none as well-built. Never quite a household name, the G-Wagen is an acquired taste but still the most individual 4x4, albeit the most expensive. Don't pay top franchise money, as you'll be quite startled at the most unMercedes-like depreciation. Post-91 models look best with black bumpers and wheel arch extensions. Bull bars, dark metallics and AMG alloys make the world of difference. Only LWB 300 GE has any sort of enduring presence or performance

What to *look for*
Engine or rear axle oil leaks, worn engine mountings, seized differential lock levers, worn track rod ends, PAS leaks, worn suspension ball joints, seized brake calipers, accident damage. Off-road abuse is common, so check for dented or damaged underside. Mercedes Benz dealer history vital

Mitsubishi Galant *old shape (84A–93K)*

Galant provides worry-free motoring and cast-iron reliability.
Hard to find and often pricey – worth it though.
Mitsubishi dealers try hard

For
Competent, strong, refined and reliable

Against
Uninvolving, bit soulless, anonymous image

Best **b**uys
1800GLS, 2000GLS

Avoid
1.6 saloons, hard driven 16vs, fast depreciating 4x4 4WS

Overall
Extremely well built and able family saloon with high equipment levels and low depreciation. Parts and service on the pricey side, not too many dealers and insurance high. 1800/2000 GLS best sellers. Turbo unwanted. GTi 16v 4x4 4WS big on ability but won't impress the neighbours. Diamond Option Pack desirable. Rare GLS turbo-diesel much sought after. GTi 16v fast and silky smooth. Litany of rally successes speaks volumes for performance and engineering strength. Hardly any advertised privately, so dealers tend to be expensive. Good used warranty, though

What to *look for*
Leaking water pumps, missing service histories, leaky power steering rack and pump. But that's about it as Galants are one of the most reliable and enduring cars in this class. Problem is, they're also one of the most boring with little or no image

Mitsubishi Colt *new shape (92J–95M)*

Clever and competent Escort chaser, but only three doors...

For
Useful and perky Escort-beater with comely Euro oval styling. Well made, impressively finished and widely respected

Against
Hard to find and usually expensive

Best **b**uys
1.6 GLXi 16v

Avoid
1.3, white a duff colour

Overall
Rare and exclusive town tearaway with hidden strengths. 1600 GLXi quick. GTi 16v even quicker. Three-year warranty best in the business. Sky-high residuals. Useful automatic. Electric sunroof option worth having. Containable insurance and ownership costs. Most jealously guarded and expensively retailed by Mitsubishi dealers. Worth paying a premium

What to *look for*
Parking trauma, never warmed-up town-bound examples, well thrashed GTis. Most initially bought by responsible types, so a low-risk secondhand buy

Mitsubishi Shogun *(83A–95M)*

Mitsubishi's best model. The Shogun lasts well, holds its
value and sells instantly. Only trouble is they're hard to find
and always expensive. Dealer purchase often the only option

For
Trendy image, reliability record, piffling
depreciation, off-road talents

Against
Slow diesel, synthetic '70s interiors, sky
high used prices, V6 thirst

Best *buys*
2.5 TD, V6 auto LWB, 1800 Diesel,
2000 GTi 16v

Avoid
Soft-tops, really high mileage diesels,
over-priced early SWBs and LWB V6

Over*all*
Range Rover without the snob value. Tough,
reliable with strong resale. Smooth V6,
imposing long wheelbase model, fast selling
diesels. Diamond Option Pack adds value.
Power steering after 89. 5-dr diesel prime spec.
V6 auto values going through a jittery stage.
Post-May 91 new shape V6 still big money.
Pre-85 soft-tops not so popular. Look smartest
in dark metallic colours with alloys and bull
bars

What to *look for*
Underbody and panel damage from off-road
use, sloppy gear change, leaking power steering
pump, damaged wheels, scruffy load areas, big
end rumble on 2.5. Service history a must. No
reports of major mechanical failure

Nissan Micra *old shape (83A–93K)*

Micras are simple, straightforward and sensible. They're
cheap to run and sell well too. Unexciting but reliable

For
Unerring reliability, simplicity,
practicality

Against
Boring, stodgy handling, pedestrian
image

Best *buys*
1.0LX, 1.2LX, 1.0 Colette

Avoid
Driving school cars, 1.0L, 4-speeders,
3-drs

Over*all*
Undeniably sensible but ultimately
unrewarding. Frumpy lines and indifferent
road manners, but will run on charity. Five-
speed GL best of early bunch, B and C plate
GL/SGL go well, post-89 1.2s quicker,
automatics in demand. Spartan equipment
levels. Colette models are sound buys. New
nose treatment March 89. Low rear loading sill
very practical. GSX has sunroof

What to *look for*
Baggy seats, torn trim. Rust on valances, door
bottoms and hatchback tailgate; clattering oil
and water pumps; blue smoke on over-revved
four-speed cars, overheating from cars without
anti-freeze, clutch wear, graunching gear
changes. Cam belt must be renewed at 36,000
miles. Vibration from auto gearbox, knocking
CV joints, split CV gaiters. Oil leaks on 85–87
models. Tired looking over 70,000 miles, full
history, low mileage examples best bet

Nissan Bluebird (96C–90G)

For
Reliable, well made, easy to maintain

Against
Stodgy, uninteresting, bland

Best buys
1.6LX, 1.8GS, 2.0 GSX

Avoid
Turbo, automatics, high-spec variants unless cheap, non power steering models, ex-taxis, high-mileage, saloons

Bluebirds are cheap to buy, easy to mend and rarely go wrong. Dull but very worthy

Overall
Sensible, undemanding family transport. Getting quite cheap now as residuals fall in wake of replacement Primera. 1.6 and 1.8 models sell quickest. Late cars most refined. Estates vast and workmanlike. 2.0 GSX a nice package. Hatchbacks sell better than saloons. All need power steering. Autos and turbos not wanted

What to look for
Valve guide smoke, appetite for brake pads, blown turbos, inoperative handbrake, worn interiors, paintwork chipping, soft suspension, soggy brakes. Service intervals are long, so many private owners skimp or do it themselves, which makes dealer history a premium

Nissan Primera (90H–95M)

For
Relatively unusual, well built, British made, efficient image

Against
Some market resistance, patchy resale demand, diesels a bit sluggish

Best buy
2.0i LX

Avoid
1.6 L, ex-taxis, some early cars had paintwork and electrical problems, quite a few ex-fleet high milers about, so watch for clocking

Fine family transport but not as desirable as Cavalier or Mondeo. Worth a look though

Overall
Underrated and smart Mondeo/Cavalier alternative. Low spec models sell best and lose least. ABS after 93. Autos worth slightly more. Diesels and Estates rare and sought after. No PAS on 1.6 L after 92. 2.0i LX best for resale

What to look for
Stone chips, flaking metallics, sticking electric windows, worn brake discs, uneven front tyre wear, failed heated rear window switch, dodgy relays, accident damage. Main agent history preferred. Not that many about so watch fancy franchise prices

Nissan Patrol (84A–95M)

Patrol is built like the Albert Memorial but looks like it too. Doesn't have the restrained elegance of Range Rover or Discovery rivals

For
Lowish prices, Gobi desert-crossing abilities, lots of dealers

Against
Garden shed styling, not that thrifty, wannabe image

Best buy
Patrol Diesel Turbo 5-dr

Avoid
Early 84A–87E 3-dr, anything showing hectic use, wishy-washy colours, pre-89 models can be rusty

Overall
No eyebrow-raiser and held back by perpendicular styling. Unfairly unregarded nonetheless. Used prices not as strong as competitors, so cheap to buy. Turbo diesel models favoured much more than petrol variants. 5-dr sells best. Metallic paint preferable. Watch depreciation and don't pay top money

What to look for
Tailgate rust, panel denting, crankshaft rattle, diesel leaks, sticking diff lock, accident damage, mismatched paint, tatty load areas, broken springs, soggy shockers. Not the easiest thing to sell used as most buyers go for more predictable choices like Shogun, Jeep, Disco and Trooper. Definitely the 4x4 poor relation. Mind you, in Saudi Arabia they won't drive anything else

Peugeot 205 (83A–95M)

205 makes a fine all-rounder

For
Chic image, supple chassis, huge model range, Pininfarina shape, go-forever diesels, rock solid used values

Against
Pricey to buy, flimsy feel, expensive dealer parts and servicing

Best buys
1.1GL, 1.4GL, 1.4GT, GLD, XLD, 1.6CTi, 1.9GTi

Avoid
3-dr 1.0, Junior, pre-85 4-speeders, thrashed GTis, anything much over 70,000, clocked and overpriced diesels and phoney special editions

Overall
One of the world's best small cars. Firm values and stylish associations continue on all but GTis. Very quick 1.9 model values hard hit. Diesels and Cabriolets enjoy legendary demand and top prices. Gearbox synchro problems on early cars. Can be tricky to start when hot. Susceptible to damp. Trim can feel fragile but mechanicals are hardy. 1.4GL well regarded. 1.1GL lively seller. 1.4GT fun. XLD and GLD fetch big money. Auto friendly and popular. Special editions not worth much more than standard item

What to look for
Rust on early cars, especially round window seals, corroding alloy wheels, crash damage on GTis, crumbling interior trim, difficult gear selection, loud tappet noise, camshaft wear, rattly engines, non-Peugeot oil filters, gearbox whine, clutch wear, tired rear shockers, scored brake discs. Cambelts must be changed at 50,000 miles

Peugeot 309 *(86C–93K)*

309 is cheap because of geriatric image. Makes sensible buying though, especially diesels and great value GTi. Colour choice important

For
Comfortable, roomy, versatile, useful

Against
Plain looks, middle-aged image, indifferent resale values

Best **b**uys
1.4i, 1.6GLX, 1.9GTi

Avoid
1.1 3-dr, ex-minicabs, very high mileage cars, hard driven SRi and GTi, anything without power steering

Overall
Much better than it looks and cheap to buy. A sensible range with long-lived diesels, capable hatchbacks and very interesting GTi. 1.6 good all-rounder, 1.3 bit slow, 1.1 definite no-no. 1.4i pleasing package. XSi a budget GTi. GLD and GRD very rewarding. GRTD fast for a diesel. All 309s need power steering. Lowered rear sill after October '89. Paint finish can be flawed. Image now fading in the wake of smooth 306

What to *look for*
Stone chips, rust, corroded alloy wheels, hissing power steering pump, split CV (constant velocity joint) gaiters, thin brake discs, water leaks in load area and around sunroof, worn rocker and camshafts, hot and cold starting problems on 1.6, fuel vaporisation, drive line shunt from injected cars, electrical problems. Camshaft belt must be changed every 36,000

Peugot 405 *(88E–95M)*

405 so much nicer to drive than most fleet cars. Latest 405s are best buys especially 1.9 injection. Autos good news too

For
Fluent handling, class-leading ride, stylish looks, plenty of equipment

Against
Some French fragility, fleet car image, only average depreciation

Best **b**uys
1.6 GR, 1.9 GR, GRD Estate, GTD Estate

Avoid
Early non-power steering 1.6s, ex-taxis, high mileage ex-company cars, well worn estates, mileagey diesels

Overall
Much more engaging than Sierra/Cavalier competitors. Estates and diesels hold value longest. 1.6/1.9 GR best for resale. All need power steering. Diesel estates sought after and expensive. Engines tend to smoke and use oil. Hot and cold starting problems. 4-speed auto pleasing. Injection GRi/SRi/GTXi smoother than carburettor cars. Mi16 4x4 unloved. 1.9 diesel better than turbocharged 1.8. 90-on GTXi and SRi have ABS. All 94-on 405s have air con

What to *look for*
Carburettor car starting problems, gear selector bushes, cambelt that must be changed every 24,000 miles, stiff steering, rattly trim, wind noise from sunroofs, flimsy switchgear, water leaks, stone chipping, windscreen washer failure, front tyre wear, cracked headlights, worn steering joints, blue exhaust smoke signalling heavy oil consumption

Peugeot 605 *(90H–95M)*

Unfairly unregarded the 605 makes a fine big car choice.
Don't pay retail money as depreciation not clever

For
Fine ride and handling, deft performer, rare and handsome

Against
Heavy depreciation, tricky resale, jerky drive train

Best buys
605 SRDT, 605 SVE 24v

Avoid
Poverty spec SLi manual, hard-driven V6s, white doesn't flatter those Pininfarina lines

Overall
Mysteriously mistrusted. An excellent luxury cruiser. Super-swift 24-valvers tremendous bargains. Infinitely superior Carlton/Granada competitor. Alluring prices after punitive initial depreciation. High spec cars make shrewd and rewarding buys. Diesels best sellers, especially SRDT. Autos drive better than manuals. All merit serious consideration as BMW/Merc alternative

What to *look for*
Crankshaft rumble, stone chipping on nose, weak synchro on 3rd, electrical maladies, grinding wheel bearings, cracked headlamps, catalytic converter failure. Resale tricky, so don't pay top money. Insist on a Peugeot service history

Porsche 944 *(83Y–91J)*

Not as expensive as you'd think, ultra reliable too. 944 is very docile and untemperamental. Often Porsche dealers offer the best deals and nicest cars. Warranty important

For
Performance, handling, quality, accessibility, looks

Against
High insurance and servicing costs, anti-social image

Best buys
944 Lux, 944 S2, 944 Turbo

Avoid
Early Lux cars without power steering, tatty pre-85 cars, anything that's been modified, over-priced Cabrios, high mileage Turbos, cars without history unless very cheap

Overall
Chic, bullet-proof and poised supercoupe. Tidy early cars great value. Entry level £4,000. Main agent history important. Air con, sunroof, sports seats and leather trim preferred. Some tat about so be very fussy. Values waning now in wake of 968 especially Cabrio and Turbo. Autos worth less. Turbo extremely fast and polished. Stock 944 Lux good buy. High-revving 944S has 16v engine. S2 has 3.0 power and much greater mid-range heave.

Standard power steering after 84. ABS after 88. Post-88 Turbos have 250 bhp engine

What to *look for*
Accident damage, stone chipping on nose, panel gaps, camshaft belt needs replacement every 48,000, worn engine mountings, cylinder head gaskets on Turbos, overheating, leaking power steering rack seals, fictitious service histories, stolen cars, clutches usually fail after 50,000. Tyre wear can be heavy. Brake pads £250 a set!

Porsche A-Z

Used *Cars*

Porsche 911 *(68F–95M)*

Find a good 911 and you'll wonder why you waited so long. A bad one will make you weep

For
Almost viceless no-nonsense supercar. Outstanding build, power, looks, flat-6 sound effects

Against
Ageing rear-engined design, high envy factor, twitchy in wet, disorganised cockpit, vicious insurance

Best **b**uys
77 to 83 cars, Late Carreras, Carrera 4, Mint 911 SCs

Avoid
Rusty 64–73 cars, semi-auto Sportmatic, Targas, anything up-specced, 4-cyl 912, 2.2 models, high mileage examples esp. cheap-sounding Turbos

Over*all*
Porsche history paramount. Only mint warranted mileage 911s make sense. Buy with extreme caution and seek expert advice. Post-77 Carrera and 911SC make fine buying. Targa and Sportmatics worth much less. Turbo too fast – superb road rocket though. Super Sport and Turbo-bodied cars hard to sell. Cabrios sought after. Carrera 2 and 4 most refined. Early 911s down to £4,000, buy only best, don't pay classic prices. 76-on cars have galvanised bodies. 84-on cars most fuel-frugal. Brilliant 2.7 RS attracts collectors' money. Guards Red the colour

What to **look** *for*
Signs of abuse, missing or false service histories, paintwork repairs, frontal accident damage, damaged alloy wheels, worn clutches, smoking or noisy engines, blown turbos, pronounced and uneven tyre wear, warped brake discs, damaged leather interiors, stolen cars. Porsche dealers offer peace of mind warranties. Prices going up of late

Porsche 928 *(77S–95M)*

928 is tremendous package of strength, performance and reliability

For
Definitive grand tourer. Huge on value, style, looks and grunt

Against
Hair-raising ownership costs, fat-cat image, cramped cockpit, wearying road noise

Best **b**uys
928 S4 auto, Mint 928 S2 autos, 928 GT manual

Avoid
Nasty, worn out, early 80s 928s with garish striped seats, anything without history, very high mileage cars, manuals except GT and GTS

Over*all*
Awesome mile-eating ability and German build quality. Manuals unloved, S4 most refined, early cars down to £5,000 can be a nightmare. Hide trim, sunroof, electric seats desirable options. Virtually impossible to sell without history. Leech-like grip and G-force acceleration. 928 GT a real stunner. Hunky 928 GTS the dog's twitcher. ABS after 83. 928 GT manual only. Servicing likely to be £700 a go. Prices softening, so value realistically. Some horrible cars about. Porsche dealer purchase with warranty is safest option

What to **look** *for*
Panel gaps, body damage, vandal damage, scruffy interiors, engine wear, fuel injection problems, warped brake discs, slipping auto box, failed electric window motors, head gasket failure/overheating, signs of poor paintwork repairs, forged service histories, more than five owners on registration document, cracked windscreens, worn door hinges, high oil consumption and blue smoke on hard acceleration

Proton 1.3/1.5 *(89F–95M)*

Tough, cheap and lots of warranties but ditch water dull.
Usually bought by retired eldely types so image non-existent

For
Thrifty, strong warranty, tougher than you'd think

Against
Faceless, little street presence, iffy resale

Best *buy*
1.5 GL 5-dr

Avoid
1.3 4-dr, finance repos, anything without a history, scruffy examples, high milers hard to sell

Over*all*
Tight economy shuttle with proven Mitsubishi power units. Budget-aimed marketing means many are bought on finance and never see a spanner. 1.5 GL best of bunch. Aeroback five-door strongest seller. 1.3 has no PAS. Auto only on SE. Special editions worth £100 more. Best bets are 91-on cars with 12v engines

What to *look for*
Camshaft wear on 1.5, water pump failure on 1.3, 2nd and 3rd gear synchro, kerbed wheels, wonky steering geometry, uneven tyre wear, leaking hoses, water leaks in boot

Renault 5 *(77S–95M)*

R5 still makes a good buy despite its age. Cheapish too

For
Value, charm, refinement, willing engines

Against
Used values fading, rust-prone, Renault dealers expensive

Best *buys*
1.4 TS, Campus, GTX 5-dr

Avoid
Early rusty cars, 3-dr, thrashed and crashed Turbos

Over*all*
Nippy, cheap and convenient with soft, cosseting ride. Campus evergreen seller, 5-dr preferable, GT Turbo difficult to work on, has high insurance and boy-racer image. Rare Monaco special edition has leather. Older cars very rusty. GTX has high spec. Phase 2 cars most refined. Autos desirable. TS practical. 850 surprisingly lively. Many special editions not worth much more. Early Phase 1 Turbos unwanted. Diesels rare and very popular

What to *look for*
Blown and abused Turbos, rust on left-hand front wing, rear torsion bar mounts, floorpan, rear wheel-arches, split CV (constant velocity joint) gaiters, worn half shafts, shock absorbers, rattly engines, blown head gaskets, failed radiator fans, clutch slip, mushy gear linkages, fragile auto boxes, collapsing interior trim on Phase 1 models, clicking speedometers, engine pinking, hot starting problems on Turbo variants

Renault 25 (84A–92J)

Had its time now and falling in value fast. Image on the skids too. Only buy dirt cheap with history, if you must. A Granada makes more sense

For
Affordability, comfort, room, big on value, cosseting ride

Against
Wicked depreciation, expensive servicing and spares, not that reliable, slow resale

Best buy
GTX

Avoid
Anything pre-88 Phase II, V6 versions, ex-hackneys, high milers worthless, average cars not worth the trouble, TS and GTS a bit basic

Overall
Not really in the game any more. Don't even think about paying main agent prices. Autos worth more. GTX spec best seller. V6 and V6 Turbo highly complex and costly to maintain, so depreciation painful. Special edition Monaco with leather trim worth a look. Facelift in April 90 with colour-coded bumpers. TXi has ABS and cruise

What to **look for**
Worn camshaft belt on 2.2, clanking timing chains on V6, engine oil leaks, head gasket failure, worn and poorly serviced turbos, auto gearbox computer malfunction, failed shockers, scored discs and worn pads, leaking PAS, broken trim and switches

Renault Clio (91H–95M)

Twinky, trendy, lively and fun, the Clio has sharp image, low costs and painless depreciation. As superminis go Renault's smallest makes a charismatic and practical long-term buy

For
Pretty face, dependable resale, low cost ownership, youthful image

Against
Pricey parts and service, strong used values

Best buys
RT 1.4 with PAS, RN 1.2/1.4, 16v

Avoid
Base spec RL 1.2, high milers or town runabouts, anything scruffy and unhistoried

Overall
Smoother-riding, trendier and more modern Fiesta alternative. Uncomfortable driving position but no-one cares. Energetic used prices, especially RN, which sells instantly. Autos with PAS good news. 1.2/1.4 best for resale. 16v has cult following. Diesel values off the clock. RT 1.8 with PAS intriguing GTi competitor

What to **look for**
Kerbed wheels, stone chipping, flimsy trim, odd electrical problem, duff rear wipers. Generally though, build quality is better than most other Renaults

A-Z Renault
Used Cars

Renault GTA (86D–92J)

Mega-unusual and wonderfully Gallic but lousy sellers and a bit gimcrack. We wouldn't

For
Looks, brilliant handling, rust-free body, 4 seater, energetic turbo

Against
Not much room for the luggage, unpredictable secondhand values, second division image

Best **buy**
V6 Turbo

Avoid
Pre-1990 cars which can have engine fires, anything mileagey and tatty. Only mint historied small mileage cars worth bothering with

Over**all**
Almost as much fun as a 911 but not an aspirational choice. Very few people have heard of them, so selling a struggle. Cheap for what they are but very much a compromise car. GTA buffs love them but the trade don't. Can be shoddily made with annoying gremlins. Find a good one and you'll enjoy it

What to **look for**
Overheating, accident damage on grp body, weak 3rd gear synchro, dicky engine management system, petrol leaks, bent chassis, clonking diffs, unreliable digital dash, iffy electrical switchgear. Engine fires…!

Renault Espace (85C–95M)

Espace is versatile and dependable, but hard to buy cheaply. Most go to franchised dealers who ask the earth

For
Versatility, space, strong used values, handles like a saloon

Against
Expensive to buy, some French tinniness

Best **buys**
2.0TXE, 2.0RXE, 2.9RT

Avoid
Ex-taxis, high mileage ex-fleet Espaces, early GTS, overpriced dealer examples

Over**all**
One of the best people carriers you can buy. Used values traditionally high owing to perennial demand. Stylish, capacious, pleasing to drive. Limited boot space when full of people. Engines noisy, gearboxes notchy. High insurance. New shape Espace has improved dash and potent V6 engine option. 2.0 TXE finest package. Renault dealers ask mad money, so private buying best if you can persuade the owner to sell. 100,000 miles a legitimate expectation

What to **look for**
Flimsy switchgear, intermittent electrics, well worn interior and load area. Few rust problems as chassis is galvanised and body is glass fibre. Suspension mountings, worn clutches, gear linkages, gearboxes, roof damage, worn shock absorbers. Much clocking so verify mileage before you buy. Privately owned examples are safest bets

292

Rover Mini *(1959–95M)*

Mini still makes sense. Cheap to run, buy and mend

For
Cute, nippy, cheerful, enduring image, minimalist fun

Against
Old as the hills, rust-prone, tiny boot

Best **b**uys
Mayfair, Cooper and higher spec variants

Avoid
Clubman, City, auto unless desperate, rusty pre-80 cars unless mint low milers, 850 variants

Over*all*
35 years old and still a sweetie. Disarming to drive. Go for specials like Mayfair or Ritz. City models a bit basic. Autos hilariously frenetic. Loose change running costs. Older cars hold price well. New Cooper has trendy image. Earliest pre-60 cars can make £5,000. Floor starter cars are collectors' material. Woody Countryman much admired. Convertibles popular

What to *look for*
Rust in seams, front wings, A panel, sills, subframe, floorpan, wheel-arches, boot floor and lid. Blown head gaskets, timing chain rattle, worn trailing arms, faulty alternators, leaking radiators, worn clutch release bearings, CV (constant velocity) joints, very troublesome automatic gearbox that slips

Rover Metro *old shape (80W–90H)*

Far from excellent in any department, the Metro can be a risky buy. Only low mileage mint examples worth the effort. Buy with care

For
Cheap, easy to fix, roomy, thrifty

Against
Unreliable, poor build quality, rust-prone

Best **b**uys
1.3 HLE, Mayfair, Vanden Plas, GTA

Avoid
MG Turbo, rusty pre-84 facelift cars, automatics, City, 1.0, expensive VDPs, vile colours such as yellow, brown, navy blue, lime green, beige

Over*all*
Not as good as people think, but plenty about at bargain basement prices. Decent transport if you're prepared to put up with the niggles. Go for high spec cars and limited editions. Only well maintained, carefully driven cars worth the trouble. Post-87 cars better built. Rust the problem. Much sub-£1,000 rubbish about, so buy latest you can afford. MG Turbos hopelessly unreliable with collapsing used values. MG 1300 quite popular. 5-dr best for resale. Colour choice important. Vanden Plas has leather and walnut

What to *look for*
Rust in wings, valance, bonnet, doors, sills, floorpan. Leaking hydrolastic suspension, rattling timing chains, blown head gaskets, worn gearboxes and radius arms, disintegrating trim, leaking radiators, water pumps, leaking and potentially dangerous petrol filler caps

Rover Metro *new shape (90G–95M)*

A much better proposition all round. Lovely engines, taut handling, absorbent ride

For
Excellent K-series engines, fun to drive, better built than its forebear

Against
Cramped rear space, high depreciation

Best **b**uys
1.1 S, 1.4 S, GTA

Avoid
High milers, ex-driving school cars, basic 1.1 C, over-rated 1.4 16v GTi

Over*all*
Lively and zesty urban runabout. Built the way the old one should have been. Splendid PSA diesel, taut handling and smooth ride. 1.1 and 1.4 S useful, GTA quick and insurable, GTi has hard ride, CVT auto in demand. 5-dr with metallic paint desirable. Ex-rental tiny mileage Channel Island cars make sense. Steady demand for all models except high milers, which the trade doesn't like. Easy to live with and plenty of dealers with low ownership costs. 16v values weakening

What to *look for*
Stone chipping, body damage, kerbed wheels, scruffy interiors and broken trim, engine pinking, front tyre wear on 16v, clocked diesels

Rover 200/400 *(89G–95M)*

Highly regarded among fleet buyers

For
Sweet engines, frugal diesels, handle well, classy big car feel, proven integrity

Against
Only average ride quality, all need power steering, expensive

Best **b**uys
214 SLi, 214 Si. Cabriolet, 218 SLD, 416 Si, 416 GSi, 418 SLD

Avoid
214 S, 3-dr, GTi, ex-fleet high milers, autos, non-power steering cars

Over*all*
One of Rover's top sellers with high-revving and smooth 16v engine. Much loved by the fleets, who know a thing or two about reliability. GSi popular, high milers difficult to sell, used values firm. 214 SLi strong seller, 416 GTi quick and competent. Solid middle class image helped by luxury interiors. Service history essential. Auto and coupe not popular. Cabriolet much admired. GTi demand poor. Most demand for Si, SLi spec. Plenty of ex-rental stuff about, so don't pay fortunes

What to *look for*
Stone chipping on bonnet, roof and wings, abused company cars, smoky 16v engines, juddering clutches, recalcitrant gearbox synchromesh, tatty trim, scuffed load areas, leaking power steering pump, camshaft wear, engine management system gremlins

Rover Montego *(84A–95M)*

Pre '88 reg specimens only for the brave. Generally fragile, dated with groan-inspiring depreciation. Only late diesels and 7-seater estates worth saving

For
Roomy, simple to fix, economical, loads for sale

Against
Early cars a bit brittle, fuddy-duddy image, MG versions a joke

Best **b**uys
1.6 LX, 2.0i LX, 2.0 GTi, Countryman Estate, 2.0 DS LX Turbo Estate

Avoid
1.3, all base models, hard driven 2.0, ex-taxis, dull colours (navy blue, beige, white), autos without PAS, shagged MGs, ruined estates, high milers can't take it so make 60,000 your threshold

Overall
Past its prime now with vanishing street cred. Estates and diesels best sellers. MG hard to insure. Little demand for overpriced Vanden Plas. Countryman Estate good news. Special Editions worth roughly £200 more than stock item. 2.0 fuel injection goes well. Most had sunroof after 88. VW-sourced auto box makes it a pleasant driver. Optional PAS handy too

What to *look for*
Oil leaks on 1.3/1.6, rattly dashboards, high incidence of speedo replacement (check mileage is accurate), head gasket failure, engine management unit on 2.0, rattly valve gear, cambelts should be changed every 36,000, reluctant gearboxes, rumbling wheel bearings, cracked plastic bumpers. Service history a must on all Montegos

Rover 800 *(86D–95M)*

Used Rover 800s need great care. All models need low mileage and service history to be worth anything come part-exchange time. Don't pay retail either

For
Very cheap to buy, big on comfort and room, impressive street presence

Against
Appalling depreciation, dire early build quality, expensive to maintain

Best **b**uys
820 Sli Fastback, mint Sterlings, cheap manual 825s, 827 Fastback, 825 diesels

Avoid
Early 87–88 cars, pre-90 non-16v 820s, high-mileage examples especially 827, anything without a dealer history, 820 autos, ex-taxis, 800s with bodykits, hard driven Vitesse models

Overall
Unrivalled value but needs to be bought carefully. Not as well built as Granada competitor. Steering lacks feel, suspension clonks. Sterling has leather, looks the part in black but don't pay all the money. Autos preferred on bigger-engined variants. 2.7 V6 goes well but value plummets like a falling girder. Post-90 820s have livelier 16v M16 engine. Vitesse values shaky. Older 825, 827 very difficult to sell unless mint. SLi best value. Fastback more desirable than saloon

What to *look for*
Cracked plastic bumpers, head gaskets on 820s, noisy auto boxes on 825 models, leaking exhaust ball joints, weeping water pumps, leaking cam bearing seals, heater and speedometer failure, noisy power steering, driver's seat wear, wheel bearings, engine management system, slow electric windows. Service history essential and don't pay anything near book price. All 800s should sell for significantly behind book value, so buy with care. Warranty desirable

Saab 900 *(84A–95M)*

Reliability personified. 200,000 miles not unknown. Unusual interesting family machine with a smudge of class. Parts and service pricey, but turbo versions huge fun

For
Last for decades, mammoth mileage ability, big on safety, brilliant in the snow, Herculean build quality

Against
Lacks refinement, no icon, costly ownership

Best *b*uys
900i 16v 5-dr, 900 GLi 5-dr, 900 SE, 900i 16v Convertible

Avoid
Ailing turbos, 3 doors in dull colours, cars without sunroofs, sketchy history

Over*all*
So reliable that the punter always comes back for another one. 5-dr versions best. Professional image. 900i 16v 5-dr best for retail. Values always steady. Early B-F plates in short supply. Convertible good news. Turbos can give problems. Turbo 16v S quite a package. New shape 900s gaining large following

What to *look for*
Overheating, noisy crankshafts, timing chains, cambelts, turbo failure, water leaks, blowing exhausts, accident damage, clocking. Bodies last for centuries, mechanicals pretty good too. Only a hydrogen bomb could wear the interior

Saab 9000 *(85C–95M)*

Saab 9000 is a solid and able performer, but depreciation will hurt. Saab dealers very pricey. Value carefully or you'll lose a mint

For
Value, comfort, lots of room, safety, built to last forever

Against
High depreciation and ownership costs, pricey parts and service, Turbos complicated

Best *b*uys
9000 2.3i 5-dr, SE models, Turbo 16v SE, 2.3 CDi 5-dr

Avoid
Early 2.0 models, hard driven early Turbos, over-priced Carlssons, high mileage Turbos

Over*all*
Smooth, agile and comfortable with cerebral professional image. Low spec models are good value, high spec cars depreciate fast. All-round demand for low mileage older models. 2.3 better bet than 2.0 CD but is unloved at high mileage. 2.3 CD auto rare and desirable. Turbo must be mint and low mileage. Ex-company high milers, need to be very cheap. Saab dealers usually expensive, but offer watertight warranties. Classified ad cars much more competitive.

What to *look for*
Leaking door and window seals, intermittent warning lights, faulty wiper motors, front tyre wear on Turbos, blown turbo units, ticking hydraulic tappets, sludged up oil galleries, fuel injection problems. Warranty desirable. Some very cheap cars at auction. Service history essential. Saab dealers offer greatest peace of mind

Seat Ibiza *(87D–93L)*

Look better than they are. Spanish engineering not the finest. Depreciation severe and most bits rust or fall off. Need to be really, really cheap

For
Modest outlay, quite easy on the eye, practical, straightforward mechanics

Against
Bizarre dash layout, fragile switches, unsteady used values, silly name

Best *buys*
1.5 GLX, 1.7 D

Avoid
Anything that isn't mint with an unbroken history, pre-90 cars with dodgy build, 900cc models, 3 doors

Overall
Economy shuttle but seriously flawed in the build quality department. 1.5 GLX makes best buying sense. 1.7 D rare and thrifty. 1.2 cheap. Off-focus image and tricky resale, so value with considerable care. Not a trade or retail favourite. Decent ones offer sensible value if bought right

What to *look for*
Timing chains, worn 900cc engines, valve guide smoke, camshaft ticking, kerbed wheels, uneven tyre wear, badly fitting interior trim, rust blistering

Skoda Estelle *(80V–91H)*

For cheap, reliable motoring you can't go wrong at this money

For
Tough, reliable, very cheap, couldn't-give-a-damn image

Against
Crude, basic, rattly, heavy depreciation

Best *buys*
120L, 135 Coupe, 130 Rapid

Avoid
Pre-85 bangers, 105L and S, never serviced finance repossessions, dealer special editions

Overall
Fine buy if you understand their limitations. Pennies to run and maintain, practical too. Estelle 120L and Rapid 135 Coupe amazing value. Buy latest and best you can find. Privately advertised cars cheapest. Rare and unhappy-looking cabriolet unpopular. 87-on have 5-speed gearbox. 89-on Rapid and latest Estelle Two make decent transport. Earlier cars just bangers. LSE/LXS more comfortable. Engines and gearboxes last forever

What to *look for*
Blue smoke from worn cylinder head, blown head gaskets, blocked radiators, worn steering joints, heavy steering, sloppy gearbox linkages, abused interiors, rust on bonnet and engine cover, broken interior switches

Skoda Favorit *(89G–95M)*

No longer a joke especially now that Volkswagen makes them. Has come surprisingly high in the Top Gear J.D. Power Car Customer Satisfaction Survey

For
Better than you'd think. Decent build quality, ride and handling. Great value

Against
Heavy depreciation, unrefined, noisy

Best **b**uys
Favorit Forum, 136 LS

Avoid
Finance repos, high milers, early 89–90 models with suspect assembly quality

Over**all**
The best car to come out of Eastern Europe. Practical, hardy with plenty of dealer support. Will sell if priced sensibly. Steady demand. Handsome estate holds value longest. Shortage of clean, low mileage examples. Forum cheapest. LS most comfortable. Some hideous colours. Growing following. One-year-old low mileage buy the shrewdest move

What to *look for*
Falling away trim and plastic mouldings, notchy gearbox synchromesh, faulty earths on electrics, spongy brakes, parking dents, kerbed wheels, rattly engines, blue smoke on acceleration, collapsing seats, jammed door handles, leaking door and boot seals, poor paint finish, ill-fitting body panels

Suzuki Vitara *(88F–95M)*

Vitara is in danger of becoming dead trendy with sky-high used values and year-round demand

For
Very trendy, car-like handling, low depreciation

Against
Limited off-road ability, wearing on long distances

Best **b**uys
JLX estate, JLX SE auto

Avoid
Non-injected 1.6, soft-tops, over-priced dealer cars loaded with knick-knacks

Over**all**
Pretty off-roader designed for on-street profiling. Civilised, interesting teenage 4x4 with dependable resale. Lively 16v engines, long wheelbase estate has most space. SE automatic most valuable. Option packs add desirability. Look mean with bullbars and wide wheels. Dark metallics best. Soft tops not favoured. Few cheap ones about. The cream goes to dealers. All models in brisk demand, particularly low-price examples

What to *look for*
Signs of off-road abuse, parking damage, heavy steering, oil-burning blue exhaust smoke, whining differentials and gearboxes, tired interiors, salt-induced underbody corrosion from beach work, roof scratches, vandal damage, any with evidence of limited servicing, unpaid finance

Subaru - Toyota A-z
Used Cars

Subaru Legacy *(89G–95M)*

All those farmers can't be wrong. Legacy is terribly able but not an image-builder. Not fast sellers but handy when it's deep and crisp and even. Mega-quick Turbo can worry Cosworths

For
Leech-like four-wheel drive grip, awesomely quick turbo, vast estates

Against
Unprepossessing image, higher than average depreciation, ugly saloons, too few dealers

Best **b**uys
2.2 GX Estate, 2.0 Turbo

Avoid
1.8, punished turbos, worn out estates, accident grief

Over**all**
Finely finished and highly regarded but still too soberly suited to woo the aspirational buyer. Turbo is Cosworth competitor. Estates hold value best. Saloons not generally favoured. Autos worth less. ABS standard only on 2.0 Turbo and 2.2 GX. Not many in the classifieds so Subaru dealers await you

What to *look for*
Uneven tyre wear, clonking four-wheel drive, panel damage, incipient underbody rust, turbo lag, stone chipping, knackered load area on estates

Toyota Corolla *(87E–95M)*

Corolla is seriously bland but bomb-proof. Rather like a very good washing machine. Drives like one too

For
Reliability, build quality, limited depreciation, predictable trade-in

Against
Anonymous, faceless image, expensive

Best **b**uys
1.3 GL 5-dr

Avoid
Saloons, 1.6 Exec, high milers, ex-taxis

Over**all**
Characterless but competent with very strong used values. Hatches preferred to saloons. Auto sought after. 1.3 GL 5-dr most wanted. 1.6 Exec and GTi harder to sell. Evergreen seller if clean and low mileage. Few bargains about. Dealers have all the nicest examples but they don't come cheap. 4x4 estate unfavoured. Power steering after 89. Check that 3-year warranty is still current

What to *look for*
Low mileage, few-owner, service history cars only. Front tyre wear and signs of hard driving on GTi. Power steering leaks, wheel bearing wear, sloppy gearbox linkage, gear whine

Toyota MR2 *old shape (85B–90G)*

Latest cars best buys. Decent enough transport if bought cheaply, don't pay top money – you'll regret it later when dealers bid low

For
Neat, nimble, reliable, fun

Against
Frequently thrashed, expensive to insure, girlie image

Best **b**uys
Late MR2 coupe

Avoid
Very high-mileage cars, over-priced dealer stock, anything with signs of accident damage or paintwork, tatty T-Bars

O*verall*
Well specified, fine handling, engaging to drive, values not as strong as they were, especially T-Bar, well screwed together and capable of big mileages. Engines need to be revved hard, so many abused. Once stylish image beginning to fade in the wake of new model so used values look threatened. Metallics best, service history important. Desirable leather on T-Bar after 88

What to *look for*
Accident damage, lack of servicing, broken door pillar aerials, headlight motors, failed electric window motors, rust round sunroof and front valance, worn wheel bearings and shock absorbers, blown exhausts, leaking CV (constant velocity) joint rubbers, oil sludge

Vauxhall Nova *(83Y–93K)*

Useful and reliable small car choice. Nova is cheap to buy and thrifty. There's a Vauxhall garage in every town, so repairs are easy and inexpensive

For
Nippy, cheap to run, plenty of dealers, quite sturdy, good resale

Against
Can feel tinny with miles, hard ride, small boot

Best **b**uys
1.5 TD, 1.3 L, 1.4 L

Avoid
All saloons, earliest Y, A and B cars unless proper, SRi and GTE, 3-dr, high milers, duff colours such as navy blue, pond green, china blue, dark brown

O*verall*
Ageing noticeably, but better value than a Metro. 5-speed 5-dr 1.3 best. Saloons not liked at all. SR and GTi model values down. 3-dr Merit and Luxe hatch will sell if clean and low in miles. Early variants always in demand. Disappointing colours. Special editions worth only £50–£100 more than standard. Rare 1.5 TD a cracker. Plenty in the classifieds. Service history worthwhile

What to *look for*
Camshaft ticking, fuel pump malfunction, worn wheel bearings, 1.0 engine smokes and rattles, sloppy gearbox linkage, tatty interiors, rust in front valance, doors, sills, front wings, engine oil leaks. Water leaks into interior, front tyre wear on SRi. Latest cars best, dealer purchase expensive and unnecessary. Go for few-owner cars privately advertised

Vauxhall Astra *old shape (84B–91J)*

Astra is dated but very dependable

For
Plentiful, unobtrusive, reliable, cheap to run, legions of dealers

Against
Dumpy shape, rear blind spots, road noise, becomes creaky with miles

Best **b**uys
1.4 LX, 1.6 SX, 1.6 LD Estate, 1.8 SXi

Avoid
All 4-speed cars, overpriced CDs, hammered SRis and GTEs, any sports variant with a bodykit, 1.2s, accident damaged 16vs, stolen recovered convertibles, Merit 3-dr, tired ex-company cars, weak colours

Over**a**ll
Decent Escort chaser but old hat now, though continues to sell surprisingly well. 1.3 and 1.4 LX in demand, SRi and GT and 16v hard to insure. Much clocking so service history and warranted mileage essential. Diesels last forever. 1.6 LD Estate particularly useful. Merit spec too basic. 5-drs sell best. 16v handling wayward at the limit. Innumerable special editions worth little more except Tiffany (add £200). SXi makes sound SRi alternative. Convertible rare and quite sought after. CD generally unloved. 88-on GTE has power steering. Performance models much favoured by joyriders and thieves

What to *look for*
Rusty pre-86 cars, camshafts last only 60,000 miles, oil leaks, worn fuel pumps, seldom serviced examples, engine bearing failure at big mileages, driveshaft/CV joint ticking, split CV boots, worn clutches, nearside rear tyre wear, front disc wear, poor cold starting, cracked headlights, scruffy load areas on estate. If well maintained with regular oil changes, Astras can do 100,000 miles without major work

Vauxhall Belmont *(86C–91J)*

Booted Astra is ugly with inert image and less than brilliant resale. Some nice ex-pensioner low milers around though, but don't pay all the money

For
Earnest, reliability, loose change ownership

Against
Ugly, unrefined, dodgy resale

Best **b**uys
LD/GLD, LXi Estate, 1.4 LX

Avoid
1.3s, anything from the fleets, high milers. Earliest C platers noisy and nasty. Some dull colours, so metallics make best buying

Over**a**ll
Cheerless booted Astra that never caught on. Hard ride, boomy engines, steady image and skittish handling at the limit. 1.6/1.8 and diesels sell best. CD and SRi hard to move. Only 1.8 LXi Estate good news with some cult following. Minor facelift in 89 but still too dreary to sell in quantity. Most bought by steady private types, which means some real minters in the lineage ads. Generally slightly cheaper than Astras. Special Editions worth £50–£150 more. A sensible if uncharismatic small car choice

What to *look for*
Camshaft failure, oil leaks, poor running from dodgy carbs, weeping fuel pumps, hot starting on injection variants, front CV joint clonking, nearside rear tyre wear, crankshaft rumble on seldom serviced examples. Evidence of regular oil changing (6,000) essential

A-Z Vauxhall

Vauxhall Cavalier *old shape (81X–88F)*

Old Cav is on the skids now, but still makes a half decent hack.
Last of the F platers make good bets but rare now with history.
£1500 buys the best, but don't expect to impress anyone

For
Cheap to buy and run, easy to mend, quite willing, fast SRi

Against
Not many nice ones left, rough engines, stiff gearboxes, low-rent image

Best **b**uys
1.8 LXi, 2.0 GLSi, 2.0 SRi, GLD Estate

Avoid
1.3, hard-to-sell convertibles, noisy 1.6, ex-hackneys, some dire solid colours, many were clocked (some several times), shabby interiors

Overall
Tried and tested but really banger territory now. Clean, last-of-the-line E & F platers good value. Hatches sell better than saloons. Engines get rattly with miles. High spec GL and CD well regarded. 1.8i drives nicely. Bizarre convertible never caught on. Estates useful and popular. Diesels still strong sellers. Silly special editions not worth a light. SRi 130 very quick. Five-speed essential. Rare with a decent service history

What to **look for**
Camshaft noise, main bearing rumble, oil leaks, gearbox rattle, slipping autos, track rod end wear, brake pads, scored discs, failed auto chokes, duff shockers, electric mirror and window switch malfunction, faded metallics. Rust on front valance, wings, doors, rear dog-leg, worn wheel bearings

Vauxhall Cavalier *new shape (88F–94L)*

Cavalier is well-proven and much-loved

For
Predictable running costs, solid resale, economical to own, quick and comfortable

Against
Rep's car image, boomy engines, excitable handling at the limit

Best **b**uys
1.6 L Hatch, 2.0 GLi Hatch, 1.7 DL, GSi 2.0 16v

Avoid
All 1.4s, saloons unless significantly cheaper than hatches, 4x4s, flogged SRis, clocked ex-company dogs, flat colours

Overall
Well entrenched fleet favourite. Fine build, looks, detailing, economy. Engines noisy and chassis could be better. 1.6 L sells fastest. Saloons usually worth less. Colour exerts significant financial effect: for metallic, red and black add £150. 1.8 and 2.0 GLi premium spec. GSi 2.0 16v nice car. SRi not so strong. 1.4L dead duck. 4x4 and CD unwanted. Diesels in demand. Sluggish autos not favoured. Deadlocks give good anti-theft protection. Ex-rental one-year-old small-mileage cars make sensible buys. Clocking rife

What to **look for**
Water in boot, creaking dashes, gear linkage on 2.0, oil-burning blue smoke from worn valve guides, scuffed wheel trims, worn camshafts, appetite for brake pads, oil leaks on 4x4, brake light switches, throttle lag on injection models, broken accelerator pedal mechanisms and clutch cables, flimsy switchgear, worn shock absorbers, electronic relay failure

Vauxhall Calibra *(90G–95M)*

Couthy coupe with an awful lot to recommend it. Swish, smart, good sellers, low depreciation and the servicing costs of a Cavalier. The odd horrid one about - buy with care

For
Matinée idol looks, generous room for a coupe, firm used values, brisk performance

Against
Some handling histrionics from unrefined chassis

Best **b**uys
2.0i 16v, 4x4 Turbo

Avoid
2.0i, accident damage

Over**all**
Vauxhall's supermodel. The Calibra is pretty, practical and pacy. 2.0i less popular - more of a Cavalier in a party frock. Best buying comes from 16 valver with alloys. 4x4 models very capable. Red is the colour. Stock Cavalier interior disappointing. Plenty about, so don't give the earth. Good long-term resale prospects. Trade love them. Early 90–91 cars best value

What to *look for*
Clocking, HP default, stone chipping, signs of regular servicing, camshaft rattle, oil leaks, worn gear selector, brake pad wear, driveshaft leaks on 4x4, kerbed front wheels. Beginning to seep onto the second-hand market in numbers with some high-milers and accident damaged cars about. Don't let those drop dead looks fool you

Vauxhall Carlton *(82Y–94L)*

Carlton makes good caravan tower

For
Value, low prices, reliability, straightforward mechanicals

Against
Caravan club image, heavy depreciation, stodgy feel

Best **b**uys
2.0i CDX auto estate, 3.0 GSi 24v, 2.0 GLi

Avoid
All 1.8s, especially autos, and pre-86 2.0 and 2.2, ex-taxis, particularly diesels

Over**all**
Well assembled Granada rival. Fairly unrefined but unbeatable value. 1.8 under-powered. 2.0 GLi most wanted. 3.0 GSi rapid. 3.0 CDX estate huge. 3.0 24v very brisk indeed. CD and CDX nicely furnished. July 86-on cars facelifted. Lotus Carlton rare Ferrari chaser, but difficult to drive in town and values beginning to wilt. Switchable auto good news. Muscular 2.6i good load-lugger

What to *look for*
Oil-burning blue smoke from worn valve guides, oil leaks round fuel and oil pumps, ticking camshafts, fuel injection system air leaks, auto choke failure, spongy brake pedals, worn discs, worn manual gearboxes, electrical malfunction, noisy hydraulic tappets on 6-cylinder engines, rocker cover oil leaks, blocked fuel filters, front tyre wear, worn power steering pump, steering box and ball joints. Auto gearbox slow to engage. Electric window winder failure. Best bought privately with service history, but watch for hard use from the caravan brigade

Vauxhall Senator (87E–94L)

Senator is outrageous value for money

Overall

Poise, power and presence. Awesome value. Manuals despised, so don't bother. 3.0 CDi the one to have with standard leather, air, switchable suspension and ABS. 3.0 24v sublime machine. 2.5i and 2.6 taxi material and unregarded. 88-on have standard ABS. Velour no-cost option undesirable. CD player after 90. Digital instrumentation not popular. 4-speed switchable auto best in the business. White 24v manual cars may have seen service with the police. Service history essential

For

German build quality, tremendous value package, sybaritic luxury, loads of standard equipment, dealers everywhere

Against

Chip-cutter front grille, serious depreciation

Best buys

3.0 CDi, 3.0 CDi 24v

Avoid

Ex-taxi 2.5/2.6, ex-police cars unless for nothing, high mileage cars without service history, digital instruments, all manuals, CD with velour trim

What to look for

Worn shock absorbers, oil leaks, fuel injection and air conditioning malfunction, loose steering boxes, leaking fuel pipes, uneven rear tyre wear, rocker cover oil leaks, scored and warped brake discs, kickdown failure on auto box, faulty electric window motors, cooling fan failure, worn wheel bearings, power steering leaks. Value with care as prices tend to run considerably behind retail book

Vauxhall Frontera (91J–95M)

One of the scores of wannabee off-roaders. Image getting a touch common so future depreciation and desirability uncertain. Diesels awfully slow

Overall

Value and versatility. Sport best buy. Long wheelbase models preferred. Options can dictate values. Bonnet badge precludes membership of the snooty off-roader club. Black, bull bars and mean alloys look the business. Enthusiastic following, so you'll pay retail or near it

For

Butch looks, gentle depreciation, easy spares and service, a lot for your money

Against

Lethargic diesel, parvenu image, strong used seller

Best buy

Frontera Sport

Avoid

Off-road battering, very high milers, hard-worked diesels with signs of towing use

What to look for

Stone chipping, underside and body damage, oil leaks, wheel bearings, valve guide smoke, rattly cam gear, crankshaft rumble

Volkswagen A-Z

For
Tough, high-mileage strengths,
reliability, economy, high resale

Against
Heavy steering and brakes, stiff
suspension, expensive parts and service

Best *b*uys
1.3 CL, 1.3 GT, 1.3 Coupe S

Avoid
Saloons, early 82–83 cars, hard-driven
1.0s, over-priced special editions,
4-speeders

Volkswagen Polo *old shape (81X–94M)*

Polo is hardy and lasts well. Few owner, small mileage
examples in demand

Over*all*
One of the more solid superminis with big car
quality. 1.0 cruises well but not exactly nippy.
85-on have 5-speed gearbox. 85–86 45 bhp
engines best value. Saloons undesirable. Rare
factory-fitted steel sunroof nice to have.
Formel E very thrifty but make sure it's a post-
85C with 4+E gearbox. CL best-selling spec.
Basic C model rather spartan. Usual VW high-
mileage ability so watch for clocking. Service
history a plus point. G40 difficult to insure.
GT Coupe sensible compromise. Fuel
injection after Nov 90 on Fox, CL and GT

What to *look for*
Rust spots on front valance and door bottoms,
dented rear valance, worn clutches, front
suspension, ball joints, seeping rocker cover
gaskets, alternator oil contamination, leaks
around fuel pumps. Big end failure, worn
brake discs, clocking, interior wear, faulty oil
pumps, worn gearbox synchromesh, clicking
driveshafts, worn CV boots. Polos tend to be
used as shopping shuttles and never warm up
properly. Don't be afraid of a well-driven and
regularly serviced high miler – it could be a
better bet and cheaper, too

For
Bomb-proof, thrifty, very high resale,
goes on forever

Against
Gloomy cockpit, low standard spec,
heavy unassisted steering

Best *b*uys
1.3 Ryder, 1.6/1.8 GL, Golf CL Turbo
D, 1.8 GTi 3-dr 16v, Jetta CL Turbo D

Avoid
Thrashed or accident damaged GTis,
GTis with tacky bodykits and big
wheels, 1.3 Jetta, Syncro models

Volkswagen Golf/Jetta MkII *(84A–92J)*

Jetta as good as Golf but cheaper

Over*all*
Still one of Britain's best used cars. Very rust-
resistant, unbreakable mechanicals. Booted
(saloon) Jetta not so chic, so values muted. 1.3
4-speed only, but surprisingly competent. 1.6
and 1.8 5-dr Golfs preferred. CL/GL best
retail spec. Golf Syncro unloved. 90G cars
with big bumpers make best buys. Post-
October 90 standard power steering on GL,
GTi and 16v. Service history, sunroof and
metallic paint required. Service and parts
prices can hurt. High-revving and torquey
16v terrific value for money

What to *look for*
CV (constant velocity) joint wear, ticking
hydraulic tappets, broken headlights, sticking
door handles, gearbox wear on high milers,
front tyre wear on GTi, clutches last for
80,000 miles, VAG exhausts can last 4 years.
Much clocking. Speedometer failure, excessive
oil consumption on early 16v, stone chipping
on bonnet lip, worn wheel bearings, bullet
holes in windscreen, distorted alloy P wheels,
arcing HT leads, seized rear brake calipers on
GTis. The Golf/Jetta is one of the most
reliable and well-built medium-sized cars on
the market. Value Jetta models 10 per cent less

A-Z Volkswagen
Used *Cars*

Volkswagen Golf *new shape (92J-95M)*

Still the ultra-desirable used car. GTi a class leader in the blue-chip image

Overall
Not as engaging as the Mk II. Reputation sullied by quality control problems. Dealers could try harder and charge less. Umwelt Diesel impossibly slow. Still a fast seller though with pleasantly slow depreciation

For
Confident resale, money-in-the-bank image, high mileage strength, muscular VR6

Against
Not as reliable as they say, four cylinder variants a bit sluggish, GTi not that quick either, some wild retail prices

Best buys
1.4 CL, VR6

Avoid
Overpriced GTis, high mileage diesels, some early J plate cars less carefully built. Vento not a strong seller in the UK. 5-drs sell better than 3-drs. Steer clear of white and navy blue

What to look for
Broken headlamps, kerbed wheels, frayed seats, electrical failure, broken switches, camshaft ticking, accident damage on GTis, high milers tend to slip out of fifth. Service history essential for retail sale. Tornado Red and Calypso Green best selling colours

Volkswagen Scirocco *(82X–92K)*

Scirocco not so popular as Golf but goes and lasts as well, good value. Interesting coupe

Overall
Golf-based bargain coupe. All the usual VW virtues, but cheaper. Rust-resistant with hardy mechanicals. Non-injected GT Coupe makes fine buy. GTi even better. Scala special edition looks smart except in white with all-white seats. Surprisingly quick but non-servo brakes need a pause for thought. Autos undesirable. Early cars always in demand. Later models need to be well behind book. VW dealers usually expensive. 150,000 miles a breeze.

For
Italian styling, cheap to buy, tough as Doc Martins

Against
Heavy steering, cramped, disinclined to stop

Best buys
Scala 1.8, GTXi, GT, Mint GTis

Avoid
Early 1500/1600s, GTL and GL, white Scala, over-priced dealer cars which will depreciate instantly

They actually go better with big mileages - just run in at 50,000. Metallics and Tornado Red prime colours

What to look for
Gearbox and clutch wear in high milers, camshaft and hydraulic tappet wear, CV joints, gearbox linkages, oil consumption in big-mileage cars, worn shock absorbers. Traditionally, Sciroccos have always sold behind retail book, so don't pay fancy prices

Volkswagen A-**z**

Volkswagen Corrado *(89F–95M)*

Corrado is long lasting and not Japanese. VR6 is wicked fun. Won't be produced for much longer, which is a shame

For
Performance, handling, build quality, stonking VR6

Against
Cramped, slightly camp image, usual VW pricey bits

Best *buy*
VR6

Avoid
Emetic yellow, slowish (relatively) 16v, some very silly dealer prices, cars without VAG history, smoking G60s, crashed and thrashed VR6s

Overall
16 valve good, G60 better, VR6 best coupe money can buy. Quite a rare sight, so exclusive. Well finished and well mannered. Early depreciation heavy. Relatively expensive to run. Resale can be tricky because of market ignorance. Vastly underrated

What to *look for*
Noisy gearboxes, weak synchro, leaking shockers, rattling G60s, bonnet stone chipping, stolen recovereds, damaged alloys, missing roof aerials, which cost a mint. Easily clocked so verify mileage before you buy

Volkswagen Passat *new shape (88E–95M)*

Strong, hardy, roomy and lasts for ages but Passat is still a bit dull. VR6 Passat is swift, sensible and comodious

For
Long life, practicality, excellent estates, roomy, dependable VAG build

Against
Drab image, heavy depreciation especially on saloons, costly parts and service

Best *buy*
CL

Avoid
Ragged estates, very high milers unless really cheap, cars without sunroofs and PAS, some sorry solid colours like white and navy blue, 16v saloon depreciates most quickly

Overall
Prosaic but respectable. Unaggressively marketed and expensively priced, the Passat never sold in huge numbers. Estates much more popular than saloons, especially diesels. Beware of basic cars without PAS. GT and 16 valve hard to insure and not that desirable. CL best for retail. Best bargains come in price range F–G plate examples from non-franchised dealers. Big mileage cars usually still quite fit

What to *look for*
Blue smoke on start-up, hunting from injection system, shock absorber leaks, warped brake discs, groaning wheel bearings, leaking PAS rack, worn cam gear, ticking camshaft, sagging rear suspension on estates, towbar means it's been a workhorse. Main agent prices usually very high. Best buying comes from private ads

Volvo 340/360 *(81X–91H)*

340 usually well cared for by blue rinsers but hideous to look at and hideous to drive. Not a car but an apology

For
Sensible, safe, cheap and undemanding

Against
Geriatric image, uninspiring to drive, bouncy ride

Best buys
340 GL 1.7 5-dr, 340 1.4 5-dr

Avoid
All autos, saloons, 3-dr, anything tatty without a service history, hard worked ex-caravan cars

Overall
Hardly exciting and very dated safety-conscious family hatchback. Five-speed standard on GL from 83. 85-on have excellent 1700cc Renault engine option. 360 GLT SE has impressive spec but can be hard to sell. 2.0 360 toughest engine but thirsty. 360 injection makes good tow car. Autos weak sellers. Saloons ugly. GLT and GLE standard power steering from November 87. Steady demand at all years for low mileage examples with some history. Scruffy cars very difficult to sell to earnest private buyers

What to **look for**
Exhaust manifold fracture on 360, engine mounting failure, faulty water pumps, overheating, blown cylinder head gasket, broken belts, faulty carburettors, clutches on autos, gearbox linkage and oil leaks, distorted brake discs, worn suspension struts

Volvo 400 *(89G–95M)*

440 no match for Sierra/Cavalier/405

For
Solid, comfortable, roomy, safe

Against
High depreciation, a bit dreary to drive, breeze block styling

Best buys
440 GLi, 460 GLi, 1.6 Li, 1.8 Xi

Avoid
Turbos, autos, early G platers with iffy fit and finish. Auction specimens which can be 'problem' cars sent there by despairing Volvo dealers

Overall
Eminently workmanlike Escort alternative that's never really caught on. Early cars had assembly problems. November 91 carburettor models have 1800cc Renault engine. '92 models have 92 bhp 1600cc engine and standard catalyst. 1.6 Li able all-rounder. 1.8Xi has power steering and split seats. GLEi and GLT have more power and spec. All models need power steering. Turbo out of favour. Higher spec cars slow sellers. Strong Volvo dealer warranty

What to **look for**
Panel gaps on pre-November 91s, rust in body seams, rattles from doors, sunroof and rear load area, rear parcel shelf hinges fragile. Electrics can be troublesome. Abnormally loud hissing from power steering pump on full lock. Worn gear shift linkages. Oil-burning blue smoke from cold start, overheating. Privately advertised examples usually a good bet and quite cheap, but Volvo dealers offer no-risk Lifetime Care Warranty. Make sure the service history's been stamped up, otherwise warranty is voided

Volvo 240 *(82Y–90H)*

For
Big, practical, versatile, dependable and safe

Against
Ugly, desperately dated, passé image. Parts, service and insurance costly

Best **b**uys
240 GL estate manual, 240 GL 2.0 saloon

Avoid
Non-power steering cars, ruined estates, early 83–84 examples, autos, all 260s

The 240 was the antique dealer's carry-all, but there are now better estates. Value carefully as prices on the wane

Over**all**
Flawed but cheap enough and willing workhorses. Don't buy without power steering. Estates most popular. Heavy thirst for fuel. Catalyst from November 89. Useful overdrive. Autos sluggish sellers. High spec GLE unwanted. DL and GL sell well. Few owner warranted mileage cars the ones to go for. Volvo dealer cars expensive but tough enough to justify cheaper private purchase. Values flagging now as image fades. Sunroof and metallic paint help. Lower body galvanised steel from 86

What to *look for*
Rust on sills, door bottoms, front valance and estate tailgate, noisy engines, camshaft rattle, scuffed interiors, especially where dogs have been carried, worn wheel bearings and brake discs, blown head gaskets, engine bore and tappet wear. Values have tumbled recently, so never pay retail and go for latest and best with history

Volvo 700 *(82Y–90H)*

For
Enormous value, tank-like solidity, some street presence, built for keeps

Against
Expensive ownership, unhappy styling, fast depreciation

Best **b**uys
740 SE auto, 740 GL estate manual

Avoid
Turbos without service history, worn out estates, high-mileage V6s, ex-taxis

Volvo 7 series is a solid old thing. Some very cheap ones about but avoid tired turbos

Over**all**
Most interesting Volvo. Hardy, roomy, impressive but lacks finesse. Very cheap. £2000 buys a respectable 740 GLE with air and leather. GLT 16v and Turbo versions have few friends. No price difference between auto and manual. Metallic, sunroof and service history desirable. Estates preferred to saloons. High-mileage saloons very difficult to sell. 740 and 760 Turbos can become very pricey to fix. Parts costs will make you gasp. Low spec models easiest to sell. Diesels rare and in demand.

What to *look for*
Blown and whistling turbos, noisy and smoky V6 engines, whining gearboxes and differentials, failed electric window lifts, worn wheel bearings, ticking camshafts, worn oil pumps, leaking power steering racks and noisy pump, stone chipping on front valance and bonnet, worn rear shockers especially on estates, overheating, delay in auto gearbox selection, badly creased or worn leather seats on GLEs, discoloured head-linings, tyre wear on Turbos, failed boot gas struts, corroded alloy wheels

How to **deal** with car **deal**ers

If car dealers did their job properly, they wouldn't have the reputation they do. Professional ones are almost always fair and honest and have a fine local reputation. The shadier variety prefer to meet you in a lay-by off the M6 and insist you pay in cash. Selling satisfying cars to satisfied customers is all about detail – the little touch that means so much – and the dealer who hasn't grasped this simple truth is the one you should avoid. Sorting the good from the bad isn't easy, but there are ways to spot a rogue.

Franchised **dealer,** small **dealer** or **trader?**

Franchised dealers

Not all car dealers selling cars from showrooms are angels but, because they're fixed in one place and can't disappear overnight, you stand a better chance of winning some sort of redress if things turn nasty. Franchised dealers – garages that sell one make of new car – have much to lose from an unhappy customer. They're

allied and answerable to the relevant manufacturer who takes a dim view of sloppy salesmanship and sharp practice. If the dealership isn't up to scratch, it's not unknown for the manufacturer to withdraw the franchise. Dealer groups, holding companies who own and operate up to a dozen different franchises, have the most to lose. Big names, such as Lex, Mann Egerton, Cowies, Henlys, Dutton-Forshaw etc, don't want their reputations sullied by bad publicity and try hard to trade professionally and offer good service.

Vauxhall, anxious to establish the credibility of the used side of their dealerships, came up with an industry first – their 'Network Q' concept – marketing it under the slogan, 'Treating Used Cars Like New' and making a big thing of higher standards of used car preparation and customer care. Buying a new or secondhand car from one of the larger franchised garages undoubtedly offers one of the lowest risk factors for two reasons. First, they select and prepare all their used cars to a minimum standard and, secondly, they trade on the excellence of their reputation and don't want indignant customers walking round the showroom shouting.

Most of the big dealerships run pretty tight operations, selling cars no older than two years and 30,000 miles, and are keen to distance themselves from the shady car dealer image. But a stroll round the used car showroom or compound is never a bad idea, and a sure way of seeing how well they operate and present their stock for sale. Unvaleted cars with flat tyres and unprepared paintwork damage don't bode well. A neat and tidy site lined with shiny well scrubbed cars tends to suggest a business-like approach. Affiliation to professional bodies such as the Motor Agents' Association helps, too. Dealerships that make life easy for the customer with clear signs, parking, reception areas, coffee machines and helpful staff usually care more than most. A good dealer offers you a safe deal and peace of mind. An exceptional one makes you enjoy the transaction.

Smaller dealers

Smaller dealers usually sell only used cars and don't operate under the umbrella of a manufacturer's new car franchise. Standards vary enormously along with the type and age of stock they sell and, while many may offer perfectly reasonable cars, it has to be said that the risk is greater when you buy from one of these smaller outfits.

There's no manufacturer, wary of bad publicity, to monitor standards, and so how smaller dealers behave and prepare their cars for sale is very much up to them.

This is probably the most familiar car selling operation – there's virtually one near every high street, usually trading from a small showroom or sales pitch. Good ones are easy to spot, selling well prepared later K, J, and H reg, from an orderly and inviting site fronted by courteous and well presented salesmen. The ones to watch sell the older stuff, sometimes as old as X and Y-reg, from compounds decorated with faded bunting, with a lop-sided caravan for an office and the obligatory roaming Alsatians. Common sense should tell you which to avoid. Haphazard rows of shabby cars with poorly prepared interiors misted up with condensation, and windscreens covered with meaningless stickers like 'This Week's Star Buy' will tell you it's time to walk away.

> **Common sense should tell you which to avoid. Compounds decorated with faded bunting, a lop-sided caravan for an office, and rows of shabby cars tell you it's time to walk away**

Traders

Traders are one-man outfits who operate from home or a warehouse/lock-up. I know many expert, honest, fair-minded traders and I've bought decent cars from them, but I've also come across some of the most amoral pedlars of scrap it's possible to imagine. With the advent of the cellular telephone (watch for adverts with 0836, 0831, 0860, 0850 telephone numbers), the jack-the-lad trader can almost appear and disappear at will, and the more dishonest ones don't lose any sleep over their reputations or product quality. They buy ex-fleet cars from auctions or large companies, and retail them through local papers, the regional *Auto Trader* magazines or *Exchange & Mart*. The better ones sell late performance and prestige models, advertised in publications like the *Sunday Times,* while the more opportunist will sell anything

from a V-reg Cortina upwards from the pages of their evening paper.

By law their adverts should have a 'T' at the end denoting 'Trade', but some, the most dangerous, pretend to be private sellers, hoping to avoid their legal responsibilities, not to mention obligations to the Inland Revenue and VAT man. The trader's *raison d'être* is simple. Because he has lower overheads, he can sell cars more cheaply than garages and turn them round more quickly. Problem is, many of the disreputable ones see car trading as a get-rich-quick scam and aren't interested in taking the long-term view. One trader I met admitted to having clocked no fewer than 200 cars – virtually everything he'd sold over a four-year period. Not all traders are villains by any means, but they're best approached through a recommendation, and unless you've heard of them or they have a sound local reputation, buying blind from an unknown trader means you're exposing yourself to the highest used car buying risk of all.

> 'One trader admitted to having clocked no fewer than 200 cars. Don't buy blind from an unknown trader. You're carelessly exposing yourself to the highest used car buying risk of all'

How to **spot** a **rogue**

Look out for street-wise words in advertisements such as 'level', 'straight', 'looks well' and other tradey-sounding jargon. These suggest the advertiser could be a trader masquerading as a private seller. 'T' at the end of the ad means Trader or Dealer. Cellphone numbers mean he might be difficult to catch later.

An honest seller will answer your questions with humour and patience. A rogue will get shirty and lose his composure. Hasty and bodged attempts to beautify a car speak volumes. Interiors covered with silicone and glossily blacked tyres are not good news. Low-brow dealers who are rude and defensive mean you should walk away. Rough cars and rough people go together.

If he claims he's a private seller, do his name and address appear on the Registration Document? If not, why not? Has he owned the car long? Is there a service history booklet, current or past MoTs? Lost documents, 'service book to follow' or 'logbook at Swansea' are not promising signs.

Never accept generous-sounding offers of being met halfway in a lay-by or at your home or workplace. Inspect the car at the seller's home address, as it appears in the Registration Document, or not at all. You might need to know where to find him later.

Never buy a car you haven't test driven yourself. Forget the old insurance excuse – if he's selling he should have sorted out cover beforehand. If the seller drives the car himself he can hide a multitude of sins.

What's in it *for the* dealer?

Car dealers work in a highly profitable business where margins are measured in thousands rather than hundreds. In fact, there's almost no limit to what a dealer can earn on any one transaction – the upper ceiling being what the customer is prepared to pay. Their margins are a fiercely guarded

> **If a new car has been in the showroom for longer than 100 days, most dealers will accept a lower margin and sell it**

secret, and can be anything from £200–£5000 on each car sold. New cars offer the least profit and used offer the most, a fact well worth remembering next time you part-exchange your one-owner, low mileage family saloon.

New *car* margins

No mystery here. New car dealers make between 10 per cent and 20 per cent on the cars they sell. Some selling high value cars in short supply, like BMWs, don't offer much of a discount and usually end up with a good 15 per cent or so. Others selling run-out models (due for replacement) work on lower margins, perhaps only 8 per cent, and the figure is usually massaged by the manufacturer who can offer the dealer a bonus or incentive on top. Discounts aren't always up to the dealer as some manufacturers set a lower discount limit, but if a new car has been in the showroom for longer than 100 days or so, most dealers will take a lower margin just to move it on.

New car dealers have other profit areas as well – extended warranties, delivery charges, accessories such as mudflaps and sunroofs, even a commission from the finance company if you buy on HP. Not forgetting the tidy profit to be taken from the part-exchange most new buyers usually trade in.

Used *car* margins

There's more, much more, to be earned from selling used cars – in some cases as much as 35 per cent. There are no hard and fast rules, no industry guidelines, and the amount the dealer can take from a single deal depends entirely on what he paid for his used car in the first place. The industry price guides give an approximate margin between a buying-in price and a retail price. In the case of a one-year-old Sierra, the suggested margin is £1500, rising to over £4000 on a one-year-old BMW 735i. Some dealers ask more than the price guide recommended Good Condition Retail, while others ask less, depending on how quickly they want to turn their stock around. But these figures are gross, which means the dealer has to deduct his reconditioning costs, fixed costs, VAT and a contribution for the Inland Revenue. Let's look at a couple of examples and see how much he can end up with after all deductions:

Example 1

A dealer buys an 89F VW Golf GL for £3,200. He services it for £60, gives it a valet for £25, touches up some paintwork damage for £75, sticks six months' tax on the screen and advertises it at £4,995. A customer comes along and offers him a cash deal of £4,500, which, being a sensible bloke, he takes. So his profit margin before he deducts his VAT and reconditioning is £1,300, or £886.38 after everybody's had their slice. Pretty typical on a small used car.

Example 2

Another dealer buys a nearly new '93K Ford Granada 2.0 Litre Ghia for £9,000. He services it for £80, valets it for £30 and taxes it for a year at £110. Sitting in his showroom with £12,000 on the screen, the Granada has cost him £9,220. In comes a customer wanting to part-exchange his old high mileage F-plate Granada, for which the dealer allows £4,000. So the customer gives his Granada plus £8,000. The dealer neatly completes the deal by passing on the G-plate Granada to another dealer for a quick £4,500. How much has he made? Total in is £12,500 minus £8,000 from the punter and plus £4,500 from the sale of the part-exchange. Total expenditure is £9,000 to buy the J-reg 2.0-Litre Ghia, £120 for bits and bobs, and some £521 in VAT, so £9,741. The result is a cool £2,759 profit before tax. Not a bad day's work.

VAT on used cars

VAT at 17.5 per cent is already included in the dealer's gross margin under the special VAT Second-Hand Car Scheme. Trouble is he's not allowed to pass on the VAT by tacking it on the price of the car so he has to deduct it from his margin. It works like this:

> *If he makes a profit margin of £1,000, he owes the VAT man £148.93 of that £1000. (For the mathematically inclined that's £1,000 x $^7/_{47}$ because the £1,000 is treated as 117.5 percent not 100 percent of the output he's making.)*

Where do *dealers'* cars *come from?*

Secondhand car dealers source cars in two ways: part-exchanges and buying in for stock. Buying in part-exchange is self-explanatory. Buying in for stock means that a dealer buys a car from another dealer or from an auction and he's confident it will catch a passing buyer's eye, so he can sell on at a profit. Sometimes he'll also buy to order, where a customer asks for a particular model and colour, and the dealer buys it specifically for that customer. Part-exchanging is fairly easy because the dealer more or less sets the price and rarely pays more than he knows he can sell it for. On paper he may seem to be paying a higher than average price, but he can 'write it back' against the profit margin from the car it was part-exchanged for.

Buying for stock is speculative and can be risky as the dealer's investment is based on the hope that a customer will appear from nowhere and buy. There's a time investment, too, since some cars can take an age to sell and need to be advertised and held in stock for several months. Not to mention loss of interest on capital tied up in the dealer's stock. Good ones know from experience which cars sell quickly and which don't – one of the reasons you may see five Golfs or 10 Sierras on any one forecourt – dealers like selling the cars they know.

Buying for a customer is a breeze because the car is, in effect, pre-sold and, as soon as the dealer has serviced and valeted it, he can sell it almost immediately. This is good business as the car's sold the same week, there's no risk involved and the car doesn't have to sit on his forecourt dropping in value every time the monthly price guides appear.

Dealer **price guides**

There are just two industry price guides available to bona fide motor dealers – the long-established *Glass's Guide* and the more recent *CAP Black Book*. Each lists the values of most of the new and secondhand cars sold in this country, suggesting different prices for different ages and mileages. Both work on roughly the same principle but, *Glass's* tends to be used more in a retail showroom situation, reflecting windscreen prices and part-exchange prices on the forecourt. *CAP* is used more at the auction and traders' end of the business, so tends to offer the knock-down price at auction. Both contain two sets of prices – 'Basic Trade', which is the price a dealer will pay for a car he intends to retail, and 'Good Condition Retail', the price the dealer will sell the car on at. The dealer's margin is simply the difference between the two.

But these two guides are exactly that, only guides; their values aren't written in tablets of stone and can vary enormously. Some cars, such as the Fiat Croma or Lancia Y10, can sell for 'behind book', or less than the guides say, because they are unfashionable, while other more aspirational cars, such as the BMW 3 Series and Mercedes-Benz 190E, can sell for 'over book'. Some dealers, however, ignore the guides completely and indulge in creative pricing on a 'know-what-I-can-get-for-it' basis. For example, a large Renault dealership I visited recently had a Renault 5 Turbo priced at a shocking £2,000 over retail. A dealer will nearly always consult his guides, but there's nothing to stop him asking more or less, depending on what his experience tells him.

*Understanding **dealer advertisements***

Reading between the lines of dealer ads can tell you a lot about a car, not to mention the people selling it. Not unnaturally, dealers want to make their merchandise sound as attractive as possible, and it's quite common for the some to be economical with the truth. They rarely put complete falsehoods in print, but prefer instead to leave out vital information or include subtle qualifications. Let's look at an example:

> 15,000 mils, full
> ring, alloys, cent
> 7499
>
> **TURBO CAT**
> d, Red, 1 owner
> g but full SAAB
> s/roof, a/l/brakes,
> vs/mirrors, cent
> eats £7399 (0456)
>
> RA 1.3 LX 5-DR
> n/shape) 1 owner,
> full s/hist, 5 spd,
> g £6999 (0123)

> owner, 11,000 miles from new.
> r/cassette, h/rests, rear w/wipe
> etc. Virtually as new and only
> £6,595 (0123) 678901
>
> **SIERRA 1.8LX** '91 model,
> 30,000 rcm, resplendent blue
> coachwork, good condition for
> the year. £4995 (01230) 4567T
>
> **SIERRA 2.0 GLSi 1993**
> Black, 1 owner, p/steering, elec
> winds, s/roof (0123) 456789
>
> **1992 NISSAN SUNNY 1.4**
> 16v Only 10,000 miles with
> full s/history. One owner. Red
> c/work, b/alarm, r/cassette

> Alpine white c/wor
> full s/hist, 5s g/
> s/roof, alloys, r/cass
> e/windows, u/used
> Imac condition £12,
> 012345
>
> **PRIMERA 1.6 L**
> Morello metallic,
> windows, PAS, cent
> £5,995 (0123) 89012
>
> **L REG TOYOTA M**
> Coupe. Only one
> and a mere 7,000 m
> s/history. Total
> throughout and v

At first glance, this sounds quite alluring, but look closer and there's some naughtiness. For instance, 91 model' means that it may have a 91 specification, but the car was actually registered in 1990. '30,000 rcm' sounds like a low mileage but rcm means 'recorded mileage' which may not be genuine. The dealer has covered himself by saying that it's only an indicated mileage. 'Resplendent blue coachwork' is pure flannel; it probably means one of the least desirable Sierra colours – dark Galaxy Blue. 'Good condition for the year' is a highly revealing qualification. It implies that the car isn't bad, but, by the same token, isn't brilliant either. And where's mention of a service history or number of previous owners? Remember that if a dealer knows of any positive features about a car he's selling, chances are he's going to shout them from the roof-tops. In this case the fact that his advert is lukewarm tends to suggest the car in question might be too.

Here's another:

F-REG GRANADA 2.9 Ghia. Met gold with beige cloth. Supplied by ourselves to previous owner. Ghia spec throughout. Usual selling price £6900. Save £1000 with us on this one. Only £5995 (0456) 789012

A real dog's dinner this. No mention of mileage, condition, service history, number of previous owners or even the date of registration. All we know is that it's an F-reg 2.9 Ghia Granada in gold with matching cloth trim and they've sold it before. More serious is the statement that you'll be saving £1000 because the usual price for such a car is £6900. Says who? If we don't know the mileage or year, how can we possibly guess what the normal price should be? If this Granada was a low mileage few-owner car in mint condition with a full service history, the dealer wouldn't be shy about telling us. He's got to be hiding something.

How to **spot** an ad from **an honest dealer**

✓ Look for a quality emphasis: 'Cartwrights – A Family Commitment to Customer Care'.

✓ Is there a straightforward mention of mileage and date of registration?

✓ Do they guarantee all quoted mileages?

✓ Are descriptions factual or flannel?

✓ Are finance details and APRs quoted clearly, or are they hidden in the fine print at the bottom?

✓ Is there any mention of service history?

List of commonly used **abbreviations**

A/C	Air conditioning	**LHD**	Left hand drive
ABS	Anti-lock brakes	**LRM**	Low recorded mileage
C/A	Central armrest	**M/Seats**	Memory seats
C/C	Cruise control	**PAS**	Power assisted steering
C/L	Central locking	**PDM**	Passenger door mirror
E/W	Electric windows	**R/H/R**	Rear head rests
E/S/R	Electric sunroof	**R/C/L**	Remote central locking
E/M	Electric mirrors	**SE**	Special equipment
F/F/S/R	Factory-fitted sunroof	**S/H**	Service history
FSH	Full service history	**T&T**	Taxed and tested
HFS	Heated front screen	**X Spokes**	Cross-spoke alloy wheels

Negotiating with a dealer **over price**

In America they call negotiation 'Give-Get Orientation', and the man who bargains is not only culturally acceptable, he's also admired. In Britain we behave differently and find assertive negotiation an uncomfortable business. In fact, rather than revelling in a pricing structure that allows us a degree of movement, most of us would prefer uniform fixed prices, so we know where we stand and don't have to face the onerous task of bartering.

But negotiation is a profit opportunity and, while you might worry that you're being too hard on the dealer, remember two things – it's your money you'll be giving away and you'll probably never see the bloke again. Far better to be thought of as mean and save yourself several hundred pounds, than be remembered as that nice push-over who paid full whack.

Getting **your** head together

This is rule number one, and it's essential: the world is full of new and used cars and thousands just like the one you want. Ignore this important fact and you'll drive home in a very expensive car. Be ready to turn, walk away and look elsewhere if you can't strike a satisfactory deal. There's no dishonour in agreeing to disagree.

Never become emotional. When you're in the buying mode you must be detached and realistic, and not let the thought of taking your new car home that evening cloud your judgement. If it's not the right price, just relax and wait until another car comes along, because it will.

You're going to **make an offer**

The first job is to make sure the dealer understands that you're going to offer less than the screen price. The best time to do this is when you make the initial phone call and say something like, 'Of course, you're negotiable on the price?' Most dealers expect spirited offers and price their cars up to take in a degree of haggling. Occasionally, you'll come across someone who feels his car is cheap enough already, or pleads poverty, or tries to tell you there are only three other cars like it in the country. If that's the case, don't bother.

Set a **target price**

Say you're interested in a Ford Orion, priced at £5,995, and want to pay cash with no part-exchange. You'll need a realistic negotiating objective – how much you think you can knock the dealer down. Don't be silly and assume you can battle him down by £1,500 because you'll be wasting his and your time because £1,500 is probably his entire profit margin. A sensible discount to aim for would be more like £600 or 10 per cent of the screen price.

Keep your **cool**

Be calm, polite and charming at all times and never lose your composure. Smile, look the dealer in the eye and offer a firm handshake which should establish you as a confident, decisive type. Under no circumstances show tetchiness, impatience or any form of animosity, otherwise you'll blow the whole deal.

> **Take a measured pace, appear unruffled by it all, bargain at your own speed and sit down with a cup of coffee**

Don't rush it, either – there's nothing to be gained by hurrying the act of negotiaton. Take a measured pace, appear unruffled by it all, bargain at your own speed and don't be pressured by the dealer. Nor should you bring your children along. They will only distract you, and the dealer or salesman will see you're more vulnerable because your attention is elsewhere.

It's worth remembering, too, that any form of negotiation is better done sitting down with a cup of coffee – don't be shy about taking the initiative here. Standing up in the showroom glowering at each other with arms folded makes everyone uncomfortable, so choose a relaxed environment if you can. Try it sitting in the car if you like.

Establish your **credibility**

Before you talk numbers, make any seller realise that you have looked at and are considering several other cars as well as his. A bit of healthy competition never hurts and it establishes you as a serious buyer who has been out there doing his homework. By appearing to know the current market, and lacing your conversation with impressive facts and figures, you rob the salesman of his greatest weapon, your ignorance, and you start to assume control of the situation.

The **opening offer**

Keeping your negotiating objective well in mind, you should make your opening offer. Be very careful here and make sure you pitch it well away from where you want to end up. The first offer is the most important of the whole negotiating process and has more effect on the outcome than any other move. Start too low, however, and you'll be summarily shown the door. If you're too high, you won't get near the price you want.

In the case of our £5,995 Orion the opening bid should be in the region of £5,000, neither too low or too high. If the dealer or salesman accepts this opening offer, you should be very suspicious indeed. Normally, he will take a sharp intake of breath, shake his head and counter your offer with something like £5,500.

The **moving phase**

This is where both parties give and get concessions, justifying and defending their positions. A clever customer would remark that he'd seen a similar Orion for £5,000 elsewhere and, while he didn't like the colour of that one, he'd be prepared to take it seriously if he wasn't happy with the price of this one. Having defended your position it's time to make another offer. This time, make the offer you want to end at – £5,250. You're effectively splitting the difference between £5,500 and £5,000 and arriving at a compromise figure.

The **closing phase**

The dealer may still hum and hah but this is the stage where the 'What if…' concession comes into play, and both parties are near to closing the deal, the idea being to tip the scales in your favour and make it easy for the seller to complete the transaction. Here the 'What if…' technique centres on payment or collection. By offering to pay for and collect the car the same day, or to pay in cash instead of a cheque, it's possible to close the sale quickly. (If the thought of carrying large amounts of money around worries you, you could suggest a banker's draft or building society cheque.) Faced with a typical deal like this, £5,250 and a lump of cash the same day to boot, most dealers would shake on it.

Negotiating **rules**

- ✓ Be calm, polite and courteous at all times
- ✓ Don't emotionalise the transaction
- ✓ Never hurry when you negotiate
- ✓ Set yourself a realistic objective
- ✓ Pitch your opening offer below where you want to finish
- ✓ The opening offer determines the final outcome
- ✓ Use the 'What if…' technique
- ✓ Good negotiation is won or lost on planning

Paying
for **your**
car

Cash is king and paying ready money is the cheapest way to buy your car. But if you can't afford to stump up the whole amount or would prefer to spread the cost, you'll have to think about a loan. Borrowing money is expensive and shopping around for the deal offering the lowest interest always pays.

Every year UK car buyers borrow around £12 billion. Assuming an annual interest rate of between 10 per cent and 15 per cent, that's close on £2 billion in interest paid annually to financial institutions. Yet few private buyers know how car finance works.

The finance boys have indeed made borrowing simple: paperwork is virtually instantaneous, credit checking doesn't take long and, if you're a clean risk, you can walk out with the money in your hand in no time. But, in the heat of the moment, propelled by the desire to own, few of us go into the subject in anything like enough detail.

> Every year UK car buyers borrow around £12 billion. Yet few private buyers understand how car finance works

The costs of an unhappy finance deal can be huge, and the misery can last for as long as three years. You can dramatically improve your finance deal by taking simple and straightforward precautions and shopping around for the cheapest charges. Before you start trawling through piles of car brochures, your first priority is to work out how much borrowing the money to pay for it is going to cost.

Hire Purchase

This is the most common financing arrangement used by private buyers. You pay a deposit (around 20 per cent on new cars and 25 per cent on used) and pay off the balance in monthly instalments, usually over three years. The motor trade affectionately call HP 'the drip'. The finance company keeps title to the car until the whole loan has been repaid. In certain circumstances, if the borrower can't pay, the finance company can repossess the car or sue for the outstanding amount.

Remember, too, that if you use finance arranged through a dealer, he'll receive a commission from the finance company. If it's an expensive car, say £10,000 worth, he could earn as much on the finance as he does on the car. So his advice is not necessarily impartial. Interestingly enough, the major players in the finance game are owned by none other than the high street banks. Mercantile Credit is owned by Barclays, Lombard by Nat West, while UDT belongs to TSB.

For:

Many people think this is the most expensive type of borrowing, but occasionally it can be cheaper than a personal loan from a high street bank. Like any commodity, finance rates can be negotiable and it's perfectly possible to strike a deal with the finance company to lower the APR. But beware – the average finance company APR usually starts a couple of percent higher than banks or building societies. If you've a good rapport with a finance company, it can pay to stay with people you know rather than shop around for a tiny additional discount. In the event of a problem they're likely to be more sympathetic.

Against:

You can't sell your car without settling the finance first and, if you default, the finance company can either repossess the car or take you to county court for what you owe. You can buy cars on finance only through dealers who have a Consumer Credit Licence. In other words, you can't buy from a private seller using an HP agreement.

Bank **loan**/Personal **loan**

This is a loan without security obtained from a bank or building society, usually made to borrowers reckoned to be a good risk who have an established financial background and credit history. The lender doesn't own the car but can take the borrower to county court if he or she defaults.

For:

You don't need a hefty deposit, you've got the cash in your pocket and aren't tied to using dealers. This improves your negotiating position.

Against:

Interest rates are usually higher than hire purchase to reflect the greater risk and convenience. You'll also need some sort of established relationship with the bank or building society before they will hand you a pile of money.

Leasing

You never actually own the car. You are effectively renting it for an agreed period for a fixed monthly sum. At the end of the lease term, usually two or three years, the car is sold (probably at auction) and any proceeds go to the leasing company. Business users registered for VAT often take this route. For the private buyer who can't reclaim the VAT there's little advantage.

For:

No capital is tied up. You've no responsibility for selling the car when you've finished with it. There are also tax benefits for business users.

Against:

You never own the car. Leasing may be convenient but it's an expensive way to finance a car.

Lease purchase

Essentially hire purchase. Usually six payments in advance followed by 30 monthly payments – the same as a 20 per cent deposit. The thing to watch is that HP interest is calculated on the amount borrowed i.e. 80 per cent of the purchase price, whereas lease purchase interest is calculated on the whole amount. So 11.5 per cent on HP looks more than 7.5 per cent on lease purchase, but actually they're the same thing.

For:

You own the car at the end.

Against:

The charges are more than for either HP or a personal loan, yet appear to be less.

Contract Hire

Again you're borrowing the car – you don't own it. But servicing and repair costs are included in the charges. Usually there's an annual mileage limit. If you exceed it, you pay a penalty *per mile*. The extra cost can be heartbreaking.

For:

Lots of convenience. You don't have to service or maintain the car, and you often get breakdown cover as well.

Against:

Very expensive. You pay for the convenience and at the end of the lease period you come away with nothing.

Balloon Payments

The finance or leasing company agrees to low payments in the short term if the borrower makes a 'balloon payment' at the end of the agreement. On a £12,000 HP deal the balloon payment could be as much as £4,000.

For:

Your payments are lower, so you can afford a better car for a smaller monthly outlay.

Against:

Interest costs are usually higher and you have to find a large amount of money at the end of the term, when the car is worth the least.

Mortgage top-up

If you've got a mortgage, you can increase it to buy a car. You add the amount onto your mortgage and the building society adjusts the monthly payments.

For:

Easy to get if you're a house owner. Interest rates are probably the lowest you'll find anywhere.

Against:

On a 25-year mortgage period it can take an eternity to pay for your car and cost a fortune in interest. You also place your house at greater risk.

0% **Finance**

Often a manufacturer's incentive on particular cars, sometimes run-out or old models. The manufacturer and the dealer meet the whole cost of the interest from their profit margin. Essentially a clever way of offering a discount without appearing to reduce the screen price.

For:

If you pay the loan off within the year, the borrowing costs you nothing.

Against:

Huge deposit (sometimes 50 per cent) and short-term repayment (often 12 months). Often available only on deals done at list price and on one particular model, so you won't get any discount and your choice and negotiating position are limited.

The **three** most popular **finance options**

✓ For flexibility, reasonable rates and good back-up, see the man at the high street bank.

✓ For the lowest interest rate but longer administrative lead-time, try the building society.

✓ For convenience, one-stop shopping, but usually the greatest expense, ask your dealer to go through a finance company.

Some commonly **misunderstood terms**

APR

The annual percentage rate is a specially calculated form of interest rate set down by the Consumer Credit Act for purposes of comparison. Simply put, the APR is a monthly percentage interest rate times 12; so if the APR is 24 per cent you're paying back 2.0 per cent of the whole amount borrowed per month on a reducing basis.

Rate *of interest*

This is the charge made for borrowing a sum of money expressed as a per centage of the total loan made over a fixed period, usually 12 months. A rate of interest of 15 per cent a year means that for every £1,000 borrowed, the borrower has to find £150 interest on top of the original £1,000 that has to be repaid.

Flat *interest* **rate**

Usually the rate on which HP and personal loans are calculated, which remains constant for the duration of the loan despite interest rate fluctuations. So £5,000 borrowed over three years at 12 percent flat means you pay back 12 per cent of £5,000 for every year you repay. That's 3x12 per cent or 36 per cent of £5,000, which works out at £1,800. So your £5,000 car actually costs you £6,800.

Credit **checking**

Every finance institution lending money to private individuals or limited companies will check their past financial record against a database of known debtors and defaulters. The two main agencies are Infolink and CCN Systems Ltd. If you have a County Court Judgement (CCJ) against you or have gone bankrupt in the past, your record will show it and you may be refused finance. You can, under the Data Protection Act, pay a fee to find out what's recorded against you.

Payment **protection**

This is a shrewd form of insurance that covers your monthly repayments against redundancy, disability or illness. It tends to work out at around an extra £20 per month for £5,000 borrowed over three years. Well worth the peace of mind.

Cooling off *period*

If you decide to back out of your finance deal, the 1974 Consumer Credit Act says that on some agreements you have five days from the day of receiving a copy of your agreement to pull out. This doesn't apply to all deals, and some garages and car dealers don't mention cooling off periods in their agreement. Check your rights before you sign.

Arrangement *fees*

If you source finance through a bank, remember that they charge arrangement fees. These can be quite high – up to 1.0 per cent of the amount borrowed. Make sure you include this in your sums.

*Paying for **your car***

Repossessions

Not all cars on finance can be repossessed. If a limited company signs an agreement, the car can be repossessed for non-payment. But if a private individual borrows less than £15,000, the car can be repossessed only with a court judgement. If it's more than £15,000 it can be repossessed regardless. The car can't be repossessed if you've already paid two-thirds of the loan, unless of course you surrender it voluntarily.

Motor loan certificate

This is a certificate given to you by a bank or building society to show sellers that you have funds available.

How to **cut** the **cost** of **finance**

✓ Always compare APRs and shop around.

✓ Work out the total of the whole amount payable, including charges, and compare one against the other.

✓ Try to negotiate interest rates down.

✓ Watch lease purchase – the interest rates are usually charged on the full principal, not just the amount borrowed.

✓ Watch out for high street bank loan arrangement fees.

✓ Avoid balloon payments – if you have to sell during the loan period, you can be left with little or no equity in the car.

✓ Watch mortgage top-ups – if you get into trouble you could lose your house for the sake of your car.

✓ If you take the zero interest route, make sure you're not sacrificing discount or other benefits.

The **cost** of **borrowing**

Borrowing period	Amount of loan		
36 months	£2,500.00	£5,000.00	£10,000.00
Total to repay	£3,851.64	£7,703.64	£15,408.36
Includes Payment Protection	£377.88	£755.76	£1,511.57
Monthly repayment	£106.99	£213.99	£428.01
Typical APR – 21.9%			

Servicing your **investment**

Once you've paid for your car the bills don't stop. Every car needs regular servicing and even the very best cars break down. How well or badly your car is repaired can colour the whole enjoyment of ownership. Finding a good garage that will look after your car properly is crucial.

There are **four** traditional **ways** of **fixing your car:**

✓ Franchised dealer or main agent

✓ Non-franchised garage or reputable specialist

✓ Fast-fit centre

✓ Back street garage

Franchised *dealers or* main agents

If your car is a couple of years old, you'll probably still be taking it to the garage that supplied it, or at least to a franchised dealer. It's important, in the first couple of years of a car's life, to have it serviced by a main agent because its service record is a key part of its resale value. Keeping the service history booklet up-to-date with main agent rubber stamps adds literally hundreds to the value of a secondhand car. If your car is, say, three to four years old, it's not so vital. Buyers won't be as fussy about its service history, and its age and mileage will be reflected in a lower price.

Consumers tend to think that main agents and franchised garages are the best option. They're certainly the most expensive but they're not infallible. We've used as many as 20 different Ford main agents and have found the quality, levels of attention and servicing work disturbingly inconsistent. Finding an efficient and reliable main agent comes down to pot luck and recommendation. Behind the swish reception area it's like any other garage – it's staffed by people. And people make mistakes.

Non-franchised *specialist* garages

These can be a good bet, if you've a three- or four-year-old BMW, Mercedes, Audi, Jaguar, etc. Non-franchised specialists are exactly that – experts in a particular make or prestige or luxury car, and they normally have all the correct tools, servicing schedules and plenty of experience. The mechanics can be refugees from main agent operations and therefore factory-trained. Again, reputation is all and it's wise to speak to someone who's used their services before making a commitment.

Invariably, they'll be able to undercut the sometimes jaw-dropping labour rates of luxury car main agents. What you won't get is potted palms and neon-blonde receptionists. You'll be able to talk to the man actually wielding the spanner and often get a more conscientious job as a result. We service all our Volkswagen GTis at just such an operation, and they go through the cars with a microscope, finding minor defects a hurried main agent might overlook.

Fast-fit

There's a fast-fit centre in every major town. These are usually tyre and exhaust specialists who have moved into low-cost and fixed-price car servicing. But fast-fit outfits aren't a good idea for every car. Complicated makes like BMW, Saab, Audi and Mercedes need the correct tools and dedicated diagnostic equipment of the main dealers. The more sophisticated the car, the less likely it is that the fast-fit boys can cope. However, for things like Escorts, Sierras, Cavaliers, Metros and Golfs, fast-fit centres often do an admirable job. They'll be cheaper and more convenient without being burdened by the sometimes lengthy 'booking in' procedure of larger garages. You may well be able to leave your car, do some shopping and return to find it ready to go.

There is, however, a shadow over some fast-fit operations. There have been celebrated cases of monstrous overcharging, and parts being claimed as faulty when they were not. The mechanics are often paid a basic salary with commission earned from sales of extra parts. We know of a firm that claimed a customer's car had a slipping clutch and quoted £400 for a replacement. The owner called in the AA who categorically stated there was nothing wrong with the clutch. So beware of dropping your guard for the sake of convenience. If in doubt, go somewhere else for a second opinion.

Back street garages

An endangered species. Soon the traditional small garage will become obsolete as cars become ever more complicated. Effectively, they're selling labour rather than technical expertise and their methods of fault diagnosis can be hit-and-miss. They rarely use the latest expensive diagnostic equipment and specialist tools and won't be able to give you a firm quote for a job they haven't done before. They're often messy, disorganised, opportunist and can be more expensive than the main agent. We've heard of cars taken to back street garages coming out worse than when they went in, and generating a bill for several hundred pounds to boot.

Here are some ways to ease your car's passage through the workshop:

✓ Signs of AA or RAC recommendation, affiliation to the MAA or other official body are encouraging.

✓ Always give the servicing receptionist a written list of jobs to be done. Any faults, untoward noises or intermittent problems should be explained as clearly as possible.

✓ Get a firm quotation in advance for the work, preferably in writing.

✓ Make sure you're informed in advance if extra work needs to be done. Leave a daytime contact phone number.

✓ Ask the servicing garage to keep any old parts. That way they'll think twice before making replacements that aren't absolutely necessary.

✓ Leave your service history booklet on reception and ensure it's stamped up with the mileage and date of service.

✓ Fast-fit centres are best entrusted with routine jobs on less sophisticated cars.

✓ Don't be told you need a complete exhaust when only the back box is blowing, or four new tyres when you've asked for one. If in any doubt, get a second opinion from an MoT test centre.

✓ Fast-fit operations sometimes use after-market parts and not those recommended by the manufacturer. If your car is still under guarantee or extended cover, fitting copy parts can void your warranty.

✓ Steer clear of back street garages offering general servicing.

What **if**?

What if your new or used car deal turns sour? The motor trade's reputation isn't exactly one of blameless rectitude, and with nearly two million new registrations and nigh on four million used cars changing hands every year, there's room enough for dodgy tactics. Trading Standards people reckon they get about 100,000 consumer complaints a year on the supply of vehicles. Only five per cent of unhappy buyers complain officially, they say, so the real level of dissatisfaction is huge – there are around 1.5 million disgruntled punters out there.

The amount and type of redress you can seek depends on whether you bought the car at auction, privately or from a dealer. Method of payment is also important, particularly with a new car. Legally speaking, the safest new car purchase is on finance from a franchised dealer. That way you have just about every bit of existing consumer legislation on your side.

The relevant laws are usually found (apart from the general law of contract) in one or more of the following Acts:

Consumer Credit Legislation
The Sale of Goods Act 1979
Trade Descriptions Act 1968
The Misrepresentation Act 1967
The Road Traffic Act

1 Consumer Credit Legislation

Applies where a vehicle is bought on credit (finance), usually under a Hire Purchase or Conditional Sale Agreement. If you've bought this way and something goes wrong with the car, you can chase compensation from the finance company as well as the dealer.

This legislation also helps if certain undertakings are given to you beforehand and on the strength of them you sign the agreement to purchase the car.

2 Sale of Goods Act 1979

The three important sections of this Act are 12, 13 and 14, covering title, sale by description, and merchantable quality/fitness for the purpose.

Section 12 (Title)

When you buy a car, whoever it's from, the seller must be legally entitled to sell it (i.e. he must be the rightful owner or carry the owner's authority). Also, the vehicle must not be subject to any charges such as outstanding finance agreements, *unless* you've been told about them beforehand and you've bought subject to them.

Section 13 (Sale by description)

Where you agree to buy after reading a description of a car – for example, in a classified ad – then the law implies a clause into the sale that the car has been accurately described.

Section 14 (Merchantable quality/fitness for the purpose)

This is the most important section of the Act. It applies only when you buy from a dealer or someone else selling in the course of his business. There are two major points: merchantable quality and fitness for the purpose.

Merchantable **quality**

This means the car must be free from defects when you buy. There are two exceptions however: firstly, where the dealer points out the faults and you go ahead anyway; secondly, where the defects are ones you could easily have spotted on examination – for example, a cracked headlight, missing wing mirror, no spare tyre or rust spots. Although you're not expected to be as thorough or as knowledgeable as an expert, you are expected to show some common sense and inspect the car for obvious defects, especially if it's secondhand. And, of course, when you're checking it over, the description and price are relevant to whether or not it is of 'merchantable quality'.

Fitness for the purpose

If, during negotiations, you tell the dealer you need the car for some unusual purpose then the law implies a clause that the car sold will be fit for that purpose. The same rule applies if you make your needs clear to any agent arranging finance for you, or who introduces you to a dealer from whom you buy a car on finance.

3 Trade Descriptions Act 1968 and Road Traffic Act

The Trade Descriptions Act makes it a criminal offence for a dealer to sell a car that's falsely described: for example, 'low mileage, one owner, a good little runner' if the car is a clapped-out ex-fleet nail with 80,000 miles on the clock. Investigation and prosecution under the Act is the responsibility of Trading Standards officers operating through county councils. While a criminal conviction won't get you compensation or your money back, it can be used as evidence in any civil claim.

Remember this, however – the Road Traffic Act says *it's an offence not only to sell an unroadworthy vehicle but also to drive one.* That gives added relevance to the business of inspecting the car to the best of your ability (or getting professional advice, from an RAC or AA officer, for example) before you buy.

4 Misrepresentation Act 1967

If you're persuaded by *anyone* (not just a dealer) to buy a car, and the claims made for it turn out to be false, negligent or mistaken, then you generally have a right to rescind the agreement. In some circumstances you can also get your money back or compensation for losses you've suffered as a result of the misrepresentation.

The list below of relevant laws is not exhaustive, but it is a handy reference table. If in doubt, you should seek clarification from a Citizen's Advice Bureau, Consumer Advice Centre or even a solicitor.

Remedies

Here's a simple guide to the remedies available in the event of breach of contract.

Act	Dealer	Private seller	Auction
Consumer Credit	YES	NO	NO
Sale of Goods	*	*	*
Section 12	YES	YES	Generally NO
Section 13	YES	YES	NO
Section 14	YES	NO	NO
Trade Descriptions	YES	YES	NO
Misrepresentation	YES	YES	YES

Remedy		
Breach of	**Dealer**	**Private**
Sale of Goods Act		
Section 12	Rescission *(rescinding the contract)* Refund/Damages	Rescission Refund/Damages
Section 13	Rejection/Repudiation Damages	Rejection/Repudiation Damages
Section 14	Rejection/Rescission	N/A
Misrepresentation	Rescission Damages	Rescission Damages

Private *sale*

Buying privately means you enjoy some protection under the Sale of Goods Act. If the car's been advertised as being in 'excellent condition, mechanically faultless' or other such flannel, it could well have been misrepresented in law. If it's downright dangerous, has defective brakes and a dodgy MoT, for example, then it's a matter for the police under the Road Traffic Act, because it's a criminal offence to sell an unroadworthy car. The only exception would be if the car was being specifically sold for parts or scrap. The police might prosecute the seller if the car's not safe for road use, but you can still sue the seller for breach of contract.

Remember

You will have a real claim against a private seller only if:

✓ There is an actual breach of contract where the seller has not complied with what you both agreed at the time of sale

✓ The car has been inaccurately described or misrepresented in some other way

✓ The car is unroadworthy and perhaps even dangerous

✓ The seller does not own or is not authorised to sell the vehicle

Auctions

Auctions levy an indemnity fee on each car sold, which covers the buyer if the car has been stolen, written off, or is still subject to HP or other finance agreement. Auctions offer a warranty on some cars, but it gives limited cover that lasts only an hour after the end of the sale and covers major mechanical defects such as engine, gearbox, back axle and clutch. After you've paid for it, you have to test the car within one hour, and, if you find anything major wrong, you can reject it and get a refund. It doesn't cover trim, body, electrics, ancillaries or other minor faults.

To make use of an auction warranty you really do have to think and act quickly.

Remember

✓ You have no contract with the auctioneer, who is acting as agent for the seller, so you can't sue the auction company

✓ Finding the seller may be difficult, as auction companies provide a certain degree of anonymity

✓ To pursue a claim you must prove that the seller deliberately misrepresented or falsely described the car

Dealers

Don't forget that the Sale of Goods Act, which applies to dealers and traders, implies three fundamental terms (see page 000) in the contract struck when you agree to buy a car.

'Fitness for the purpose' is rarely a good reason for rejecting a new car because it's assumed you know, from the manufacturer's brochure, what the car can and cannot do. Unless it simply doesn't work, it's deemed to be fit for the purpose for which it's intended. If you do reject a new car, you must do so immediately, ideally on the day of purchase, while it's still a brand new car.

'Fitness for the purpose' is an effective weapon for rejecting secondhand cars, however. If you tell the salesman that you want to commute 500 miles a week on motorways, and you end up on the hard shoulder, you could well have a case. Unfortunately, life's rarely that simple, and the mileage, general condition and the way you've looked after the car will all have a bearing on the success of a claim.

As for compensation from a dealer, if you bought a Cavalier with a warranted 20,000 miles and it turned out to be a saggy old rep's hack with an actual mileage of 95,000, you'd be able to claim compensation for the difference between the price paid and the actual market value.

Remember

✓ If you buy a car from a dealer which is not of merchantable quality or is unfit for its purpose, you will have a civil claim

✓ The Trade Descriptions Act (1968) protects you from misleading written or verbal descriptions

✓ A successful criminal prosecution by Trading Standards officers against a dealer does not automatically guarantee you financial compensation

✓ Buying on hire purchase gives you more protection under the terms of the Consumer Credit Act (1974). The finance company shares liability with the dealer if anything goes wrong

New cars

If a major problem occurs in the first few days (and this probably means no more than three or four days), do not drive the car again. Instead, immediately inform your dealer in writing that you're rejecting the car. Say why, and tell him you're contacting your solicitor. If your new car is a real lemon, the contract between you and the seller is deemed to be broken and, by notifying the dealer, preferably in writing, you may be able to rescind the contract. If you can rescind, then you'll get your money back and the seller will take the car back. In other words, the sale never took place. Trouble is, if you've racked up a few thousand miles and there are obvious signs of wear and tear, 'rescission' (rescinding of the contract) is impossible, because the car isn't in the same state of 'newness' that it was when you bought it.

Remember

✓ Always reject a seriously faulty new car *immediately* if you are not prepared to live with a vehicle that needs a major repair so early in its life

✓ Notify the dealer in writing that you're rejecting the car, and keep a copy of your letter

Questions and answers

Q How can I prove my new car wasn't of merchantable quality?

A To claim a full refund the car must be virtually unusable. Most faults on new cars are relatively minor and don't add up to 'unfitness'. Usually, you'd be expected to allow the garage at least one shot at putting things right. On secondhand cars there's a bit more protection. If your engine blows shortly after you've bought the car you've got a case for non-merchantable quality, although you'll have to prove you've used the car reasonably and not caned the life out of it.

Q What is reasonable use?

A If you bought a small family estate, used it for humping bricks for six months and the rear suspension collapsed, you'd be laughed out of court. But if you told the salesman that this was what you were buying the estate for, and he said it would be OK, then, subject to proving what was said, you'd have a reasonable case for compensation.

Q Can I sue the car manufacturer if anything goes wrong?

A Generally speaking, no. Your contract is with the dealer, not the manufacturer, and it is the dealer who must be sued for breach of contract. If, however, the dealer is no longer around or simply refuses to co-operate, then you may be able to chase the manufacturer if the car carries his guarantee or warranty. But examine the small print first.

Q Can I sue the new car dealer?

A Yes. But only if your new car is not of merchantable quality, or some other contract condition is broken, for example wrong specification, but the problems are not sufficiently serious to justify a rescission.

Q Can I sue the used car dealer?

A Yes, but again there needs to be a breach of contract, such as the car being of unmerchantable quality, although standards of quality are deemed to be lower on a used car (unless the car's been misrepresented). You can't reasonably expect 20,000 trouble-free miles from a car costing £595.

Q What are my obligations?

A You must examine the car as far as is reasonably practical. That doesn't mean whipping off the cylinder head to check the valves, but it does mean making a visual inspection and taking a test drive before you buy. Any declared faults like electric windows not working or a jammed sunroof are your problem and not the seller's. If in doubt, have an independent inspection carried out by an expert.

Q What about mileage?

A Every used car dealer is legally required to verify the mileage of any car he sells 'showing due diligence'. If he sells a car without taking reasonable steps to check the mileage and it turns out to be false, he may be liable. If he believes, because he's done his homework and exercised due diligence, that the mileage is genuine, he probably has a defence. Mileage disclaimer stickers cover dealers against misrepresentation – they usually say something like 'we cannot guarantee the mileage of this car'. In that case, just accept that you have no redress in this respect, and go into the deal, if at all, with your eyes open.

Q What help can I get if my car proves to be clocked?

A Go to your local Trading Standards Office. They will investigate the mileage and contact previous owners for verification. They may prosecute the seller, but that's no guarantee you will receive compensation. Trading Standards never involve themselves in recovering compensation for a buyer.

Q What if I buy a car which has outstanding finance?

A If you're a private buyer, the law assumes that not everybody is able to check a car's financial background, whereas dealers can. So if you bought a car with outstanding finance from a dealer, he's liable for the debt, because he could have, and should have, checked it out. If you buy privately and not enough payments under the HP agreement have been made (normally 50 per cent) the HP company cannot repossess the car and will have to look to the seller for what's due. If they can recover, however, your remedy is to chase the seller, but he may well have no money to pay.

Q What happens if I buy a stolen car?

A Usually the buyer of a stolen vehicle can never become the legal owner. The original owner can recover his property from the purchaser (or any subsequent purchaser), however well intentioned. The law allows an unsuspecting purchaser to sue the seller, who could also be the thief, for return of the purchase price. The trouble is, this is obviously only of value if the seller has any money that you can recover.

Q What happens if I inadvertently buy a rebuilt write-off?

A You're not automatically entitled to your money back just because a car's been rebuilt. It's not a criminal offence to sell a damaged/repaired car. You've either got to prove it was unroadworthy when you bought it, or that you were misled about its history. You are best advised always to question the vehicle's accident history and, if the seller is not the registered owner, to speak to the previous owner. Preferably get a signed written statement from the seller confirming what he tells you about its accident history.

   When a vehicle is written off it is normally registered on the VCAR (Vehicle Condition Alert Register). Ring HPI on (01722) 422422, have your credit card to hand as there's a £15 charge, and they'll tell you if the car's been damaged or owes outstanding finance.

   Unfortunately, not every written-off or seriously damaged car is so registered because it's possible that no insurance claim was made, for instance, if a car was insured Third Party only and was driven into a ditch or tree.

Q My car's been serviced and it's not right. What do I do?

A Take it back to the garage, leave it with them along with a written list of defects (keep a copy). If you get no satisfaction, call the AA, RAC or other independent body and have the car inspected and get a written report. Often this is enough to galvanise the garage into some form of activity. If there is a fault or signs of shoddy workmanship and the garage still won't budge, go to the Trading Standards Office. They'll pursue the complaint on your behalf and you may also be able to sue for any additional expense involved in settling the problems.

Q The car's fine but the bill's enormous. What do I do?
A Again, if the bill has not been agreed in advance, you'll need to
   consult an independent arbiter. Call in the AA or RAC, get them
   to check the work, examine the replaced parts and decide if you've
   been ripped off or not. If you haven't had value for money, you'll
   have to contact the Trading Standards Office and possibly even
   pursue the claim through the courts yourself. Remember, it's
   always best to get an estimate before work is undertaken.

   N.B. *Always bear in mind that, when seeking compensation or
   repayment from the seller, you may have to give credit for your use of
   the vehicle.*

Before you hand over money

✓ Make sure you get a receipt stating date of sale, price, seller's name and
  address, your name and address, car registration and chassis number,
  any declared faults, whether the recorded mileage is genuine or not and
  the seller's signature.

✓ Check that the name and address appearing on the V5 or registration
  document is the same as the seller's actual address. Ask to see some
  identification.

✓ Check the chassis number against the V5.

✓ Try to speak to the previous owner to confirm the car's history and
  mileage. Get his name from the V5 and his telephone number through
  Directory Enquiries (tel: 192).

✓ For a small fee, private buyers can ring HPI (Hire Purchase Information
  Plc on 01722 422422) to find out whether a car is still on finance or has
  been written off by an insurance company during its life. This is not,
  however, fully watertight.

✓ If you think a car may be stolen, don't hesitate to contact your local
  police before taking things any further.

✓ Keep a copy of the original advertisement.

✓ Take a witness with you. He or she should preferably be independent, so
  not immediate family. Their evidence may carry more weight because it's
  more likely to be seen as unbiased.

General note

The examples and principles discussed in this chapter are inevitably general in
nature and for guidance purposes only. Each case or problem will depend on its
own merits and you should take advice before taking legal steps against any party
you feel you have a grievance with. No liability is or can be accepted for any party
acting or failing to act as a result of anything contained in this chapter.

Reference information

Glossary of **abbreviations**

A/C	Air Conditioning
ABS	Anti-lock Braking System
ALB	Anti-lock Brakes
C/L	Central Locking
C/C	Cruise Control
CDL	Central Door Locking
CT	Cherished Number Plate Transfer
DOHC	Double Overhead Camshaft
DOR	Date Of First Registration
E/W	Electric Windows
EFi	Electronic Fuel Injection
ESR	Electric Sunroof
EDM	Electric Door Mirrors
FSH	Full Service History
FFSR	Factory Fitted Sunroof
4WS	Four Wheel Steer
GCR	Good Condition Retail
HFS	Heated Front Screen
HWW	Headlamp Wash/Wipe
HRW	Heated Rear Window
LWB	Long Wheelbase
LHD	Left-hand Drive
LM	Low Mileage
LSD	Limited Slip Diff
NWO	Not Written Off
ONO	Or Nearest Offer
OVNO	Or Very Near Offer
OTR	On The Road (Price)
P/PLATE	Private Plate
PDM	Passenger Door Mirror
PAS	Power Assisted Steering
P/EX	Part-exchange
PDI	Pre-delivery Inspection
PAB	Power Assisted Brakes
RHR	Rear Headrests
RM	Recorded Mileage
RWW	Rear Wash/Wipe
SE	Special Equipment
S/REC	Stolen Recovered
SWB	Short Wheelbase
TSO	Trading Standards Officer
V5	Registration Document
VLM	Very Low Mileage
WHY	What Have You? (to part-exchange)

Some **motor trade phrases** explained

Block	Auction
Behind Book	Under trade guide price
Blow-over	Poor respray
Booked at	Trade guide value
Bottom Book	Trade guide buying-in price
Clag / gob	Filler
Clocking	Winding back mileages
Copy Parts	Non-manufacturer-approved spare parts
Delivery Charges	Dealer charge for number plates, PDI etc
Delivery Mileage	Nominal mileage recorded during delivery
Ex-Channel Island	Ex Jersey/Guernsey rental cars
Late Plate	Registered after August (eg '88F not '88E)
Level Car	Car without bodywork damage
Not Recorded	Not on HPI damaged or finance register
Oil Burner	Diesel car
Over Book	Above trade guide price
Pitch	Car sales lot
Price To Change	Cash balance to pay after part-exchange
Proper Car	Car fit for retail sale
Rent	Road tax
Repo	Finance repossession
Ring	Auction
Ringing	Changing identity of a stolen car
Same Plate	Current registration letter
Self-Shifter	Automatic
Swapper	Part-exchange
Ticket	MoT certificate
Total Loss	Car written off by insurance company
Trade Sale	Dealer wholesale price without warranty
Zeroing	Winding back mileages to 00000

Useful **names** and **addresses**

HP Information plc (HPI)
Dolphin House,
PO Box 61,
New Street,
SALISBURY SP1 2TB
01722 413434

Institute of Trading Standards Administration (ITSA)
4/5 Hadleigh Business Centre,
351 London Road,
HADLEIGH,
Essex SS7 2BT
01702 559930

Driver and Vehicle Licensing Authority (DVLA)
Enquiry Unit,
SWANSEA SA99 1AL
0839 858585

Automobile Association (AA)
Fanum House,
BASINGSTOKE,
Hampshire,
RG21 2EA
01256 20123

AA Vehicle Inspections
0345 500610

Royal Automobile Club (RAC)
Legal Enquiries,
RAC Motoring Services,
PO Box 700,
Spectrum,
Bond Street,
BRISTOL BS99 1AB
0345 300400

RAC Vehicle Inspections
0800 333660

Association For Consumer Research
2 Marylebone Road,
LONDON NW1 4DX
0171 486 5544

ADT Auctions Ltd,
Off Tower Road,
HINDHEAD,
Surrey GU26 6ST
01428 607440

Central Motor Auctions plc (CMA)
Central House,
Pontefract Road,
Rothwell,
LEEDS LS26 0JE
0113 2820707

National Car Auctions (NCA)
Fulwood Industrial Estate,
Common Road,
Huthwaite,
Nr MANSFIELD,
Notts
01623 554232

Retail Motor Industry Federation (RMIF)
201 Great Portland Street
LONDON W1N 6AB
0171 580 9122

Society of Motor Manufacturers & Traders Ltd (SMMT)
Forbes House,
Halkin Street,
LONDON SW1X 7DA
0171 235 7000

Recommended **reading**

The Top Gear Magazine
(Published monthly. New cars, used cars, classic cars, consumer problems,
investigations, data tables)
BBC Enterprises
101 Bayham Street,
LONDON NW1 0AG
0171 331 8000

Autocar & Motor
(Published every Wednesday. New car launches, forthcoming models, road tests)
Editorial
38–42 Hampton Road,
TEDDINGTON
Middlesex TW11 0JE
0181 943 5013

What Car?
(Published monthly. High consumer content. New and secondhand car buying,
road tests, legal problems, useful car comparison tests)
Editorial
38–42 Hampton Road,
TEDDINGTON
Middlesex TW11 0JE
0181 943 5637

CAR Magazine
(Published monthly. New models, road tests, industry news, performance cars)
EMAP National Publications Ltd,
Abbot's Court,
34 Farringdon Lane,
LONDON EC1
0171 216 6200

Auto Express
(Published weekly. New car news, road tests, used car buying)
Ludgate House,
245 Blackfriars Road,
LONDON SE1 9UX
0171 922 2991

Reference information

Trade only price guides

Published monthly:

Glass's Guide
Glass's Guide Service Ltd,
Elgin House,
St George's Avenue,
WEYBRIDGE,
Surrey KT13 0BX
01932 853211

CAP Black Book
CAP Nationwide Motor Research Ltd,
CAP House,
Carleton Road,
SKIPTON,
North Yorkshire BD23 2BE
01756 700666

Retail used price guides

Published monthly. Available from newsagents:

Parker's Guide
Parker Mead Ltd,
45 St Mary's Road,
EALING,
London W5 5RG
0181 579 1082

Motorist's Guide
Foxpride Ltd,
67 Tyrrell Street,
LEICESTER LE3 5SB
0116 2511393

Used Car Prices And Information
Greenlight Publishing Ltd,
The Publishing House,
Hatfield Peverel,
CHELMSFORD,
Essex CM3 2HF
01245 381011

General Index

References are to the non-A–Z sections.

General Index

E

electrial equipment *32*
electric windows *20, 236, 245*
engine size *19*
engineer's reports *213*
engines *236*
    defective *225, 226, 230, 231, 232, 233, 235*
    reconditioned *224–5*
estates *19, 220*
executive cars *see* prestige cars
exhausts *225, 226, 231, 233, 235, 329*
extras *see* options

F

family cars *29, 245–6*
fast-fit centres *329–30*
faults *see* condition
filler, repairs with *225, 229*
finance *27, 215, 323–8, 331–2*
    outstanding *337*
finance companies *218, 324, 326, 332*
'fitness for the purpose' *332, 334–5, 336*
flank *225, 229*
fleet cars/sales *203, 211, 212, 213, 218, 220*
4 X 4s *28, 29, 220*
franchised dealers *25, 26, 30–1, 203, 204–6,*
   311–12, 329, 331
front-wheel drives *234*

G

garages *329–30, 338*
    see also dealers; traders
gear knobs *219, 232*
gearboxes
    automatic *20, 21, 31, 226, 231, 247*
    manual *31, 230, 231, 234, 247*
    reconditioned *224–5*
Glass's Guide *317, 346*
guarantees *see* warranties

H

hatchbacks *19*
head gaskets *230*
hire purchase *216, 324, 325, 326, 327, 332, 337*
HPI (Hire Purchase Information plc) *338, 339, 343*

I

ignition timing *226*
image *1–9, 18–20*
imports *25, 26–7, 228*
indemnity fees *216, 334*
independent dealers *see* dealers; non-franchised
dealers; traders
Infolink *327*
inspections
    post servicing *338*
    pre-purchase *229–35, 337*
Institute of Trading Standards Administration (ITSA)
343
insurance *220, 221, 227, 327, 338*

interest rates *325, 326, 327*
    see also APR
interiors *210, 224, 232, 236*

J

Japanese cars *11, 13, 27*
JD Power Survey *11–16*

L

'landmarks' *212*
lease cars *212, 218*
lease purchase *325, 326*
leasing *325*
leather trim *20, 21*
lights, warning *225, 232, 233*
limited editions *33*
liquidation sales *203*
loans, bank/personal *324–5, 326, 327*
luxury cars *see* prestige cars

M

main agents *see* franchised dealers
manual transmission *see* gearboxes, manual
manufacturers *25, 32, 312*
    discounts and special offers *30*
    and image *3, 6–7*
    sales/auctions *211, 218*
    warranties *26, 30, 33–4, 211, 330, 336*
mats *224, 236*
'merchantable' quality *332, 335, 336*
metallic colours *19, 21, 22, 23, 229*
mileages *219*
    clocking *216, 222, 222–3, 226–7, 232, 236*
    disclaimer stickers *223, 337*
    high *19, 207, 213, 232, 234*
    low *17, 19, 30, 203, 209, 211, 236*
    warranted *206, 213, 214, 216, 227, 319*
Misrepresentaion Act (1967) *333*
models *19, 27, 30, 315*
mortgage top-ups *326, 328*
Motor Agents Association (MAA) *34, 312, 330*
motor loan certificate *328*
Motorist's Guide *221, 346*
MoTs *221, 223, 224, 225, 227, 236, 330*

N

National Breakdown *221*
National Car Auctions (NCA) *211, 344*
nearly new cars *17, 30, 211, 220*
'Network Q' (Vauxhall) *312*
new cars
    automatic versus manual *31*
    before accepting delivery *32*
    dealers margins *315*
    depreciation *17, 18–20*
    old and new models *27*
    options *20–1, 22, 31, 33*
    prices *27, 30, 31, 32–3, 320–2*
    problems with *334–5, 335–6*
    reasons for buying *17–18*
    sale or return *31*